D0977820

Woven Hearts

Ribbon of Gold

by Cathy Marie Hake

Dedication

To all of my dear Christian sisters who long for a godly husband, yet still fill their lives with joy and service as they wait for the Lord's timing and will.

Special thanks to Rick Randall of the Boott Cotton Mill National Park. He graciously shared a wealth of information and helps keep this part of our nation's history alive as he works in the weaving room there.

"I am the door: by me if any man enter in, he shall be saved, and shall go in and out, and find pasture. The thief cometh not, but for to steal, and to kill, and to destroy: I am come that they might have life, and that they might have it more abundantly."
JOHN 10:9–10

Chapter 1

Eastead, Massachusetts—1846

A scream pierced the loud roar of the steam engines and clack and whoosh of the looms. Isabel Shaw whirled around as she yanked the ten-inch shears from the cloth sheath at her waist. Four hasty, desperate hacks freed Mary's brown cotton skirt from the take-up gear on the machine.

Kathleen hurriedly snatched the ragged scrap before it stopped the loom or caused an unsightly flaw in the cotton cloth. "Whew!"

Isabel gave Mary a quick hug and half-shouted in her ear, "You did fine! You're one of us now." She glanced down at the ragged hole in Mary's dress, then meaningfully at her bun. "Aren't you glad you pinned up your hair?"

Mary nodded and accepted the bobbin Kathleen grabbed from a box by their feet and thrust into her hands.

"Keep up, Honey. We'll help you." Every word they spoke had to be shouted to be heard. Isabel guided Mary's shaking hands, steadying them as they popped the old bobbin out of the nearly empty shuttle and deftly thrust the new one in place.

Mary lifted the alderwood shuttle that was shaped like a bottomless canoe to her lips, then sucked the loose thread through the small hole near one of the copper-tipped ends. After she placed the shuttle firmly into the far right-hand side of the race, she gave Isabel a wobbly smile.

"You're catching on quick!" Isabel carefully held in her own deep blue calico skirt as she turned back to her own machines. Closely packed as the looms were, she'd learned to mind her skirts when she moved in order to prevent being snared.

In unison, the trio resumed weaving the thirty-inch-wide shirting at Steadman Textiles. Machines continued to roar, and they put off a greasy odor that mixed oddly with the smell of the thread. Since untreated thread snagged and broke, they dressed the cotton thread with potato starch to make it stronger. The odor saturated the brick walls and wooden floor, and Isabel longed for a breath of snow-fresh air.

Beneath her skirt and single flannel petticoat, she felt her stocking slip down. *I can't take the time. I'm already in trouble for helping Mary.* Isabel considered herself lucky to have stockings at all. When she went to help the girls at Kindred Hearts Orphanage with their sewing after church the previous Sunday, its headmistress, Amy Ross, discreetly passed the paper-wrapped black stockings to her. Amy explained that a wealthy woman had generously left a few charity baskets. Isabel knew the extra-long stockings wouldn't fit petite Amy or any of the older girls. Since she was tall and her last pair of stockings looked far beyond redemption, the sagging new stockings reminded her of how God provided for her needs. She just wished she had tied her garter tighter.

Nimble fingered, Isabel replaced her own bobbins and saw to setting the hooks attached to a leather strap weighted with a bell-shaped metal piece. The temple hooks kept the web of her fabric snug. Down the line she went, only to start again as soon as she finished her last. A bobbin lasted just five minutes. It took rhythm for her to keep up with the speed of the machines, and the mishap made it hard to catch up.

Eleven year olds lugged in baskets with more thread, and empty bobbins went into one bin to be dragged away by slightly younger girls. Isabel took care not to step on them when they crawled past to pull those heavy bins.

The warm, filling porridge from breakfast sat heavily in her stomach. Though known for being a pinchpenny, Ebenezer Steadman had considered feeding his workers well to be a sound business investment. He'd arranged for the boardinghouse tables to groan beneath the weight of good food for his workers. When she'd first come to work at the mill two years ago, Isabel enjoyed the same hearty breakfasts she'd eaten back home—eggs, bacon or sausage, freshly baked bread, and plenty of creamy milk. Since Mr. Steadman passed on—ostensibly to be with the Lord—the mill's overseer had ordered severe changes in how things ran. Delicious meals and extras at the dining tables disappeared overnight. Pasty porridge, stews made with gristly meat, cheap corned beef, and day-old fish now dominated the menu. Though Isabel didn't approve of gossip, she couldn't help wondering if Mr. Jefford was tucking the saved money into the pocket of his expensive, new, double-breasted coat.

She shook her head to rid herself of the uncharitable thought. Instead, she continued to diligently tend her looms and pray for Mama and each of her siblings in turn. Originally, Isabel had left her family's farm in New Hampshire and come to work at Steadman Textiles so money could be put aside for her brother's education. David hoped to be a doctor someday. A bright boy, he showed every promise of bettering himself with advanced learning.

Then Papa died, and her plans had changed. Isabel sent almost all her pay home so Mama could keep food on the table, and David set aside his dreams and took an apprenticeship with a cooper. The beat of the machines rang out a cadence to her prayer. *Lord, be with them. Take my love to them. . . .*

Carter Steadman sauntered down the long catwalk. He sensed his snail's pace tried Harlan Jefford's patience. Though aware his overseer was a busy man, Carter didn't consider it too much to expect a thorough inspection. He'd arranged in advance for this tour of the mill, and he didn't want to rush from room to room. After the improvements and innovations he saw in England, he wanted to institute several changes at his family's mill. He'd have to be selective about which alterations to make first. Changes, he'd discovered, were best accepted if introduced gradually. Judging from Jefford's scowl, Carter decided those changes would have to be presented with a shipload of tact.

Below him, the looms operated in mesmerizing synchronicity, creating fabric at a dizzying rate. His brows knit. Carter stopped and counted the stroke speed. Tapping the toe of his sleekly polished boot, he kept beat with the rhythmic machinery.

Whale oil lamps overhead cast a dim glow upon the workroom. For fear one might cause a fire, buckets of water sat at the ready by the windows. Warp threads strung from the backs of one hundred metal-and-wood looms, looking like a million harp strings. They protested loudly each time the rear beams clanked up and down. Shuttles carrying the weft threads zoomed across the warp threads, and beater bars slammed the weave tight. Finished cloth wound onto the front beams of the machines into fifty-yard bolts.

Here and there, weavers had tacked or pasted pages to their looms or the windows so they could read a quick snippet as they worked. With the looms operating at top speed, no one truly had an opportunity to read, so those pages stood as a reminder of dusty, forgotten dreams.

Jefford propped his forearms on the metal rail and nodded toward the floor. "I've kept everything running just as your father ordered."

"Even the speed?"

"Ayuh. Upping the speed yields three hundred more bolts of cloth from No. 14 yarn each day." He drummed his palms on the rail proudly. "I get 250 yards from each loom each week."

Carter strove to appear unruffled as he leaned against the rail and watched the women tend the looms. Speeding up the machinery was a simple matter of adjusting a few levers; speeding up the workers took more finesse. If the overseer occasionally issued the command to accelerate work to meet a special order, Carter might consider it, but he counted it unsafe to push the workers at this pace on a daily basis. "So you run the looms at maximum capacity at all times?"

"A mighty poor overseer I'd be to do otherwise."

Tamping down his temper, Carter reminded himself Jefford boasted working for the mill for a fair length of time. During those years, he'd obeyed the mandates given him—but those orders had come from an owner who rarely troubled himself over the needs of others. If Jefford displayed that same loyalty to Carter's plans, the mill would benefit. *I'll give him a chance.*

Watching the bustle below, Carter realized the workers seemed to cover a fair distance in their movements. His eyes narrowed. "How many looms apiece?"

"Three, most often. Some, I can stretch to four."

Carter's molars grated. "Three or four?"

Jefford shot him a bland look, then added, "Beginners are on two for the first week or so. If they can't handle three by the second week, they're turned out."

Some changes can't wait. Carter watched the women scrambling to keep pace with the machines and decided he'd finish the tour, then demand speed and loom assignment adjustments.

Just as they prepared to continue, a cry sounded. A quick scan of the floor revealed a flurry of activity among three women who then rapidly separated and got back to their weaving. Carter suspected the middle one had gotten snagged in the machinery and her friends hastily freed her.

Jefford squinted and read aloud, "Row Sixteen." The tone of his voice promised retribution. He turned to Carter. "Mr. Steadman—that is, your father—made the policy no one could leave her loom for any reason without permission."

"Frivolous causes, I agree with. In this case, however, they rescued a worker. I consider the purpose quite reasonable."

"Begging your pardon, Mr. Steadman, but you cannot expect these women to think the matter through. We'll have pandemonium if we let them start to decide for themselves when they can stop working!"

"Row Sixteen did a fair job helping the center worker and resuming duty. Since I approve, you needn't take any action against them."

The overseer nodded curtly. His face reflected disagreement.

Carter crossed his arms and studied him for a long moment. "You've served at Steadman Mills a long while, haven't you?"

"Seven years." Chest puffed out with pride, Jefford added, "And every year's turned a better profit than the last one!"

Carter headed down the catwalk again. "If you have weavers handling three looms apiece, we must have fewer workers and the boardinghouses must have vacancies."

"No, Sir. While you was away, your dad replaced the old looms with modern ones. Faster, better technology—more profit in that, you know. He scooted the looms all up a bit tighter and added in six more rows. I've kept every machine busy, so the boardinghouses are full."

No wonder that woman got caught in the machine. Carter

stopped. His hands tightened around the metal rail. "How often do the workers get snagged in the works or injured?"

"Haven't bothered to count." The overseer shrugged indifferently.

Carter hit his limit. Before the day was done, he would let Jefford know that as the new owner, he expected changes. He wasn't going to delay them, after all.

Chapter 2

Carter saw blatant disregard for the workers' safety from the room where the raw cotton was cleaned, to the thread room, through the weaving room, and on to the fabric finishing. He didn't expect the mill to be a Sunday picnic, but he refused to allow the current situation to continue.

He stood at the doorway to the kitchen of one of the boardinghouses and watched the women wolf down their mid-day meal. Accustomed to refined dining, he felt a bolt of disbelief. These women engaged in no gentle conversation and never paused between bites. The meal of corned beef, cabbage, and bread seemed simple but plentiful. They'd not return to work hungry. Still, he couldn't help thinking that eating so fast might well cause indigestion.

The contrast between this meal and the feast he and Jefford shared just an hour before jarred him. Admittedly, duckling might be far too difficult to roast for this many women, and Jefford might well have ordered an especially fine meal to impress the new boss. . . .

The bells chimed, interrupting his musings. All of the women rose and carried their plates to wooden boxes at the end of each table. Like a chain of postulants in a nunnery, they obeyed the bells that regimented their lives.

Carter drew a gold pocket watch from his paisley silk waistcoat pocket and noted the time. Twenty-five minutes. He cocked a brow and looked at Jefford, then shot a meaningful glance at his timepiece.

"No use wasting daylight by having them dawdle over their meal."

Just then, a tall brunette passed by and captured Carter's attention. Fine-boned and graceful, she looked and moved like a queen. She carried her own plate and another, as well.

He smiled. Seeing her was the first pleasant thing he'd experienced all day.

Her voice lilted softly as she promised the pale teen beside her, "Tomorrow, your fingers won't be so stiff and sore. You're doing fine."

Unaware of his presence, the younger girl plucked at a sizable, ragged hole in her brown skirt. "But my clothes! I can't do anything about them, because I promised Aunt Amy I'd give most of my pay to her!"

"Beneath our aprons, many of us have tattered skirts," the first reassured. "You're not alone in that. Kathleen and I will help you mend it before you walk home."

"That we will," the third woman said. "And Amy would never expect all of your money."

Lazing against the doorsill, Jefford declared, "They get

along well enough. Not many troublemakers."

His attitude had grated on Carter's nerves all morning. Even if Jefford held no compassion whatsoever, couldn't he understand these women would work better if treated well? On a simple business level, it made sense to invest in a happy workforce. Even if greed were his sole motivation, Jefford should be able to see that much. Carter refused to accept such an attitude, and he was about to show this pompous man just how different things were going to be. He paced off and stopped the trio. "A moment, please."

The youngest looked stricken and blurted out, "It was my fault, Sir. Please don't punish them for helping me!"

The other two drew closer to her in an instinctively protective move and stared up at him. Their somber expressions sliced through his heart. Something inside twisted. He'd frightened her. Carter asked the pretty brunette, "Are you from Row Sixteen?"

"Yes, Sir, we are."

"Your names?"

She blinked, and he noted how her huge brown eyes glistened. The others huddled closer still. *All of them are frightened, as a matter of fact. These women are so accustomed to harsh management, they expect me to castigate them. They did nothing I wouldn't have done myself.*

"I'm Isabel Shaw, Sir." The plates in the dark-haired beauty's hands rattled a bit as she tilted her head to the right. "Mary Tottard," then to the left, "Kathleen McKenna."

"Don't you think I didn't see what happened this morning."

Jefford set his hands on his hips and scowled at them. Other women hurriedly slid by and left the boardinghouse's dining hall.

Isabel wet her lips. "Sir, it's Mary's first day to mind her own loom."

"She understood the rules. She also knows the penalty—as do both of you," Jefford asserted.

"But in this case," Carter inserted smoothly, "you were right to react so quickly." He cast a glance at Mary's ruined skirt. "You're not wearing an apron. On your way back to the floor, go help yourself to a remnant."

All three women rewarded him with relieved smiles, but Isabel cast a wary glance at Jefford.

Carter gave the overseer a cool look, then turned to address the women. "You other ladies are welcome to a piece, as well."

Isabel blinked in astonishment. "Sir, I can make do just fine with my apron; but if you don't mind, I'd take a scrap so we can make a few dolls for the girls at the orphanage."

Her charitable response took him by surprise. Carter tilted his head to the side and stared at her for a long moment. "Miss Shaw, I'd be pleased if you'd take a length for yourself and some for the orphans. How many dolls are you making?"

A beautiful flush painted her cheeks. "Mrs. Ross has sixteen girls, Sir. A bit over a yard of cotton would be enough for us to make sure each of the young ones has a Christmas doll."

"Take an additional yard apiece for them—not just the plain solids, either. Make them fancy pieces from printworks. That way, the girls can learn to stitch some pretty little clothes and blankets. . .and," he stressed, "be sure to take a piece for yourself."

She almost dropped the plates. "Oh, Sir, you're being so generous, but I wouldn't want you to get in trouble."

Carter wanted to chuckle. Clearly, Miss Shaw didn't know his identity—a surprising fact since the Steadman males bore a strong resemblance to one another. Tall, broad of shoulder, and square-jawed, he resembled his father with the exception that his dark brown hair hadn't a single hint of silver to it. Had she never seen his father? He set those thoughts aside and found her concern for him quite charming. So was her selflessness.

He didn't want to embarrass her, so he turned to the overseer. "Mr. Jefford is more than able to approve of this."

"Oh, God bless you, Sir!"

"Yes, God bless you!" the other two said in unison.

Once they were out of earshot, Jefford heaved a deep sigh. "Mr. Steadman, that was a terrible mistake. You've been abroad and don't understand the way of things anymore. Every last woman on the floor is going to be looking for a handout now. This is a business, not a charity!"

Carter reined in his temper and strove to face his overseer with a modicum of civility. Getting him to institute changes would likely be difficult, and inspiring him to cooperate would require finesse. "You've shown me the mill all morning, Jefford. The productivity of Steadman Textiles would stagger smaller minds than ours. A few paltry yards won't be missed, and as it aids orphans, it's a worthwhile charity."

"Your father believed charity began at home." Jefford's

thinned lips made it clear he agreed with that theory.

"Farmers in the Old Testament left grain in the fields so the widows and orphans could glean. God blessed them for it. So far as I can see, the Lord's blessing will carry me a far sight better than hoarding a few remnants."

Jefford hitched his left shoulder in a gesture that might have looked careless, had the motion not been so tense. "Whatever you want, Sir. You're the owner now, since your father stuck his spoon in the wall."

"Nice, white muslin, Kathleen! Look at this." Isabel held up a two-yard length of fabric from the rainbow stack on their bed in the boardinghouse. The remainder of the pile gaily tumbled across the colorful nine-patch quilt that covered the double bed they shared. "Why, the girls will be delighted."

Kathleen laughed. "Amy is going to be more excited than all of her little ones."

"I know. Let's tell Amy we'll make the dolls, and we'll let her have three yards so she and the older girls can sew doll clothes for the young ones. That way, they'll all have a part in the gift."

Kathleen sat cross-legged on the other side of the bed and took the pins out of her twisted coronette, releasing an abundance of black curls that bounced down her back, then sprang back up to curl in abandon around her shoulders. At times like this, Isabel knew her Scottish friend must have left a trail of swains behind when her father decided to sell his New England farmhouse and move the family to Indiana, sending

Kathleen to the mill to help them financially until they got settled in their new home. Oblivious to Isabel's admiring look, Kathleen stared at the fabric and wondered aloud, "What about the older girls? Some of them are beyond doll age."

"We'll use some of the fabric to make them aprons. Ginger can help us decide who'd like which piece best."

"Aye, and ye can use the scraps to teach the wee girls to quilt dolly blankets," Pegeen said as she plopped down on her bed. She yawned deeply. "I dinna ken how the both of you find the strength to sit there by the lamp in the evenin' to work. I'm worn down to a nubbin' by the day's end."

After slamming the lid down on her lap desk, Grace blew on her letter to dry the ink. The dark expression she wore promised a biting comment. "Didn't you listen to the sermon on Sunday? Christians are obliged to do good works."

"Ach! I sit there the whole while, daydreamin'. Spinnin' in her grave, she is, my mama—her daughter darkening the doors of any church not named after the Virgin or a saint. If the dragon who runs this boardinghouse didn't herd us all out to her verra own church, I'd not go, and well you know it." Pegeen wrinkled her nose. All of the mill workers had to attend church, or they lost their positions. "I need every last cent so I can bring me sister o'er."

Isabel and Kathleen exchanged a quick glance. They made no secret of their faith, and they had made a pact to pray for their two roommates since neither sought salvation. Instead of arguing, Isabel simply said, "The idea of having the girls quilt is lovely, Peg."

"She just goes to help at the orphanage so she won't miss her little sisters so much." Grace folded her letter with a savage sweep of her hand. "Face it—we're all here because our families need money. Nothing like being a beast of burden so someone else's life improves."

When the boardinghouses designated for the Irish lasses filled to capacity, Isabel and Kathleen offered to take Pegeen into their room. Grace arrived a year later, and she pitched a fit when she learned she'd have to share not only a room but a bed with an immigrant. Disgruntled because her stepfather sent her to the mills to earn funds for his son's education, she'd been alternately rude and sullen. Others felt fortunate to have their positions, but Grace grumbled constantly. Close quarters and the differences among the four roommates made for some challenging moments.

After Grace left the room, Kathleen leaned forward. "We're not going to let her sour tongue get to us, Isabel."

"We haven't, yet," Isabel whispered.

Kathleen picked up a length of mauve cotton that had a wispy green vine every few inches. "Who does this remind you of?"

"Mauve—Amy. Definitely Amy." Isabel sighed. "There's not enough for an apron unless we piece the straps."

Kathleen folded the length and carefully set it aside. "We'll do that. If I don't miss my guess, Amy's spent every last cent she has on those girls. It's well past time she got something new for herself."

"I made my sisters dolls last Christmas. I still have the

papers I used as a pattern." Isabel knelt by the small oak chest of drawers all four of them shared and searched for the pattern she'd made. For a moment, her heart ached to cuddle her sisters again. It had been two long years since she'd seen them, but she couldn't spare the dollar it would take to travel home and back again. The thick packet of letters in the drawer testified to the passage of time and served as a reminder that Mama loved her and needed her help.

A glittering gold ribbon wrapped around the letters. Grandma carried that ribbon in her bridal bouquet, and Mama did, too. By rights, Isabel's older sister should have gotten the ribbon; but Hannah and Abe surprised everyone in church one day by standing up and asking the parson to wed them. Hannah carried no bouquet to tie with the cherished ribbon. She'd happily pledged her vows and gone home to live in the little cottage on the outskirts of the village where her husband sharecropped.

Last Christmas, Mama sent the precious ribbon with a sweet, sweet letter—she'd apologized she hadn't managed to scrape together a few cents for a gift, but postage would add on a cost she could ill afford. Instead, she'd tucked her beloved ribbon of gold into the letter with the pledge to pray for Isabel as the sun's first rays streaked the morning sky.

Each time Isabel touched that ribbon, she felt close to her family. Her three little sisters and Mama would need her to send money home for many years to come. Isabel's heart grew heavy when she realized she probably wouldn't ever carry the ribbon in a bridal bouquet.

Chapter 3

Carter pulled his thick, black wool greatcoat tighter and headed across the courtyard toward the office. The five o'clock bell chimed, calling the employees to work. He hoped Jefford would be self-indulgent enough to sleep a bit later. After all, the last thing Carter wanted was for the overseer to hover while he examined the books.

Last evening, Carter's mother expressed her irritation when he stated his plan to return to the mill again today. "Your father paid others to see to that. So do you. Indeed, you pay them exceedingly well. The profits are such that we've been able to live comfortably. Stay home. Belinda Atherton and her daughters are coming to tea tomorrow."

Another good reason to be at the mill. Carter had hastily turned down the invitation.

He left the house early, before his mother could involve him in her matrimonial machinations. Her idea of a suitable wife revolved around wealth and breeding. She'd be delighted to match him with a brainless, simpering girl whose only interests were shopping and attending soirees. Carter wanted nothing to do with a "biddable" socialite; he had more important issues to mind. Mother, bless her compassionate soul, would understand—especially if he went home for supper tonight and shared with her his plan to wait on God's timing instead of rushing to the altar. At the present, cotton—not courtship—demanded his attention.

Virtually nothing had changed since he left except that Jefford ran the mill even more harshly. Carter and his father parted on less-than-comfortable terms. Father felt betrayed when Carter stated he fully understood and supported the mill workers in Lowell, who went on strike and took other actions to protest low wages, long hours, and poor working conditions. His father's anger rose even higher when Carter stated that he held similar concerns about Steadman Textiles. Mother soothed Father's fury by suggesting Carter merely hadn't enough knowledge of the world to understand the situation. They'd sent him to Europe with the expectation he'd go on a Grand Tour, rub elbows with idle, rich young men, and come to see the benefits of his station in life. Instead, he'd spent his time visiting other textile factories and making notes of techniques and labor management.

When he received word that his father died at a card table from a violent heart spell, Carter knew the time had come for him to return to Eastead. For all of Father's wealth, he'd not been able to take a cent to his grave. Carter mourned the fact that his father stayed so busy seeking wealth, he'd never sought the Lord. The young man resolved to set a different course for his own life.

Then, too, Carter felt a heavy burden weighing down on his shoulders. It fell to him to recompense his father's wrongs. God was the God of justice. The Bible clearly warned the sins of the father were visited upon the son. Aware he bore the responsibility of making restitution and appeasing God's pending wrath, Carter vowed to do all that was in his power to cancel the curse and receive God's blessing.

The office building door was unlocked, so Carter pushed it open and hastily lit an oil lamp on the small table beside the door. Half a dozen strides carried him to the bookkeeper's office. He inserted a key into the lock and let himself in. He'd not let Jefford know he possessed a key. At first, he'd been willing to believe the overseer had tried to be a diligent steward of the responsibilities he carried. Now, he couldn't be sure the overseer warranted his trust, so until he inspected the books and records, Carter chose to keep some matters to himself. The moment Jefford arrived today, he'd realize the new Steadman owner held keys—but by then it would be too late to doctor the financial records.

Carter put the lamp on the corner of the cherry wood desk and took a seat. For the next two hours, he pored over the books. Indeed, the records showed impressive business accomplishments—Steadman Textiles averaged six million yards of cloth each year. Carter knew a pound of cotton yielded three and one-fifth yards and that a bale of raw cotton usually weighed 361 pounds. Quickly scribbling on a nearby slate and using those facts, he checked the figures in the ledgers. Indeed, everything checked out as it ought.

Heavy footsteps made him aware he'd soon have company. Carter turned around in time to catch sight of the mill's overseer as he crossed the plank floor with a lumbering gait.

"Mr. Steadman! Had I known you wished to review the books, I'd have brought you here yesterday." Harlan Jefford gave him a brisk nod as he peeled out of his stylish, heavy wool coat.

"I appreciated the tour you gave me. I didn't want to take more of your time while I went through the mundane matters."

"I do my best to see to each and every detail." Having hung his coat on a brass wall hook, Jefford stepped over to the desk and jabbed a beefy finger toward the ledger. "The books prove it. Even after your father died, I kept the mill going and made sure it brought in just as much as when he'd been here to inspect the finances."

"There's no doubt Steadman Textiles turns a remarkable profit. Your zeal is noteworthy." Carter watched his overseer's chest puff out with pride. Sweeping changes would no doubt irk this arrogant man. That didn't matter. Carter had taken the reins, and he wasn't about to let someone else decide on the path. "As you're so capable, I'm counting on you to help make the changes go smoothly."

"Changes?" Jefford's shoulders stiffened.

Carter gestured toward a hard-backed chair. "This is a good time to outline the reorganization. Have a seat."

Shaking his head sagely, the overseer dragged the chair across the plank floor. Its legs scraped in loud protest, then the seat creaked under his considerable weight. He leaned back and jutted his chin toward the desk. "Those books show Steadman Textiles is turning the best profit it ever has—far and away above what the other mills are doing. Tampering with a good system isn't wise."

Carter stared at him.

Jefford shifted uncomfortably. "Begging your pardon, Sir, but you've been gone a good long while. I mean you no disrespect. Give yourself a month or so to get a feel for how things run around here. No need to rush into things."

"Your concern is duly noted," Carter said in a soft tone that would have warned anyone who knew him that he was doing his utmost to rein in his temper.

Jefford's head bobbed, and a patronizing smile accompanied his next words. "Your father and I built a good system here. He approved of how I run things."

"My father and I disagreed on some of those issues. I am now the owner. I expect your full loyalty and cooperation." Carter closed the ledger, having seen enough. He stared straight at the overseer and watched the man's jaw tighten and his face grow florid. He didn't know Jefford well enough to guess whether the reaction indicated wounded pride, frustration, or anger.

"You know Steadman Textiles inside and out. You will be pivotal in instituting the revisions."

"No one knows the mill better."

Carter couldn't be sure if Jefford had agreed with his praise or was making a point of stressing his own significance. "Several of the changes are beneath a man of your importance in the scheme of things around here."

Jefford tugged at his gold silk waistcoat. He looked more like a prosperous bank owner than a mill overseer. "Your regard does me proud, Sir. I consider it my duty to keep on top of things—everything."

"Agreed. That's why we're meeting now."

"Things changed while you was away. Used to be farmers' daughters who worked here. Nowadays, I get them Irish gals. More than a third of the workers are potato eaters." A glint lit his eyes. "Willin' to work for less, too."

"So that is why the pay dropped from $3.50 a week to $3.25?"

"Ayuh." A smug smile crossed Jefford's face.

"And you're still charging $1.25 per week room and found."

"The boardinghouses are better than what those lasses ever had back home." The overseer leaned forward. "Saving a quarter per worker each week adds up to a tidy sum. It boosted the profits. Your father came up with that notion himself."

"I am not my father." The iron in Carter's voice made it clear things would change. "Pay is to be brought back up to $3.50 a week, effective today."

Jefford's eyes bulged. "For all but the Irish, right?"

"For all of the women. The book of Ephesians says, 'Now, therefore, you are no longer strangers and foreigners, but fellow citizens with the saints and members of the household of God.' I'll not hold with treating the Irish women any differently than the others."

"If that's what you order."

Though Jefford's tone made it clear he disagreed with the decision, Carter didn't care. He suspected the overseer wouldn't be any happier with his next words. "There are other issues we need to address at once."

Chapter 4

"Mr. Jefford looks like he sat on a pincushion," Kathleen whispered to Isabel as they gathered in the aisles of the weaving room.

Isabel shot her a quicksilver smile, then turned her attention back to the overseer. Standing on an overturned salt box, he stuck out above all of the women's scarved heads. His brows beetled into a dark Vee, and he kept huffing like a steam engine coming up to speed. Never before had the women been ordered to gather for a meeting before the day began. If the overseer needed to make an announcement, he waited until mealtime so as not to lose a moment of labor.

Hands on his hips, he clipped out loudly, "Henceforth, you will all tend only two machines. . .one machine for the new laborers for the first fortnight."

Isabel drew in a surprised breath. Only two looms?

"That better not mean he's cutting pay again," the woman behind her grumbled.

Oh, if it does, I won't be able to send Mama enough to take care of everyone back home!

"Rows One through Eighteen will work their usual stations, but Nineteen through Twenty-five are to fill in the gaps formed by the reduced responsibilities."

Mary let out a relieved sigh. Isabel grabbed her hand and squeezed it. They wouldn't be separated.

"Now get to work." Jefford scowled and flapped his hands like he was shooing away a flock of pesky hens.

Weaving felt different that morning. Isabel couldn't decide what gave her the odd sensation her world had changed. Perhaps it was because she didn't have to scurry madly about to tend three looms. She still needed to work at a steady pace, but even then, it almost felt like her job had slowed from a horse race to a hayride. Mayhap 'twas that her threads didn't seem to break as often at this speed, so she didn't have to tie as many weaver's knots. Then, too, Pegeen now wove on her other side, and her cheeky smile had a way of lifting Isabel's spirits.

Midmorning, a pair of men came into the weaving room. Instead of leaving the windows closed as was customary, they opened each of them a few inches for almost an hour. The fresh air smelled and felt wonderful.

As the women filed down the stairs on the outside of the building to go to dinner, Kathleen tilted her head toward the blackened brick walls. "Now can you beat that? All along, Mr. Jefford said the breeze would dry out the room and make the threads break. Hasn't done anything at all."

"It blew out some of the hot oil and the thread's stale potato starch smell." Mary's deep brown pelisse parted as she reached around to retie the length of pink-and-white-striped fabric that served as her new apron. "I'm ever so grateful."

"The air's so wet from the snow, it couldn't dry anything out," Kathleen decided.

"Hot and humid—that's what they want," one of the women behind them said. A smash piecer, she knew more about the weaving room than anyone else. "Get a room dry or cold, and the threads snap all over the place. What with the steam heater going, they could leave the windows open on days like this and we'd all be better off."

Isabel compressed her lips, then cast a look around. "I'm worried. If we're not weaving as much fabric, then profits will fall. They'll either pay us less or dismiss some of us."

"Saints preserve us! I hope not!" The woman in front of Isabel turned and gave her a stricken look. "I'm needin' that money to fetch my sister here. I figured 'twould take me another four months to earn her passage. If they cut our wages. . ."

"And the orphanage needs money," Mary added. "Last night, Aunt Amy told me she expects me to keep a fair portion of my earnings, but if they drop our wages, I'm going to try to keep her from finding out. It costs a fair amount to feed all of us girls."

"Speaking of food," Kathleen moaned, "I hope we get something better for lunch today. You know I'm not one to complain, but we used to eat well. They're holding out the same dollar and a quarter each week for room and found, but the meals aren't half as good as they used to be."

Isabel shuddered. "I agree. I know I ought to be thankful

for a full plate, but they're buying the cheapest food they can now. I couldn't gnaw through the gristly meat in the stew last night."

"Aunt Amy makes such good food." Mary sighed. "She didn't get cross with me about my ruined dress. She just gave me a hug. I'm glad I still get to live at Kindred Hearts."

"Did you tell her about us making dolls for the girls for Christmas?" Isabel slipped into the dining hall and shed her cape.

"Oh, yes! And Ginger is so sweet. She offered some of the yarn in her knitting bag so we could make hair. If you make the dolls and faces, we'll match the hair for each of the girls."

"Oh, can't you just see red, looping curls on Patty's or brown ones on Ruthie's?" Isabel laughed as they all sat at the table. "We ought to match the color we embroider the eyes, then, too."

Moments later, the kind, dark-haired man from the previous day strolled over and stopped by the head of their table. He flashed an urbane smile. "I see you got an apron, Miss Mary."

"Oh, yes. Thank you, Sir!"

Isabel paused a moment from passing a bowl of potatoes to Kathleen. She smiled at him. "And we thank you, too, for the fabric. We'll be making lovely dolls."

"At the risk of being thought an eavesdropper, I'll confess I overheard you discussing them. It occurred to me, you might need cotton to stuff the dolls. I delivered a roll of batting to your boardinghouse."

"How thoughtful of you!"

"It was nothing. I'll be here, moving the looms for the next week. Perhaps you could bring the first one in so I can see how she turns out."

"It's the least I could do," Isabel murmured.

Kathleen twisted around. "Moving looms? Why?"

The man gave her a puzzled look for a moment. "I thought you'd been told we're removing some of the looms."

"No." Isabel gulped. "Is there a problem? Are the mills cutting back?"

His hazel eyes darkened, and he clamped his lips together.

"I don't mean to put you in an awkward position, asking you to reveal your supervisor's plans," she stammered. "It's just that we all count on every bit we earn. Most of the women here are trying to put by money to send a brother or son to school. Some are saving to bring a relative over from Ireland."

"I understand." He nodded and cast a glance about the room.

"That's me," one woman volunteered. "I'm bringing me sister over. We were hoping she'd find a job here at the mill when she came. Isabel—her mama's a widow and has a flock of bairns back home, and Mary shares her pay wi' the orphanage."

"God blesses those who see to the widows and orphans." The man's smile warmed enough to melt an icicle in an instant. "Put your trust in the Lord, ladies. He'll provide."

Once he walked off, Isabel quickly finished dishing up her meal and ate. When she went down the center walkway in the mill, she spied the kind stranger in a knot of other workmen. Tall and broad shouldered as he was, he stood out even in their midst. Throughout the rest of the day, she caught occasional glimpses of the men through the swirling lint as they unbolted looms from the floor and dismantled them.

If the mills were turning out less fabric, using fewer machines, and serving cheaper food, then Steadman Textiles must be in trouble. Before fear overtook her, Isabel thought, *Trust in the Lord. . . .* From the looks of things, she was going to have an opportunity to exercise her faith.

Two days later, Carter looked to the side as he finished rolling up a blueprint. "Miss Isabel," he said in greeting to the young woman who stood before him.

A shy smile touched her lips as she held out a doll. He didn't bother to look at the toy—he could barely take his eyes off the woman. A becoming flush tinted her cheeks, and several tiny wisps of her rich brown hair spiraled at her temples and nape. Queen Esther couldn't have been half as lovely. Realizing he bordered on being rude for staring, he focused his attention on the doll. After he set aside the blueprint and wiped his hands off on the thighs of an old pair of heavy broadcloth pants, he accepted the toy.

"Betty's barely two. Amy took in her baby sister, too." Isabel smiled lovingly at the doll. "Little Betty's hair is that same shade of chestnut, and I embroidered brown eyes to make them match hers—only hers are so big and pretty."

"The doll is splendid." Carter didn't try to hide his grin. "Can't say I ever held one before, but if little Betty is half as sweet as this, I'm surprised someone hasn't adopted her."

"She's far cuter, but she has a limp. Amy Ross gets an occasional inquiry, but folks are generally looking for a healthy older girl to watch their younger children or use as a maid. Amy won't let the girls work until they're sixteen. Most of her girls are fine, but Betty has a limp, and Ginger is nearly blind."

He thoughtfully fingered the little loops of reddish-brown yarn that made a mop of curls. "How many children did you say she has?"

"Sixteen. Mary Tottard is the oldest. You met her the other day and let her have material for an apron. She and Veronica are the only ones who work."

The pink-and-white-striped dress on the doll jarred his memory. "I see you're clever about using scraps."

"Every scrap counts." Her smile sparkled with joy. "I can't thank you enough for talking Mr. Jefford into allowing us to have the material. He always admonishes us about the little things adding up around here. This time, those little bits of fabric will add up for the orphans."

"I thought the remnants and seconds were always donated to worthy causes."

Her brows arched. "Why, no, Sir. They're sold in the company store."

Disgust twisted through him. *Why did I expect this would be any different? Every rock I pick up has slime under it.*

At every turn, Carter discovered ways his father and the overseer squeezed every last penny of profit imaginable from the mill. How much money could one man want? His family lived in luxury, yet his father cut the wages of these women, then sold them flawed goods in order not to take a complete loss. *Yet another sin of his I need to atone for. . . .*

"Look at that," one of the women exclaimed as she walked in. "Isabel, you made another doll. Will you get to take this one home to your sisters?"

Isabel's smile faded a bit. "No, I'm afraid not."

The woman patted her arm. "It's sweet of you to send Christmas gifts to them."

"We're making dolls for the girls at Kindred Hearts. If you'd like to join us, you can come to my room any evening."

After the other woman walked off, Carter gently set the doll into Isabel's arms. He watched how she nestled it close. For some reason, she looked so right with that baby doll cradled to her bosom. Tenderhearted as she was, she'd be a very loving mother. "I could get you more fabric so you could make them for your little sisters, too."

"It's kind of you to offer, but I used my fabric allotment to do that last Christmas." The steam engines started to chuff. "I need to get back to my looms. I didn't mean to take up so much of your time."

"Hey you! Get busy. I don't pay you to angle for a husband. And you—the women are off limits. Get those last machines out of here and—" Jefford's voice came to a strangled halt when he drew close enough to see around the loom's frame.

Carter stared at him coldly. The bell to begin work hadn't yet rung. He'd seen Isabel oil her looms already, so she'd prepared for the day.

"Mr. Steadman—" Jefford stammered and cleared his throat.

"*Steadman!*" Isabel's eyes widened and the color drained from her face. A second later, two bright pink spots appeared in her cheeks. "I'm sorry I bothered you, Sir." She turned and dashed off.

Chapter 5

Carter rolled down his shirtsleeves as Jefford stammered. "Begging your pardon, Sir. I didn't realize it was you. I never would have—I mean, I was just trying to make sure. I don't let the workers flirt or trifle with one another here—"

Carter lifted a single finger, and the other man fell silent. "What time is it?"

The overseer fumbled to retrieve his pocket watch, then faltered, "Five until the hour, Sir."

Just then, the bell to begin work rang. The supervisor stepped onto his stool and pulled a cord. Above him, a leather belt shifted onto a tight pulley, and every loom in the room groaned and rattled into action. The floor rumbled beneath their feet.

Carter tilted his head and squinted at the ceiling. "Am I to assume you've weaseled five extra minutes in the morning, just as you have at the dinner hour?"

Jefford had to lean close to hear the question over the din. He shouted back, "By your father's orders!"

"Ten minutes a day, six days a week." Carter glared at him. "That's an extra hour of work each week."

"We pay them by the week, not the hour," Jefford pointed out as he shifted from one foot to the other.

"I'll have to think about how to make restitution. You're to personally adjust the chimes so they ring true to time." Carter walked off, climbed the stairs, and strode across the catwalk. He looked down at the floor of the weaving room and gritted his teeth. *How do I make up for the way these women have been cheated? Dad had so much—couldn't he at least pay them and deal with them fairly?*

The looms were operating at normal speed instead of at the frantic pace of a few days ago. As he and the workmen had spaced out the remaining looms, safe room existed for the weavers to tend to their labors. Those facts should have brought him satisfaction, but they didn't.

He looked down at Row Sixteen. At their first meeting, he hadn't revealed his identity to Isabel Shaw. He'd originally assumed she knew who he was, then refrained from introducing himself once he realized differently. At some point, he should have said something, but he hadn't. Regrets assailed him.

All she wanted to do was thank me for letting her help the orphans. . .and she got embarrassed for her sweet intentions and nice manners. She didn't get to take the dolls to her own sisters last year and doesn't plan to go see them again this Christmas. How long since she went home for a visit?

The women who worked in Lowell wore clothing comparable to fashion plates. As he came home from Europe, he'd ridden through Lowell and noted how those women, dressed in their stylish designs, could easily blend into the merchant class of the Continent. He squinted as he studied the women below him. What had Isabel said? *Beneath our aprons, many of us have tattered skirts.*

Were those words mere consolation, an exaggeration, or a revelation that the workers preferred to keep their better garments to wear away from the mill?

Then again, there seemed to be two distinctly different groups of women here. Some came to benefit from the after-work classes and library and were able to save their wages for a brother or son's education. Others—like Isabel—sent almost every last cent home to distressed families.

When the bell sounded for midday meal, Carter discreetly stood off to the side and watched the women head for the tables. He specifically came to Isabel's boardinghouse, partly because the women had already seen him there, so his presence wouldn't be cause for comment. Most of all, Carter chose that house because he found Isabel so appealing, he'd take any chance or excuse to be closer to her.

From a spot beside the door, Carter studied the sleeves and hems of the women's lint-covered gowns. He meant no disrespect, but he needed to collect facts. Jefford didn't have a sympathetic bone in his body, and the women likely wouldn't be bold enough to complain to Carter, so he silently observed the condition of their clothing. Just before he turned to leave, he watched Isabel for one last moment. Weak noontime sunlight slanted from the window and brought out the sparkle in her beautiful eyes. Even dressed in worn calico and dusted with lint, she reminded him of a queen.

Isabel lay in bed and stared at the ceiling. She couldn't get to sleep. "Kathleen?" she whispered in the dark.

"Oh, so you're awake, too?"

"Likely I'm purple from pinching myself to see if I'm awake."

Kathleen muffled her laughter. "Then you'll match the material for your new dress."

"As long as I don't match the pumpkin pie we had at supper, I'll be happy."

"Could you believe that? It's been months since we had such a meal." Kathleen folded her hands behind her head and stared at the ceiling. "Fine food and new clothes. I hardly know what to think."

Isabel rolled over and knew exactly what to think. Carter Steadman's hand and heart were behind all these changes. She stared at the fabric draped over the foot of their bed. A length of plaid in plum and two shades of blue lay there, waiting to be made into a new dress. Beside it, a dove gray-and-black stripe shimmered dully in the moonlight. Isabel selected it for Mama—since she'd been in mourning for two years, gray would be proper. Right beside those pieces, the verdant green dress length Kathleen chose for herself made a cheerful swag atop the amber calico.

"Kathleen, I ought to be ashamed for asking, but could we maybe work on our dresses tomorrow instead of the dolls? We have almost a month to go before Christmas."

Kathleen chuckled. "I was trying to find a way to ask you the same thing!"

Grace sat up and grumbled, "I'm tired. Will you just hush up? Just because you were both here long enough to get two lengths, you don't have to gloat."

Two dress lengths. . .and they weren't even to be counted against the two yards the Steadmans gave to each worker at Christmas! If that weren't enough, a grim-faced young Mr. Steadman had stood before everyone that afternoon.

"You have my personal apology. I've discovered the bells were set wrong. I've calculated you all worked about an hour extra each week."

Everyone stood in the yard, uneasy with his revelation, but careful not to voice discontent for fear Jefford or someone else would note dissenters and blacklist them.

Carter Steadman went on. "I owe the workers here restitution. Pay will be brought back up to the wages noted in my ledger from two years ago. You will each be paid double this week, and tomorrow will be a holiday for you. Just as I expect your best efforts and loyalty, I'll do my utmost to deal with you fairly."

His admission astonished Isabel. If his honesty and humility weren't enough, his restitution stunned her. The whole yard rang with cheers. Once the clamor died down, Mr. Steadman added, "For those who have worked here less than a year, you may have a dress or shirt-length of fabric. Those who've worked here longer may have two."

Lying in the dark, Isabel remembered every word he'd said. Tomorrow would be like a holiday—they'd have a day off work to use at their leisure. "Imagine, we're off on a Saturday!"

Grace threw a pillow at her. "Isabel, I declare, the minute we blow out the lamp at night, you start chattering."

"Sorry, Grace. I did that back home, too." She started to laugh. "Oops. Sorry. I was talking again."

"Mother, were you aware Father was selling the seconds and remnants to the workers instead of donating them to charity?" Carter sat across the supper table and waited for an answer.

"Why, no, Dear. We rarely discussed business." She took a sip of tea, then smiled. "You could ask Mr. Jefford. Your father trusted him implicitly."

"I don't mean to hurt your feelings, Mother. You'll hear things are changing at Steadman Textiles and for good cause. Father and Mr. Jefford agreed on despicable practices."

"Despicable? Now, Carter, I know you didn't agree with your father at times—"

"Mother, word is going to get out. I'd rather tell you these things myself than have you hear gossip from others. The workers have been cheated—blatantly cheated. The chimes didn't ring true time, so they've set to work early, gotten off late, and had shortened mealtimes. Because the Irish girls are so desperate to earn money to bring family over, the wages were dropped."

"Oh, Carter!" She placed her hand to the bodice of her black bombazine mourning gown. "This is shameful."

"I agree." He gave her a grim smile. "I'm setting things right, but I felt it only fair to warn you, there may be comments about the changes being made. I also needed to ask where the seconds used to go so we can resume donating them to worthy causes."

A frown marred her brow. "I couldn't rightly say. Since Amy Ross started running Kindred Hearts, I was certain we'd been donating material to the little orphans."

He shook his head as he sliced the savory roast beef. "I made inquiries. As a matter of fact, one of the weavers offered to sacrifice taking a length for herself so she could have material to make dolls for the children for Christmas. I rode by the orphanage today, and though the girls all looked happy as could be, they wore frocks that were patched and threadbare."

"This cannot continue—we must do something at once!"

"My thoughts precisely. I'd like to gather up some material for the children to have new frocks and small clothes. Would you like to deliver it?"

"Of course I will. I'll get buttons, ribbons, and thread, too." The creases on her forehead smoothed as the serving maid carried in dessert plates. The aroma of apples and cinnamon wafted through the room, and Carter thought that was the cause of his mother's pleasure until she coyly added, "I could ask Belinda Atherton to accompany me. You missed seeing her daughters, Carter. They're both comely girls and quite accomplished."

"Mother, please don't try to play matchmaker."

"Someone has to. I want grandchildren, Carter. It's high time for you to marry a nice girl and start a family."

"I suppose you have a bevy of suitable prospects." He sighed.

"Now that you mention it. . ."

"Hold on." Carter held up both hands in a horrified gesture. "The mill is going to keep me busy for some time. I'd like to ask if you'd help me with the charity issues instead of parading eligible girls by the door at every opportunity."

"I could do both, you know."

Chapter 6

Two girls bracketed Isabel on the shabby red velvet settee in the orphanage's parlor. She worked with each of them as they cross-stitched alphabet samplers while she cuddled little Betty on her lap. "Alys, you did a wonderful job on that line. You're running out of floss. Knot that and rethread your needle. What color would you like to use?"

"Rose, please. It's so pretty!"

"Aye, now." Ginger's knitting needles clacked in a steady rhythm. "That's our Alys for you—always loving rose the best. I always know 'tis her comin' me way when I see her pink dress."

Kathleen winked at Isabel. They'd arranged with Amy and Ginger to give them hints about the girls and what colors to use for their dolls.

One of the older girls sat on the floor, whipstitching an orange patch she'd cleverly cut to look like a fish to cover a small hole in the bodice of a little dress. Kathleen sat on another settee, cradling the baby and helping the twins with their samplers.

A few minutes later, Amy lifted Ruthie onto a small cherry wood end table so she could measure her dress to see how many inches of a strip from a flour sack she needed to insert to stretch it to a decent length.

When someone knocked on the door, Mary hopped up. "I'll get it, Auntie Amy." A second later, Isabel heard her squeak, "Mr. Steadman!"

A minute later, Carter Steadman and his mother came into the parlor. He smoothly reached down, helped Amy to her feet, and greeted her warmly. "I'm so sorry to hear you lost Jason. He was such a good friend and a fine man. He'd be proud of you for opening your heart and home to all of these little girls."

Amy gave him a warm smile, and her voice barely quavered at all. "Mrs. Steadman and Carter, what a lovely surprise. I miss Jason terribly, and I'm so sorry for your loss as well."

"I should stop clackin' these needles and get tea, Aunt Amy." Ginger set aside her knitting and chuckled softly as she rose. "I recall me dear granny saying tea is better than sympathy."

Mrs. Steadman managed a watery little laugh. "Tea would be lovely."

"While you visit, I'll take care of things," Carter Steadman murmured to his mother. He then nodded politely to Isabel. "Miss Isabel, it looks like your little friends are talented with their needles."

"Yes, they are." She hoped she didn't sound too silly. Seeing him at the orphanage shocked her.

He turned and greeted Kathleen by name, then met

Veronica. To his credit, he didn't treat them as lowly weavers in his factory. His manners were impeccable, and he managed to momentarily excuse himself while they all tried to cover their surprise with small talk.

Moments later, he came back inside the parlor with two large, paper-wrapped packages under his arms. He set them down, left, and returned with two more.

Quite commendably, Amy had taught her charges fine manners. Two of the older ones took the initiative to bring in chairs from the dining room, and the twins had already hopped up so Mrs. Steadman could sit on the settee with Kathleen. Though the girls desperately wanted to know what the packages contained, none of them asked. As Carter straightened up from setting down the additional packages, Alys popped off the settee she shared with Isabel. "You can have my place, Sir. I'll go help with the teacups!"

Isabel couldn't quite imagine sitting next to her employer. Their social circles didn't overlap. She started to rise. "I'll help—"

"I'm sure Amy has plenty of help in the kitchen already, Miss Isabel." Carter smiled at her, then brushed his knuckles over Alys's cheek. "Thank you for the seat, Little One." As Alys giggled and skipped off, Carter started to lower his tall frame onto the dainty settee.

"Wait!"

He jolted up straight and gave Isabel a baffled look.

"The needle," she warned. "Alys stuck her needle in the cushion."

He chuckled. "Better this needle than one of the wicked-looking knitting needles that lively redhead was wielding!"

Isabel hugged Betty a bit closer and reached to pluck the needle from the cushion. His fingers and hers met. "Better no needle at all," she said as she pulled her hand back.

He sat beside her, and Isabel tried to tuck in her full skirts, but holding Betty made it impossible. So did the horsehair crinoline and flannel petticoats. Seemingly oblivious to the way the full skirts of her Sunday-best, cabbage rose dress brushed his pant leg, he turned his wide shoulders a bit and gently threaded his fingers through Betty's curls. "This must be Betty."

"Why, Carter, however did you guess?" Amy asked.

"Miss Isabel described her perfectly." He looked about the room. "She told me each of the girls at Kindred Hearts is very special."

Isabel let out a relieved breath. She'd feared for a moment that he'd accidentally say something about the dolls and ruin the girls' Christmas surprise.

"That's Isabel, to be sure. Always has a kind word on her lips," Amy said.

"'Specially at nighttime," Kathleen tacked on. "Blow out the lamps, and she chatters like a magpie!"

All the girls giggled, and Carter gave Isabel an amused look, then winked. "*Some* of us know when to keep quiet."

Isabel couldn't help laughing. She relaxed a bit and watched as the girls hastened to show Mrs. Steadman their sewing projects. Amy and Kathleen kept a steady patter of conversation, so Isabel decided she'd better put this lone man in a room full of women and girls at ease.

"We're so grateful for the changes you've made at the mill, Sir."

"I've done nothing other than give the workers their due." He let out a long, heavy breath. "I have a lot to atone for."

Isabel gathered Betty a bit closer and murmured softly, "Sir, you're making changes—good, fair changes. None of us holds you to account for what your father did."

"God does."

She gave him a startled look. "I don't understand—"

"The sins of the father are visited upon the son. The Bible states it clearly. I'm doing my best to make amends." His jaw hardened, and he shook his head. "I didn't mean to mention any of this. Forgive me."

Isabel blinked at him in utter astonishment. His admission caught her completely off guard. Unsure what to think of such a declaration, she shifted her hand a bit to subtly pat his upper arm. "Please don't apologize for saying what weighs heavy on your heart. The Bible tells us to bear one another's burdens."

He wound one of Betty's curls around his forefinger. "I still have plenty to do." He untwisted the ringlet and started to play with another as he changed the subject. "Do you come here often?"

"Every Sunday afternoon. Kathleen comes, too. I love children."

He looked about the parlor and studied the girls. One by one, they showed his mother their sewing projects and beamed at the praise she lavished upon them. "Sixteen girls," he mused.

"I don't know how she manages it."

"Amy has them organized and does a wonderful job. We come to help with sewing, but I always go back to the boardinghouse feeling like she and her girls gave more to me."

Betty stirred, so Isabel readjusted her a bit and smoothed down her butter yellow frock. She still couldn't quite fathom that an important man like him had remembered something as inconsequential as a little orphan's name.

"She must be heavy. Would you like me to carry her to bed?"

"Oh, thank you, but no. Betty takes her nap in my lap each Sunday. The baby Kathleen is holding is Betty's little sister. Someone offered to adopt the baby, but Amy wants to keep them together. Betty has already lost her parents. . . ."

"Excuse me, Mr. Steadman." Ginger's voice sounded over a chorus of giggles. "Susannah was asking you if you'd be takin' a wee bit o' cream or sugar in your tea."

"Now let's see. . . ." He drew out the words as he stared at the ceiling and tapped a finger on the cleft in his chin. That finger came away and delved into the pocket of his coat. He pulled out a small paper packet. A distinct, sweet fragrance wafted from it. "This time of year, I always like to have peppermint in my tea. Would anyone else like to try one?"

Like a flock of sparrows after a fistful of crumbs, the girls flitted to him. He winked and told the first, "Give one to each of the ladies for me. If you put it in the cup before Mrs. Ross pours the tea—"

"Who's Mrs. Ross?" a little voice piped up.

"Auntie Amy," whispered another.

Carter pretended not to notice and continued, "The hot tea will melt the peppermint and sweeten your cup."

"Auntie Amy," Ruthie asked, "may we do the thing for them?"

Amy gave her girls an indulgent smile. "Perhaps another time."

"What thing?" Mrs. Steadman asked.

"They've been acting out parts of the Christmas story each evening."

"Could we do it, please?" Patty begged. "The man could be Joseph. We never got a real man to be Joseph before."

Carter leaned forward and looked past Isabel, straight into Patty's big blue eyes. "I've never been Joseph. What do I have to do?"

"You have to forget what everyone else thinks and care about what Gods wants you to do. You take Mary on a trip, but you walk and let her ride the donkey 'cuz she's tired. Next, you get to kneel by Baby Jesus. Then you're 'posed to feel lucky 'cuz He's good, so He forgives you even when you done bad things in the past. See? That's God's Christmas present to us."

In a matter of moments, Carter Steadman, owner of the influential Steadman Textile Mill, had a clump of little girls surrounding him. He played his part with notable enthusiasm and skill. He didn't even bat an eye when the wagon became a donkey. With true gallantry, he lifted "Mary" on and off the "donkey," then tenderly helped her wrap a doll in a blanket. Isabel smiled as he calmly hiked one of the twins onto his shoulder so she'd stop whacking him whilst she flapped her arms as angel wings.

When he knelt at the crate that served as the manger, he didn't fold his hands in prayer. Instead, he spread his arms wide. The "animals," "Mary," and another angel all crowded in to be included in his hug. In a rich baritone, he began to sing, "While Shepherds Watched Their Flocks by Night." Everyone joined in.

Isabel mouthed the song, but the words didn't register. Instead, she ached for her employer. He knew the Christmas story, but he hadn't fully accepted its meaning. He'd been so busy trying to atone for his father's wrongs and earn his place in God's kingdom, he hadn't allowed himself to accept the gift of grace God provided by giving His Son. If only he could understand God appreciated deeds done in love, but they weren't necessary for atonement. The price was paid—and represented right there in front of him in the form of a blanket-wrapped doll.

Carter Steadman's rich baritone contrasted with the girls' sweet sopranos, and the words finally registered in Isabel's heart. "Good will henceforth from heav'n to men, Begin and never cease, Begin and never cease."

Lord, please loosen the chains in his heart and make him feel free to accept Your good will.

After Kathleen blew out the lamp that night, Isabel heard her humming that same tune. She closed her eyes and promised herself she wouldn't talk tonight—but it was so hard to stay silent. Memories of how her employer had humbly knelt on a tattered carpet and pretended with those girls tugged at her heart.

He'd been trying so hard to prove to himself and everyone else that he wasn't going to be like his father, and his methods of restitution could only be considered more than generous. In the past two weeks, he'd increased their pay, given them an extra day off, provided cloth, and made sure the meals improved considerably.

Couldn't he see he'd never be like his father? Carter Steadman displayed too much integrity, too much humility to ever put himself or greed above others. Odd, how he'd already proven the vast difference between his ways and his father's, yet he hadn't proven it to himself.

Isabel snuggled deeper under her covers. If only he'd stayed long enough to watch the girls open his packages! Instead, he'd escorted his mother from the orphanage without saying a word about the paper-wrapped bundles he'd delivered. Amy waited until the girls cleared away the teacups and plates, then she clipped the strings on the first package.

A veritable rainbow of fabrics and ribbons and a wealth of buttons spilled out. The girls squealed with glee, and Amy's pretty gray eyes went silver with tears of gratitude. If only Carter Steadman could have seen the joy his gift gave to others. . .and if only he could accept that God gave His gifts as freely. Just as the girls hadn't earned a thing from their benefactor, so he would never earn a thing from God. No matter how hard he tried, how many good deeds he performed, God's infinite grace was all that mattered.

Father, reveal Yourself to him. Free him from the bonds of his past and let him come to understand the sweetness of Your Christmas Gift. Reach his heart and teach him we are reconciled through Christ, not through our works.

"Isabel?" Kathleen propped up on her elbow and whispered, "Are you talking to yourself again?"

"Praying."

Kathleen muffled a giggle. "I'm praying, too—that no one asks you to sing a duet in church with Mr. Steadman."

Chapter 7

Production is dropping," Jefford grumbled as he walked through the weaving room. "The carding, spinning, and weaving have all slowed down."

"Quality is much higher," Carter countered. "With the No. 30 yarn, we get thirty yards of cloth per loom per day. It sells for more. Printworks are putting out extraordinary designs, too."

"Hmmpf." Jefford cast a surly look out the window. "Winter means fewer hours at the looms. During summer, we get fourteen, but now—"

"Ten now." Carter's voice went steely. "Eleven in the summer. No more."

"Profits are going to drop. Can't run a successful business like this. You cut their hours, increased their pay, and slowed production. Your father—"

Carter's hands clenched into fists at his side. "My father's choices are not mine."

Jefford shrugged. "You own the place." He cast a look about the weaving room, then said, "We're in for more change, too.

Daisy is leaving to be married. I'll need to appoint a new head weaver."

"Kathleen McKenna."

Brows furrowed, Jefford shook his head. "I had my eye on a few others."

I have no doubt you did, Carter thought sourly. He'd already considered several possibilities. Isabel was exceedingly patient—which made her an excellent trainer. Still, the women looked to Kathleen to speak for them. She'd represented them well regarding a concern over a problem with badly wound bobbins last week, and she had a level head on her shoulders. Carter wanted a Christian woman who would be diligent and loyal to him. He wasn't about to let Jefford plant someone in that position.

Jefford shifted and pushed the issue. "I know these women. Decisions like this take extensive knowledge—"

"Kathleen McKenna," Carter ordered implacably.

"Your own father passed her by last year when the position opened."

"Mr. Jefford, if one of the employees goes counter to your order, what becomes of her?"

"I dismiss her at once."

"In that aspect, we are alike." Carter stared pointedly at the overseer. "I've given you an order."

Carter walked away. Machines around them muffled Jefford's comment, but Carter made out, "just like your father." Though tempted to wheel around and fire him, Carter resisted the urge. He refused to rage as his father so often had.

His boots pounded out every step toward the office with

determination. *I will not be like my father. I refuse to. Bad enough, the sins of the father are passed on to the sons. I have enough to atone for. When I have a son, I want his legacy to be blameless.* He looked around. What more could he do to expunge his father's greedy acts?

"How are you doing on the dolls?"

Isabel looked up and gave her employer a smile as she swallowed a bite of fresh, fried codfish. He often passed by and spoke to the women. He frequently came to her table, but since he'd assigned Kathleen as head weaver, it made sense that he'd sometimes show up at their boardinghouse to contact her. Still, he must have a warm heart, because he not only checked with Kathleen about some detail about the day's order or a problem, he'd also chat for a few moments about something quite ordinary and pleasant.

He chuckled. "I caught you with your mouth full."

Isabel smiled after she swallowed. "We need to put the finishing touches on just a few more dolls, then we'll be done. The girls will be so happy, Sir."

"I've no doubt of that."

"Amy is allowing the older girls to stay up a bit later so they can make a dress for the dolls. That way, they get to be part of the secret."

He nodded, then asked, "What of those girls?"

"Aprons. We've made one for each of them." Isabel averted her gaze. Staring at this handsome man defied propriety.

He lifted her hand and ran the pad of his thumb over her

fingers. "You must be nimble-fingered to get so much done."

Isabel looked up at him, startled at his touch. Her hand tingled and her heart sped up at that light contact.

"Aye, and look at how pretty her new dress is," Kathleen chimed in.

"Very becoming, indeed."

"Thank you, Sir," Isabel mumbled as she pulled her hand free from his disturbing hold. "All of us are grateful for your generosity."

"You have laudable skills with the loom and needle." He never took his eyes off her. Though his words could have included every woman in the boardinghouse's dining hall, Isabel fought the notion that he meant to aim them specifically at her. Yet he maintained eye contact. "You earned that fabric."

"Your surprise delighted Amy and the girls," Isabel murmured.

His mouth crooked into a rakish grin. "So I gathered. She wrote me a note, and the girls got together and drew a picture of our nativity play." He turned to Kathleen. "As for you, Miss Kathleen—you displayed admirable expertise that afternoon when you organized them for the play."

Kathleen shrugged. "Amy needed to tend the baby. I'm accustomed to herding my brothers and sisters about." She accepted the bowl of succotash. "Ma always said I had a bossy streak."

His lighthearted chuckle and the fact that he'd addressed another worker eased Isabel's uneasiness. She spread butter on a slice of hot-from-the-oven bread. "You made a wonderful

Joseph, Sir. It's hard to say who enjoyed the Christmas pageant you put on more—the girls or the adults who served as the audience. Your voice is exceptional. If you attend church regularly, Parson Hull will be after you to sing a special."

He gave her a baffled look. "Of course I'll attend each Sunday."

Isabel cringed. She'd meant no offense, but since his father rarely attended, she hadn't been sure if the new owner was much of a churchgoer.

Before she could say anything, he added, "Perhaps you'd like to make that a duet with me, Miss Isabel."

She felt her cheeks go hot as she laughed self-consciously. "Sir, my singing is likely to cause parishioners to seek repentance so they can put an end to such punishment."

He chuckled as he walked away.

Kathleen nudged Isabel and murmured, "I think he's sweet on you."

Isabel dropped her fork. "Kathleen!"

"I'm serious. He's quite a catch."

"Not for me. I'm just a worker; he owns the whole place." Isabel hissed, "So help me, Kathleen, don't you dare breathe another word of that nonsense. He's far above my station, and that kind of scandal could get me dismissed. My family needs me to work—"

"If you married him, you'd have plenty of money," Kathleen singsonged under her breath.

"The day I marry, it will be for love, not money." She sighed. "But I doubt that day will ever come."

Isabel fingered the golden ribbon after she slipped Mama's most recent letter into the packet. Just because Isabel wrote and told her of the changes at the mill, Mama's letter now asked questions a simple mill girl couldn't answer about her employer. . .she hinted such a man would make a fine husband. Between Mama's note and Kathleen's teasing, Isabel worried maybe she'd somehow revealed the secret feelings she'd begun to have for him. The very thought anyone might detect she felt a special fondness for him terrified her. What if she were so transparent, she was making a fool of herself and he detected it?

In the privacy of her room, for just a moment, she allowed her imagination to fly free about Mama and Kathleen's opinions regarding Mr. Steadman's interest in her. Surely, they were wrong. Still, thoughts tumbled through her mind. *Oh, to have such a fine man interested in me, to call me his own! I long to be married and have children. . . .*

Isabel shook her head. Carter Steadman was so unreachable, he might as well be in China. He'd wed some wealthy young darling of high society. Imagining for even a moment that someone of his class would stoop beneath his station to court a mill girl would lead only to heartbreak.

Isabel shoved the drawer shut, walked over to the small bedside table, and moved the candlestick aside. She took a sheet of foolscap from the drawer and dipped her pen. "Dearest Mama," she began. A wave of loneliness washed over her.

"Carter, I'm counting on you to come speak to my Missionary

Benevolence Meeting this week."

Carter hung up his coat and gave his mother a wry look. "I scarcely think the women would consider England a heathen country. Why would my trip there be germane to mission work?"

Her smile drooped, and it caused him a pang. She'd endured months of grief alone, waiting for word to reach him and for him to return home. Even now, she permitted herself only very limited social connections. Carter crossed the floor with a few long strides and gave her a kiss on the cheek. "But for you, I'll do it."

Wednesday, Carter plastered on a smile and accepted a third cup of tea as he juggled his fork and a plate loaded with a mountain of tea cakes and silly looking confections. If the Atherton girls didn't drown him in tea, Blanche Smythe might well bury him under desserts. Every last mama and eligible daughter in town filled the main floor of the Steadman home. "Excuse me, ladies," he murmured as he swam through a sea of skirts that swirled like the colored glass shards of a kaleidoscope.

"Carter," Mrs. Henly gushed just before he reached the door, "your talk positively inspired us—didn't it, Elizabeth?"

Elizabeth's fat sausage curls bounced as she emphatically nodded her head and hastily swallowed something. The years of Carter's absence hadn't treated Elizabeth kindly. Gawky and gap-toothed, she didn't shine among the butterfly set of Massachusetts society.

Carter wanted nothing to do with this after-speech parade of prospective wives, but he'd always held a rather tender spot in his heart for Elizabeth. He forced himself to remain long enough to exchange a few inane pleasantries, and the look of sheer gratitude on her face tugged at his heart.

"Oh, Mr. Steadman!" Blanche Smythe headed toward him with another plate of food.

Elizabeth deftly swiped the first plate from Carter and handed it to her mother, then snatched his teacup and emptied it in the potted palm. Though she hid her smile behind her fan, the twinkle in her eyes let him know their childhood friendship had endured.

Carter tilted his head back, let out a full-throated laugh, and barely waited for Blanche to reach them. "Ladies, you must excuse me for leaving you, but I have matters I must attend at the mill." He nodded at Elizabeth. "It was especially nice to see you again, Miss Henly."

He made his escape and headed for the mill. That whole morning might have been a fiasco, but Elizabeth's assistance made it worth the lost time. It did him good to see her sense of humor was just as sharp as it had been when they were children. He chuckled to himself, then sobered again at the blatant truth: Mother wanted him wed, and she'd no doubt make it a crusade. He'd gotten an updated look at the girls she fancied as candidates, and not a one appealed to him. When the time came for him to marry, he didn't care for silks, pearls, and curls. He wanted a woman with heart.

A woman like Isabel Shaw.

Snow started to fall, and he lengthened his stride. Isabel. He'd been enchanted with her from their first meeting. She'd been so embarrassed when she discovered his identity, he knew full well she had no designs on him. Indeed, she'd about died ten deaths when he sat on the settee next to her at the orphanage. He walked past the buildings and headed into the office. After closing the door, he prayed, "Father, make Your will known to me regarding a wife. Give me a wife who delights in the Word and adorns herself with love and humility instead of braids and pearls."

Just then, a knock interrupted him. "Sir? Mr. Steadman—are you there?"

"Yes." He turned as the door opened. Isabel Shaw stood in the opening.

Chapter 8

"Your cousin's ship docked early," Isabel announced as she looked down at her employer, sitting behind his desk.

"Which one?"

"Maxwell." As soon as she identified which cousin, Isabel realized he wanted to know which ship. She hastily added, "This time, it's the *Resolute.* The *Reliant* isn't due for almost two weeks."

Carter nodded. "That makes sense. Last I heard, the *Steadfast* was bound for Europe. Did you come just to tell me Maxwell is here?"

Embarrassed she'd been so caught up in his presence that she failed to give the full message, Isabel blurted out, "Kathleen's busy with a jammed shuttle, so Mr. Jefford sent me. He wants permission to speed up the looms and keep us late so we can meet the order."

Isabel watched as her employer rose from behind his desk. She'd always been self-conscious about her height, but around him, she felt almost dainty.

He reached for his greatcoat and hat, then frowned. "Where is your wrap?"

"Oh." She let out a small laugh as she brushed a few errant snowflakes from her sleeve. "I just dashed over. Since Mr. Jefford, himself, tripped the levers to stop my looms, I presumed I'd best make haste."

"Going from the heat of the weaving room to the cold of a snowstorm is liable to cause you a nasty chill." He draped his heavy coat about her. "Let's go see what Maxwell and Jefford want."

Though she could have demurred and refused the coat, Isabel relished its warmth. She grabbed the lapels and held it shut as Mr. Steadman walked by her side, across the courtyard, and into the weaving room. Once there, she started to shed the coat; but Mr. Steadman rested his huge hands on her shoulders and kept it in place as he looked for Jefford. He dipped his head so his lips almost brushed her ear as he half-shouted, "Did he mention where we should meet?"

"No, Sir. Your cousin—the Shipping Steadman—"

Even over the clatter and roar of machinery, she could hear him laugh. "The Shipping Steadman?"

Isabel nodded and amusement threaded through her. "They've named each of you Steadmans, you know. You're the Cotton Steadman, Mr. Maxwell is the Shipping Steadman, and his brother is Little Steadman."

"Lucas wouldn't appreciate that. He'll be out of medical school soon. I rather doubt he'll want to be considered as anything other than Dr. Steadman."

Just then, Mr. Jefford and Maxwell Steadman came over. Isabel tried to ignore the odd, assessing looks in their eyes as they spied Carter's hands upon her shoulders and her still burrowed in the folds of his wondrously warm coat. She shed the greatcoat at once.

Before she could slip back to her machines, the Shipping Steadman bellowed above the din, "So you're Isabel. Aunt Vivian told me to send you home to her. The carriage is out by the west entrance for you."

"What's this?" Carter asked.

Maxwell shrugged. A rapscallion's smile tilted his mouth. "At sea, everyone follows my orders; on land, everyone follows your mother's."

Isabel cast a baffled glance at both cousins, then looked at Mr. Jefford. "My looms—"

"Go," he barked.

"Get your coat and bonnet first," Carter ordered.

"Yes, Sir." She scurried away, confused by this odd turn of events.

Isabel nestled the doll in her arms as she stood on a splendid Turkish carpet in the ornate Steadman parlor. Large gilt-framed portraits, elegant chandeliers, and russet velvet draperies made this place look more like a palace than a home. A handful of servants quietly set the mansion to rights in the aftermath of some sort of party, but one of the maids had shown her here. Isabel couldn't decide whether she should sit or stand as she waited for Mrs. Steadman to arrive. She'd never spoken to Mrs. Steadman other than that Sunday when they'd chanced to meet at the orphanage. *Why did she send for me, and why did the driver stop off at the boardinghouse and make me go get this doll?*

"Isabel, how lovely to see you."

Isabel spun at the sound of the dulcet voice and saw Mrs. Steadman entering the room. Isabel smiled. "Mrs. Steadman, I–I. . ."

"Do have a seat." Mrs. Steadman gestured toward an elegant floral tapestry chair by the marble fireplace and took the matching chair, which sat at a close angle. "I've asked for tea to warm us."

"How gracious of you."

Mrs. Steadman leaned a bit closer. The whisper of her black silk mourning gown and scent of her expensive French perfume underscored her social standing, yet she almost greedily reached for the doll. "May I, please?"

"Of course." Isabel handed over the little doll she'd finished making only the night before. Designed to resemble Patty, it bore blue eyes and carroty hair. "We're making them for the little girls at Kindred Hearts."

"Ohhh," Mrs. Steadman breathed, "she's adorable. Simply adorable." She played with the yarn braids, examined the embroidered features, and admired the ruffled little dress. "You sew magnificently."

"Thank you, Ma'am."

"When Carter told me what you were doing, I hoped I

might have finally found someone to help me." Mrs. Steadman carefully propped the doll beside her as if she were a treasured friend instead of a bit of yarn and remnant cloth. Then she lifted a basket from beside her chair. "I have the dolls that belonged to my grandmother and mother, as well as my own. I fear they were more loved than cared for."

Puzzled, Isabel sat and waited for her to continue.

"Here." Mrs. Steadman withdrew a porcelain-faced doll. Though the head was still in good condition, the dress needed mending, and a detached porcelain leg had been tied about the waist with some twine. "This was Grandmama's. I was hoping maybe you could repair her."

Isabel examined all three dolls. She nodded confidently. "Yes, all three can be mended. They're delightful."

"Oh, wonderful! You must begin as soon as we finish our tea."

Isabel reverently ran her finger over the belt on one of the older dolls. "My grandmother carried a ribbon similar to this in her bridal bouquet. It carried the same embossed roses, but it was gold, not silver."

"Oh, so she kept it?"

"Yes. My mother used it in her bouquet, too." Isabel forced a bright smile, though deep inside she felt a twang of sadness for the fact that for her, the ribbon would hold letters instead of a bridal bouquet. "I should be able to fix these pretty little dolls quite quickly."

"Oh, no. Don't rush. I want you to take your time. Clearly, you're deft with a needle, but I confess I'm a bit lonely these days." She waved her hand dismissively. "Missionary Benevolence met here today, yet now that everyone has gone home, the house feels all that much more empty."

Isabel gave her a sad smile. "My condolences for your loss."

Mrs. Steadman blinked a few times and took a bracing breath. Her smile trembled a bit. "Stitch slowly, my dear. I'd count it a favor."

"And precisely what schemes are you up to now, Mother?"

She laughed merrily and patted his shoulder. "Now, Carter, never let it be said I've ignored your preferences. I saw the way you looked at Isabel at the orphanage. I'd have to be blind to miss the way you lit up in her presence. When all of the young ladies were here for the missionary meeting, you didn't show a speck of interest in anyone other than Elizabeth Henly, and you've always been like a doting brother to her."

He quirked a brow and stayed silent. She hadn't wasted a moment. He'd barely escaped from that gaggle of socialites before Mother sent for Isabel.

"I'm determined to see you happily wed and make sure that I have several grandbabies to cuddle. Clearly, you cannot court Isabel at the mill, so I've concocted a perfectly legitimate reason for her to be here. You'll simply show up for supper, and after dining, we'll visit before you escort her to the boardinghouse."

"Mind you, I'm not complaining in the least, but I confess, I am surprised. I have distinct recollections of Father talking about how Grandfather disowned Uncle Esau for marrying beneath him."

Mother sighed. "That was a shameful chapter in the family history—not on Esau's part, but on your grandfather's. Esau's bride was a charming girl who came from a sound family, but your grandfather wanted him to marry to bind the Steadmans to another society family. He put money and power above his son's happiness. More the fool, he."

"I don't know Isabel well enough—"

"Which is why I'll arrange for you to spend plenty of time with her here. It will all be quite proper."

Carter bent down and brushed a kiss on his mother's cheek. "You've made my life far easier. Now instead of having to divide my time between convincing you she'd make a worthy wife and courting her, I'll have you as an ally and be free to direct my attentions on her alone."

His mother laughed. "You're already so smitten, the girl hasn't a chance."

"Yes, the last one is finished." Isabel set down her fork and blotted her lips with the napkin. After two days, she'd lovingly repaired all three dolls.

"Not quite." Mrs. Steadman shook her head. "I sent Bernice to the attic. She found Grandmama's doll trunk. There's another doll, and several of her little frocks are in dire need of restoration."

Carter chuckled. "Isabel, once Mother gets a notion in her head, it's impossible to divert her."

Beneath the table, Isabel pleated her skirts with her fingers. Though the days here were far easier and Mrs. Steadman's company quite pleasant, the best part of the arrangement was the wonderful evening meals spent with Carter. He was so interesting and easy to converse with.

Nonetheless, this couldn't continue. Isabel had obligations to meet. She ventured, "Perhaps I could take one piece back to the room with me and work on it each night after I'm done at the mill."

"Oh, I simply couldn't bear to have those taken from under my roof."

Carter frowned at Isabel. "Are you unhappy here?"

Heat flooded her cheeks. "Oh, no, Sir!" Her fingers clenched tightly together, trapping the material into a scrunched ball. *I'm never happier than in your presence. . . .* She tamped down that thought before it imprudently left her lips. She had no call to be mooning over any man—let alone her employer! Embarrassing as this was, she had to stick to business and speak up—for Mama's sake.

"Then what is it?"

Isabel trained her gaze on the handsome cleft in his chin and cleared her throat. "I need to work. For my family. Mama—"

"Just a minute." He leaned forward and locked eyes with her. The candleglow made his hazel eyes look like molten gold. "Of course you're to draw wages for sewing."

"I should have realized. . . ." Playing with a jet button at her throat in agitation, Mrs. Steadman gave her an apologetic look. "I'll send a note to Mr. Jefford at once. He'll see to it, Dear." She then turned to her son. "Our Isabel sends her wages home to her mother and three little sisters."

"I'll speak with Jefford directly." Carter must have sensed her discomfort in discussing the crass matter of finances at the table, so he mercifully changed the topic of conversation. "It occurred to me this afternoon as we reset the looms in Building Three to do toweling that if Amy's girls needed clothing, she probably could use towels."

"Sheets, too, Son," Mrs. Steadman urged.

They moved on to the parlor for a leisurely after-supper discussion, and the Steadmans asked Isabel several questions about the orphanage. Though both huge and lavishly appointed, the mansion seemed warm and comfortable. Isabel truly enjoyed retiring to the parlor with them and sitting by the fireplace, conversing for an hour or so each evening.

Carter eventually cast a look at the window. "It's not snowing now. Would you rather I take you back in the carriage, or would you like to walk tonight, Isabel?"

"Oh, I can walk alone, Sir."

"Piffle! Carter, walk her home. A bit of fresh air would do you both good. Isabel, Bernice found my mother's pelisse when she went to the attic. It's warmer than yours. I insist you use it. We can't have you catch a chill. She was a stately woman, just like you—willowy and tall. It should suit you perfectly."

When Carter helped her into the midnight blue pelisse, Isabel felt like a princess. "Oh, this is too grand," she whispered. "Mrs. Steadman, I don't think you should loan it to me."

"I don't think so, either." Mrs. Steadman smiled. "It's not a loan. I want you to keep it." She laughed at Isabel's gasp. "Dear, that fits as though it were made for you. I'm so pleased it suits you so well."

"Please explain to her," Isabel begged Carter.

"There's no one here who can wear it, Isabel." Carter gently lifted the hood over her hair and let his fingers linger on the fabric at her temples for a moment. "Besides, a beautiful woman like you deserves pretty things."

Chapter 9

As if the gift of the garment hadn't been enough of a shock, Carter Steadman's compliment completely overwhelmed Isabel. Before she could stammer out her thanks, Mrs. Steadman bustled between them and gave her a quick embrace. "I'll see you in the morning. Now off with you."

Moments later, Isabel walked alongside her employer. The scent of chimney smoke filled the crisp air. Moonlight sparkled on the new fallen snow that crunched beneath their boots. Her new pelisse warmed her heart every bit as much as her body. "Your mother is such a kind woman."

"Yes, she is. How she and my father ever wed is beyond me. For every thread of kindness she wove, he unrolled a bolt of oppression." He held aside a branch so she wouldn't snag on it.

"Mr. Steadman—"

"Call me Carter, Isabel—at least away from the mill."

She looked at him, then nodded. Was this an invitation for her to say what was on her heart? She'd felt God pushing her to tell Carter something, but if he took it the wrong way, it could ruin the unique friendship they'd begun to forge. Not only that, he was still her employer, and if she offended him, it could threaten her job. *But Carter's not that kind of man. . . .*

Isabel cast a glance at him. "Carter, might I say something personal?"

He stopped and gave her a heart-melting smile. "You can say anything you'd like."

God, please give me the words. . . . "You mentioned something back at the orphanage, and it's bothered me."

"What was that?"

"You feel the sins of the father are visited upon the son. I think you're working far too hard to try to buy your way into God's good graces."

He frowned. "The Bible is clear about the legacy a father leaves."

"True, it was. . .in the Old Testament. In the New Testament, Christ made a new covenant. God claims us as His children by grace. Any of our works and deeds are simply to be an offering of thanks and a help to one another. Your father's sins were his, Carter; God looks on your soul and knows your heart. He'd never punish you for your father's deeds."

"I'm not blameless."

"None of us are. None of us gets what we deserve. If we did, we'd all be doomed. Instead, we are saved by grace."

"Of course we are."

"I don't mean to judge you, but I wonder if you've given Him your soul, but not your heart."

He gave her a baffled look. "What do you mean?"

Isabel drew in a bracing breath as she prayed for the Lord to use her. Carter hadn't cut her off so far—in fact, he was pursuing the conversation. Had the Holy Spirit been preparing his heart for this very conversation?

Carter reached up and gently tugged her hood a bit closer about her. "Isabel, I told you, you could say anything you wanted to."

"Christ paid the price already, Carter. Nothing you do will add to His sacrifice."

"I know that. I've accepted Christ, Isabel."

"When you accepted Him, God forgave all. From the things you say, I get the feeling you claim the pardon from sin; but walking with Him can be so much more than that—it is receiving the Father's love and consolation."

Carter grimaced and let his hands drop to his sides. "My own father was harsh. Thinking of God as my Father brings to mind reproof, not compassion."

"Maybe it's time for you to leave the past behind." Isabel grabbed his hands and squeezed them. "Stop letting yesterday be an anchor that causes you pain and regret. You accepted His pardon; I'd love to see you experience His peace."

Sunday passed. Though the others all reported to the mill on Monday, Isabel went to the Steadmans' home. For the next three evenings, Carter walked her back to the boardinghouse. Each time, he offered his arm so she wouldn't slip on the icy ground; but as they neared the boardinghouse, he took care to keep his hands clasped behind his back so he'd not give anyone cause to tease Isabel or cast aspersions on her character.

That restraint cost him dearly. He'd far rather hold her hand or wrap his arm about her shoulders. The most he allowed himself was to help her with her hood—it allowed him a fleeting opportunity to feel the softness of her luxurious hair. Yielding to his attraction would put them both in an impossible position, so he governed his actions.

Each evening, they spoke more openly about a number of things. He asked about her family and she heard about his years in England. They spoke about the mill and the orphanage, but she never again brought up spiritual matters. Carter felt grateful she left him to ponder those matters on his own. Intensely personal as they were, he needed time to contemplate what she'd said and meditate over what the Bible revealed.

Now as he walked her back to the boardinghouse, he quietly said, "I need to go out of town for a few days. I worry about Mother being alone, and she enjoys your companionship. Are you going to the orphanage after church on Sunday?"

"Yes."

Carter waited for a moment, but because she made no offer, he forged ahead. "Why don't you invite her to go with you?"

Isabel gave him a startled look. "Sir, that isn't done."

"Isabel, you and she get along so well. Because she's in mourning, she isn't socializing except for church-related events. She'd be glad to have an opportunity to get out."

"But I'm just a mill girl."

Carter shook his head and tilted her face up to his. "How can you be so wise about forgiveness, yet you ignore all the verses about us all being equal in God's sight?"

"Even if I got beyond that, others wouldn't. Your mother is a fine lady. The women in her social circle are far above—"

"You underestimate your worth," he growled. Tempted to dip his head and brand her with a kiss, Carter denied himself. Instead, he gruffly took her arm and quickened his pace to the boardinghouse. When he returned home from this trip, he was going to set Miss Isabel Shaw straight.

Fired? Isabel couldn't believe her ears. She tilted her head to the side and faintly said, "I beg your pardon?"

Mr. Jefford leaned forward in the chair and set his beefy hands on top of Mr. Steadman's desk. He'd called her in to the office, and she'd wondered what he was up to. He snarled, "You heard me, all right. I told you to pack your belongings and be out of the boardinghouse by supper."

"But why?" His leer gave her the shivers.

"You knew the rules when you signed on. We demand our women be of the highest moral quality. It's come to my attention you're keeping company with a gentleman late in the evenings. Brazen hussies taint the good name of—"

"Mr. Jefford!"

He waved his hand. "I won't hear another word. All you'd do is lie. Pack and leave by supper. Now go. I have work to do."

Isabel wiped away hot tears, but more trailed down her cheeks. Her vision blurred as she folded her new plaid dress and put it into the portmanteau on top of her Sunday-best, cabbage rose dress. Last, she put in the bundle of letters from home. The gold ribbon mocked her. She couldn't even keep her job—how would she ever keep a man?

"Isabel, I can't believe this." Kathleen stormed back and forth.

"Oh, believe it," Grace sneered. "She reached too high. Thought she was better than the rest of us, going over to the owner's house. He skulked away and had the overseer do the dirty work of discharging her."

"Hush," Pegeen hissed at her. "Isabel's a good woman. You have no call to be mean to her."

"This is wrong." Kathleen spun around and shook her head. "Wait until Mr. Steadman gets back."

"I c–can't. Mr. Jefford told me I had to be gone by supper."

"Then go to Mrs. Steadman!"

Isabel shook her head. The very notion that Mrs. Steadman might hear such scurrilous accusations mortified her. The woman had such a tender heart, she'd probably blame herself. "Even if things were settled, Mr. Jefford would make my life a nightmare."

"You're one of the best weavers. What about somewhere else?"

Isabel hitched her shoulder. "Mr. Jefford dismissed me without a certificate of honorable discharge. No other mill will take me on." She didn't add on the rest. No one would hire a woman reputed to be a mill owner's cast-off mistress.

"It's been two and a half years since I saw Mama and my sisters. David, too. I'll go home and see what work I can find there."

Her last possession was her Bible. Isabel held it to her bosom, then went across the room and somberly held the leather-bound book out to Pegeen. "You've learned to read this year. I want you to have this."

"Oh, no, Isabel. I—"

"It would bring me comfort, knowing I've left it with you. Mama has a Bible I can share."

Once Pegeen accepted the Bible, Isabel pulled on her bonnet and the pelisse Mrs. Steadman had insisted she keep. Pride made her want to return it; common sense dictated she keep it and take her own cape home for Mama or her sisters to use.

A week's wages were knotted in her handkerchief. She couldn't afford to spend the money for a coach ride back home. Luckily, one of the other girls was going home to take on a teaching position, so Isabel would ride in her wagon all but the last two miles.

Isabel tried to muffle her sob. She lifted her portmanteau and whispered to Kathleen, "Write me. Tell me how the girls liked the dolls, and say good-bye to Amy for me."

Kathleen hugged her close. "God go with you."

Carter briskly strode into the weaving room just minutes before the day was to begin. While he'd been gone, he'd spent considerable time pondering Isabel's comments about God's grace. After he'd prayed and felt released from the burden he carried, Carter rushed through the rest of his business so he could come share his joy. He made up his mind, and he didn't believe in wasting his time. As soon as he spied Isabel, he. . .

She wasn't at her looms. Where was she? He scanned the area again. A new lass with hair the shade of untanned leather struggled to tie her apron about her ample waist. The wide-eyed way she gawked about made it clear she felt overwhelmed.

Mary had begun to oil the loom before them, the whole time explaining in a patient tone what she was doing.

To the other side, Kathleen looked up from preparing her own looms to glower at him.

His heart gave a sudden jolt. He'd assumed Isabel hadn't extended an invitation to his mother and had skipped church on Sunday because of her sensitivity to the difference in their social standing. Was she sick? He demanded hoarsely, "Where is Isabel?"

"Gone home." Mary's eyes welled up with tears.

"What?"

Chapter 10

"You can't be serious!" His mother quickly folded a few garments and shoved them into a black leather valise. "I hope you discharged Jefford at once."

Carter shoved his feet into riding boots. "I barely let him grab his coat and hat before I got rid of him. Maxwell delivered the cotton, and I laid out the orders for the next week late last evening. James Roland can oversee the mill, and Kathleen can keep charge of the weaving rooms for the next few days 'til I get back."

"With Isabel," his mother tacked on.

"With Isabel," he confirmed in a definitive voice. He'd gotten her address from Kathleen, and he was about to go claim his woman.

"Isabel?"

"Yes?" Isabel sat on the mattress and plaited her sisters' hair for bedtime. The threadbare flannel of their nightgowns made her heart twist. Over the past two and a half years, how many thousands of yards of cloth had she woven, yet her own little sisters went to sleep in thin-as-air gowns on a frigid night.

"Do you s'pose Baby Jesus got poked by the hay in His manger?"

She forced a laugh. "I don't know." After she tied a bit of string about the last braid, Isabel took her cape and spread it over the mattress. "This'll keep the hay from jabbing you. Now hop in and we'll say prayers."

The small cabin shook as the front door slammed. Abe probably just got back after checking the animals. He made a meager living by sharecropping, but he and Hannah had been good enough to take in Mama and the girls. Still, with him, Hannah, and their baby, that had been burden enough. Isabel knew there wasn't room for her here—but she had nowhere else to turn.

"Isabel, come down here."

She startled at the sound of Carter Steadman's voice. Peering over the loft at him, she called, "What are you doing here?"

He folded his arms akimbo. "Strange, but I was wondering the same thing about you. Come down, and bring your coat. We're going outside to talk."

"It's cold out there!"

"Which is why I told you to bring your coat," he said with excessive patience.

"We can sit by the fire inside."

Isabel wasn't sure if she heard his mutterings correctly. "Obtuse and stubborn" seemed to be mentioned, but whatever the rest of the words were, Hannah and Mama drowned them out with their muffled giggles. Abe looked entirely too entertained. Unwilling to provide more amusement for them, Isabel took the pelisse Carter's mother had given to her and tucked it under her arm.

Just as she started down the ladder, Carter growled, "Are you trying to break your neck? Drop that thing and use both hands."

All three of her sisters lined up by the loft rail and twittered.

Isabel flung the piece so it hit him square in the chest, then scurried down before he could say another word. "Mr. Steadman—"

"Carter," he corrected as he spun her about and wrapped her tight. He then nodded his head toward Mama. "Mrs. Shaw, I presume."

"Indeed." Mama smiled at him.

"Ma'am, I intend to drag your daughter outside and talk some sense into her. Before I do, I'd best mind my manners and propriety enough to declare my intentions. I'm Carter Steadman, and I can provide well for her. I love her and aim to ask for her hand, so if you have any objections, now's the time to speak up."

"Carter!" Isabel spluttered.

He kept his hands clamped on her shoulders.

Mama looked to Abe. Abe took a moment to take Carter's measure, then asked, "Are you a God-fearing man?"

"Aye, and a God-loving man, as well."

Abe nodded. Mama smiled, and all of the girls cheered.

Carter swept Isabel straight off her feet and headed for the door. Hannah opened it and before she could catch her breath, Isabel found herself sitting on a crate in the barn.

Carter knelt beside her. "Isabel, I already proclaimed my love for you back in the house. I can't apologize, because though such tender words would best be said in private the first time, I'm willing to shout them to the world. A man can't hope for a treasure better than a godly wife. I'm asking you to be my bride."

Isabel ducked her head in disgrace. "Mr. Steadman, you and I both know the gossip was untrue. You needn't be gallant and do this to salvage my reputation."

"Jefford's opinion holds no sway. Everyone who knows you knows better than to put any store by his accusations."

"Then you can see your noble proposal is unnecessary."

He gave her a tender look. "I think it's essential."

Isabel wrapped her arms around herself. "Carter, we both know your propensity for trying to cover someone else's wrongdoings with a good deed. I thought you'd grown beyond that. Proposing to me is—"

"The most selfish thing I've ever done. I want you for my own. I want to come home to your gentle words and sweet laughter each night. We'll give my mother a dozen beautiful grandbabies. Don't you understand, Isabel? I couldn't risk ruining your reputation, so my mother and I plotted a way to allow me to court you under proper, albeit contrived, circumstances."

"I can't imagine this."

"You'd better. Before I left, I'd already asked Parson Hull about the best date for a wedding. You're all I could ever hope for in a wife. Don't you hold any feeling for me?"

"Yes! But I'm just—"

"Mine." He kept her from saying another word by kissing her.

They spent the next three days with her family. Carter rolled up his sleeves and worked alongside Abe on farm chores. He gave her little sisters piggyback rides and took Isabel out on a walk to choose a Christmas tree.

David came home from his apprenticeship for Christmas. He and Carter bunked down in the barn loft. That first night, Isabel feared they'd be too cold. Hannah merely laughed. "How could you forget all of the quilts Mama made you sew?"

"Mama—I wrote and told you to—"

Mama wrapped her arm about Isabel's waist. "I couldn't sell them, Honey. See? I knew you'd need them."

Carter bedded down under three of those quilts that night and marveled that Isabel had worked so hard on such beautiful quilts, only to tell her mother to sell them off. The sacrifice staggered him. She reminded him of the widow in the Bible who tithed her last mite. *Father, thank You for giving me such a wonderful, loving woman to be my wife.*

The next morning, he took Isabel for an early morning stroll. She kept her eyes on him, a fact that pleased him no end. . .until they came upon a specific tree. They paused, and Carter finally urged, "Sweetheart, turn your head to the right."

There, the special gold ribbon dangled from a branch. Tied to it was a ring. "Merry Christmas."

"Oh, Carter, I love you!" Isabel threw her arms around his neck and kissed him.

A month and a half later, they kissed at the altar. The golden ribbon dangled from Isabel's bridal bouquet. Her heart overflowed with joy. Carter had continued to do good deeds, but they came from the fullness of his heart instead of as an attempt to appease God's wrath. His mother's support eased Isabel's entry into what might have seemed snobbish society—and a sweet young woman named Elizabeth Henly quite helpfully taught her how to dispose of the ofttimes undrinkable punches and teas in strategically placed potted plants.

Kathleen caught the bridal bouquet, and as she and Mama helped Isabel change into her going-away gown, Kathleen returned the ribbon. "Someday, your own daughter will cherish it, too. Keep it for her as a symbol of how God fills our lives with love."

CATHY MARIE HAKE

Cathy Marie is a Southern California native who loves her work as a nurse and Lamaze teacher. She and her husband have a daughter, a son, and a dog, so life is never dull or quiet. Cathy Marie considers herself a sentimental packrat, collecting antiques and Hummel figurines. She otherwise keeps busy with reading, writing, baking, and being a prayer warrior. "I am easily distracted during prayer, so I devote certain tasks and chores to specific requests or persons so I can keep faithful in my prayer life." Cathy Marie's first book was published by **Heartsong Presents** in 2000 and earned her a spot as one of the readers' favorite new authors.

Run of the Mill

by Susan Downs

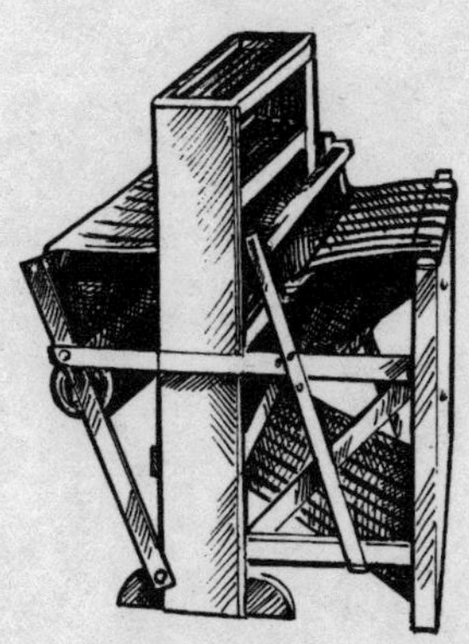

Dedication

To my daughters-in-law, Jara and Sarah.
God blessed me when He blessed my sons
with brides as wonderful as you.
No one will ever accuse either of you
of being *Run of the Mill!*

Chapter 1

"Is everything all right here?" Kathleen McKenna stood on the front porch of the Steadman mansion and craned her neck to see past the young servant girl who had answered the door. "I debated all the way over whether or not I should still come. When I saw the Steadman pew empty in church today, I worried the family might have taken ill."

Before the girl could respond, the familiar voice of Kathleen's best friend, Isabel Steadman, wafted from the dark interior. "We are all fine, Kathleen. Just unexpectedly detained this morning." Isabel stepped out of the shadows and, dismissing the girl with a smile and a nod, she swung the door open wide. "Come in. Come in. When I passed through the kitchen a few moments ago, Cook said she could serve up dinner as soon as you arrived."

Kathleen glanced down at the brown spatters on her Sunday-best dress. "My boots are a muddy mess after traveling the footpath from church. Perhaps I should leave them here on the porch." She scraped her feet back and forth across the doormat in an attempt to dislodge the worst of the caked-on mud.

Isabel grabbed the carpetbag Kathleen clutched under her arm and pulled both her guest and the bag over the threshold. "Come on in and don't you worry about a little mud. I doubt the condition of your shoes could be any worse than those." Isabel nodded to the foyer's marble-tiled floor where someone had left the most enormous pair of men's work boots Kathleen had ever seen. And the filthiest.

Just past the shoes, in the middle of the usually immaculate entryway, a higgledy-piggledy tower of wooden crates, bandboxes, and trunks reached almost to the crystal chandelier.

"If he had not come bearing gifts, we women of the house might have been furious," Isabel said with a soft chuckle. "Then again, I have never seen Mother Steadman angry with anyone."

"Oh, Isabel, you have a houseguest!" Kathleen took a step back. "I mustn't intrude. I will take my dinner at the boardinghouse with the other mill girls today."

"Nonsense." While she spoke, Isabel removed Kathleen's shawl from her shoulders and draped it over a peg on the coat tree, then she set the carpetbag on the floor. "I look forward all week to seeing you on Sunday, and your place is already set at the table. Who else would fill me in on all the mill news? Surely you don't expect Carter to provide an accurate report. He might own the place, but he doesn't know beans about the latest goings-on with the girls. Besides, Carter's cousin isn't a guest at all. Though he's not been home since Carter and I wed, Maxwell occupies the third floor of this house when he isn't traveling."

A shiver of discomfort washed over Kathleen at the prospect of dining with Carter's cousin, Maxwell Steadman. She had only seen him from afar on the infrequent occasions when he visited the mill. Still, his size, his demeanor, his commanding presence, his nomadic existence—in short, everything about him intimidated her. And as everyone she worked with at the mill knew, she was not one to be easily daunted by a man.

She didn't imagine today's noon meal at Steadman Manor would be the pleasant event she had come to expect every Sunday. However, when Isabel looped arms with Kathleen and coaxed her toward the dining room, she pasted on a smile and tried to share Isabel's enthusiasm as her friend prattled on.

"You will never guess what those crates hold—"

Kathleen looked back over her shoulder at the mountain of wooden boxes. All she could see were bits of straw poking through the slats.

Isabel couldn't wait for an answer. "Lemons!" she exclaimed.

"Lemons?" Kathleen echoed. The very utterance of the word made her mouth water, and she was suddenly able to pinpoint the source of the faint citrus smell she had detected when she entered the foyer.

"They hold *lemons,*" Isabel repeated, squeezing Kathleen's arm. "Fresh from Florida. Maxwell gives them to his sailors to prevent scurvy, but he bought more on this trip than they can possibly eat before the fruit goes bad, so he gave us these crates to sell or use as we see fit. Carter says we can deliver them to the girls at Kindred Hearts this afternoon."

"Won't they be thrilled?" Kathleen had never seen her

friend so excited. Her jubilance proved contagious.

"They will think Christmas has come all over again when we present them with flannel nighties and with lemons, too." Isabel's eyes sparkled with glee as she eyed the carpetbag. "You did bring the nightgowns, didn't you?"

Kathleen nodded in answer to the question. "Yes, dear friend. You needn't worry. Pegeen, Grace, and I finished the trim work on the last gown Thursday."

At the pronouncement, Isabel gave Kathleen's arm another squeeze.

"Your husband's misfortune at having to shut down the mill because of all this rain proved to be our gain," Kathleen confided to her friend. "I've been able to complete a number of personal projects this week. Although, come payday, I am sure to miss my usual piece rate bonus."

"Miss Kathleen, knowing the miracles you work on that loom, I have no doubt you will make up the yardage in a matter of hours," Carter Steadman said as he entered the dining room by way of the adjoining parlor. "Wouldn't you agree with me, Dear?" He bowed to Kathleen in greeting while Isabel released her hold on Kathleen's arm and moved to stand by her husband's side.

"I think I deserve a little credit for Kathleen's success," Isabel said with a mischievous grin. "Everything she knows about weaving, she learned from me." The three shared a laugh before a serious look supplanted Carter's jovial expression.

"All joking aside, Miss Kathleen, I made careful note of the fact that, despite the shutdown, you took it upon yourself to spend a good many hours cleaning the looms in your weave room. Such dedication to your responsibilities won't go unrewarded." As his litany of praise continued, Kathleen dropped her gaze and studied the intricate pattern of the dining room's Persian rug.

Her cheeks burning with the heat of embarrassment, she looked up to protest her employer's compliments, but he had turned back toward the parlor. "Maxwell, I'll have you know that, due to the efforts of my head weaver here, no time will be wasted when the rainwaters recede from the tailrace and wheelpit in sufficient measure to restart our machinery." Carter motioned for his cousin to join them in the dining room. "In light of the news you just shared with me, this could prove invaluable."

The massive frame of the man whom most of Eastead covertly referred to as "the Shipping Steadman" filled the doorway. Kathleen had to tip her head back in order to look him in the eye. She moistened her lips and schooled her features in hopes of masking her alarm. The face-to-face reality of Maxwell Steadman loomed even larger and more intimidating than her distant memory of him.

"Cousin, let me introduce you to one of my most prized employees, Miss Kathleen McKenna. It's been nearly two years now since she signed on to work for us in the mill. Her father thought our 'land of steady habits' was becoming a bit too congested for his taste, so he sold their Connecticut farmland and loaded the rest of the family in a Conestoga headed for Indiana's wide-open spaces. Miss Kathleen stayed behind to earn a bit of income for the family until the others could get sufficiently settled."

Carter then turned toward her. "Miss Kathleen, I would like you to meet Maxwell Steadman, president and principal shareholder of Steadman Shipping Company."

While Maxwell Steadman shared the same chisel-cut, square jaw and slightly cleft chin as his cousin, the family resemblance ended there. He towered a good three inches over Carter, and his tanned, weather-beaten skin testified to years of exposure to the elements. One glance at his mariner's muscular bulk convinced Kathleen that he had single-handedly hoisted many a sail. She suspected the two cousins might have also inherited the same hair color, but years in the sun had streaked the Shipping Steadman's cinnamon brown mane with shimmering strands of gold.

"Pleased to make your acquaintance, Miss McKenna." Acting every bit the part of a perfect gentleman, he reached out and took her by the hand, then dipped over it in a polite bow. When he straightened to his full height, she found herself tensing under his scrutiny. His eyes reminded her of thick molasses, yet she wondered if any sweetness lay hidden in their depths. He was, after all, a seaman and merchant by trade.

"Considering the high regard with which my cousin holds certain weavers previously in his employ," he continued, "Carter's compliment must, indeed, be well deserved."

Kathleen did not know quite how to take his remarks. His granite expression refused to reveal whether he intended to pay her a compliment—or send a subtle, barbed statement of disapproval at his upper-class cousin's choice of a working-class bride. He shot a fleeting glance toward the newlyweds, and Kathleen traced his movements. She could tell by the look on Isabel's face that her dear friend shared her bewilderment.

To throw her even more off-kilter, when Kathleen glimpsed his way again, Maxwell Steadman flashed her a slow, disarming smile. Her attempts to return his friendly overture with a smile of her own brought an unbidden and unwelcome flash of excitement fluttering through her chest and set off a ringing in her ears.

Mercifully, Vivian Steadman, Carter's mother and Maxwell's aunt, chose this precise moment to make her entrance into the dining room, thus saving Kathleen from having to formulate an intelligent response. Though the saintly matriarch never would complain, she approached them in short, wooden strides, and at once, Kathleen recognized the damp weather's ill effect on Mrs. Steadman's rheumatism.

"Children, shall we take our seats? Cook tells me dinner is getting cold."

"Well, Nephew, I see you've met Miss Kathleen." Aunt Vivian's feigned whisper carried across the room for all to hear as, in slow, measured steps, Maxwell escorted her to her seat at the head of the dining table. By the time Maxwell managed to slide his aunt's chair up to the table, Carter had already assisted both of the younger women into their places and was taking a seat next to his wife.

Aunt Vivian dropped all pretense of speaking only to Maxwell when he moved to take the one remaining empty seat—sandwiched between his aunt and their fair young dinner guest. "We count our lovely Miss Kathleen among the chiefest of the many blessings Carter's new bride brought into our lives," she said.

Maxwell could see through his aunt's innocent remarks. He had fallen prey to her matchmaking wiles before. Indeed, he had noted the loveliness of Miss Kathleen McKenna. He could not refrain from staring at the petite and comely young woman with her dark chestnut hair, pale, fair skin, and eyes the same soft green as the costly celadon he'd purchased on his last voyage to the Orient. However, as much as he admired her beauty, he considered it foolish to entertain any romantic notions concerning a subordinate member of the working class, and he saw no blessing or benefit in Carter's stooping to wed someone like Isabel, no matter how pretty or beguiling she might be.

When Maxwell took his seat directly across from Carter, he caught an interchange of affectionate glances between the newlyweds. The two appeared thoroughly intoxicated by the very presence of the other, but Maxwell shook off the prick of jealousy that needled him as he watched the lovebirds.

During his last visit, Maxwell had been taken aback by Carter's obvious infatuation with one of the mill girls in his employ. During the course of his most recent journey, he'd fully expected his cousin to come to his senses. Instead, Carter's obsession with Isabel appeared to have intensified. The realization startled and perplexed Maxwell. After all, Carter might have chosen any of Eastead's eligible debutantes as his bride—one with something to bring to a marriage besides the clothes on her back and a pretty smile.

If Aunt Vivian's enthusiastic and vocal support of Isabel were any indication, the Steadman family's intolerant position on such mismatched unions had certainly softened over the short course of one generation. According to whispered family folklore, in addition to Maxwell's and Carter's fathers, a third son had once stood in line to inherit the Steadman fortunes. However, when the fabled Esau Steadman chose a life mate considerably below his family's means and social standing, Grandfather Steadman had promptly disowned him and forbidden anyone to speak his son's name in his presence again. Grandfather Steadman would never have allowed a mill girl to dine at his table.

Maxwell cast a sideways glance at Kathleen McKenna, then shook his head to dismiss these domestic matters from his thoughts. A host of far more pressing business items vied for his attention. He didn't have time to concern himself with Byronic musings. Such affairs played little significance in his life, after all. He prided himself on his confirmed bachelorhood. He loved his carefree, vagabond ways. He never intended to marry—neither for love nor money.

Aunt Vivian called on Carter to ask the blessing, after which a uniformed maid bearing a soup tureen promptly appeared from the kitchen. Once all had been served, Maxwell waited for his aunt to commence eating before he spooned a large bite of clam chowder into his mouth.

"Maxwell, you don't mind if I share with our present company the matters we were just discussing in the parlor, do you?"

Carter's request so caught Maxwell off guard, a clam tidbit lodged in his throat and he fought to swallow without choking. He managed a raspy, "Certainly," before reaching for his water glass. He dared not argue the point here and now, but for Carter to bring up matters of trade and commerce as topics of dinner conversation seemed, at the least, somewhat ill-mannered. Far beyond that, for him to disclose such professional concerns with these members of the fairer sex struck Maxwell as downright unconventional. Preposterous.

He drained the water from his glass, yet a lingering urge to cough tickled at his throat.

Miss Kathleen leaned in toward him as she passed the bread basket. "Are you all right, Mr. Steadman?" she murmured, concern shadowing her features.

"Fine," he rasped and nodded toward his bowl of chowder. "I have been so long deprived of Cook's good food, I got caught making a glutton of myself is all."

"Perhaps you are simply trying to smother your sorrows in the soup, my boy." Carter jabbed at the air toward Maxwell with his empty spoon and chuckled. "Forgive me. I did not intend to make light of your hapless circumstances, but I have to believe the Lord has a reason for allowing this delay of your voyage to England."

Maxwell offered Carter a thin-lipped smile but kept his comments to himself. Although God might have played a part in the tempest that destroyed his clipper's sails, he highly doubted the scoundrel of an overseer, Jedidiah Drake, had consulted the Almighty before leaving Steadman Shipping high and dry.

"Ladies," Carter began, "when Maxwell landed in Eastead this morning, a messenger presented him with a packet containing two rather dire reports." He paused to give all three women sufficient time to cluck and "my-my" their condolences to Maxwell. "While none of us takes any pleasure in Maxwell's misfortune, you might find it interesting to learn that our former agent at Steadman Textiles, Harlan Jefford, convinced Jedidiah Drake, the overseer of Steadman Shipping, to enter into a new business venture with him. The two set off for California on Friday—without the courtesy of Drake serving a day's notice to poor Maxwell here."

From the little bit of information Carter had told him earlier in the day about Jefford, Maxwell well understood why Isabel, in particular, might be pleased to know she wouldn't be running into the former mill agent on the streets of Eastead anytime soon. However, his overseer's desertion to join Jefford's camp left Maxwell with no one he could trust to manage his business while he traveled abroad. Good men were hard to come by. Carter had been forced to manage the entire mill operation personally since he'd dismissed Jefford back in December and had only hired a new mill agent from Boston within the past month. Maxwell was at a decided disadvantage since his own travels kept him from making the acquaintance of any prospective candidates who might already live in the region.

"What a pity," his aunt exclaimed. "You were no doubt

hoping to set sail right away, what with warm weather coming on." She shifted in her seat to look at Carter. "Son, isn't there any way you can help?"

Maxwell leaned to one side to allow the servant to trade his empty soup bowl for a plate heaped with a generous portion of his favorite fare—Yankee pot roast and all the trimmings. Yet while the meal looked and smelled delicious, he found he no longer had much of an appetite.

"I appreciate your concern, Aunt Vivian, but according to the other report I received this morning, even if I found a new overseer tomorrow, I couldn't lift anchor until I'd outfitted the *Steadfast* with a full complement of fresh sails." Maxwell sighed and absentmindedly jabbed at a parsnip with his fork. "She's my only clipper in port right now, and she limped into harbor last week with her sails in shreds after encountering an intense gale a few miles offshore." He glanced at Carter, who was rubbing his chin in contemplation. They studied one another for a long moment before Carter abruptly turned his attention to Miss McKenna.

"Miss Kathleen, I'll run this by Agent Woolery first thing tomorrow morning, but frankly, at this point, both you and I have a better working knowledge of the mill and the weave rooms than he does. If this freshet has, indeed, blown out to sea, I can't think of any reason why we couldn't shift our production schedule tomorrow and set our spindles and looms to do a rush order of sailcloth for my cousin here. Can you?"

While Carter spoke, Maxwell rested his fork against his plate and pushed back from the table just far enough to easily observe Miss McKenna's response. He was already growing somewhat accustomed to his cousin's unorthodox business practices and odd way of dealing with subordinates—women in particular. He did not, however, expect the reaction of the young lady at his side.

The hitherto demure and soft-spoken dinner guest pushed her plate away and, with her back ramrod straight, clasped her folded hands in her lap and leaned toward her employer. She began to shake her head from side to side in calculating slowness. She paused and twisted in her chair to look at Maxwell.

"Mr. Steadman, may I ask how many yards of sailcloth a clipper requires?"

The assertive tone in her voice so took him aback, Maxwell needed a moment to register the fact that she meant the question for him. "Let me think on it for a minute." He tapped his lips with his index finger and rushed through the calculations. He could give her a close estimate immediately, but he thought in this instance he ought to provide a rather accurate figure.

Main-topmast. . .topgallant. . .mizzen. . . He mentally ticked off the various dimensions of the *Steadfast*'s masts and yards. As he did his figuring, Carter and the two younger women discussed in hushed undertones the modifications the mill would need to make to the spindles and looms in order to put this spur-of-the-moment work order into motion, while his forever-patient aunt Vivian observed their proceedings in silence. Her quiet tolerance bore testimony to the many such meals-turned-business-meetings she had sat through in her day.

When Maxwell felt confident of his total, he cleared his

throat and lightly nudged Miss McKenna's elbow to gain her attention again.

"Twelve thousand five hundred yards—thirteen thousand should be more than sufficient."

He half-expected her to cower at the daunting figure. Instead, Maxwell watched her expression brighten. Her celadon green eyes sparkled with fiery excitement and darted to and fro beneath her spiked eyebrows as though she were ciphering a complex mathematical equation without the aid of pencil and paper.

"Oh, that's nothing," she said with a swish of her hand. "We've three hundred looms each producing fifty yards a day, so we could weave that amount of yardage in a day or two without a bit of trouble. The delay comes, of course, in the preparatory setup and finish work." She spoke to him as a teacher would a thickheaded pupil. "The cotton duck you need for sail sheeting requires a denser thread than what our spindles are producing for the shirting we are weaving now, and the looms would need to be adjusted to provide a tighter, sturdier weave. In addition, the mill may find it necessary to temporarily employ seamstresses skilled in the art of sail-making to do the finish work."

She looked first at Carter, then back to him, before settling her gaze on Carter again. "With all due respect to both Mr. Steadmans, it appears to be neither a prudent use of the shipping company's finances nor of the mill's labor force to fill such a small order. Perhaps you could convince the Shipping Steadman to consider multiplying his order, say, tenfold?"

Maxwell bit his lip to keep from laughing aloud at her reference to him. *The Shipping Steadman, indeed.* Plainly, there were too many Mr. Steadmans in the room. He could see he would need to come up with a different form of address if he kept company with his cousin in the presence of Miss McKenna for any length of time. Judging from the way Carter seemed to value her opinion, the prospect could be a definite possibility, and the more Maxwell thought about it, the more he warmed to the idea.

Maxwell had never known a beautiful woman like Kathleen McKenna could also be so sharp-witted and quick with figures. She obviously had a good head for business, a thought that struck Maxwell as altogether unnatural. He could never ask anyone because his curiosity would certainly be misconstrued; however, he wondered why a beauty like Miss McKenna had not yet married. She was well into her marriageable years. He guessed her to be at least nineteen or twenty. Perhaps the reason had something to do with her having to postpone her assumption of the preferred vocation of most women—homemaking and child rearing—in order to enter into millwork as a means of supporting her family.

He generally held to the opinion that wives were better left in the dark in matters of commerce, lest they be construed as meddling in affairs they had no business concerning themselves with. The man who had to live with a woman as assertive and sure of herself in economic issues as Kathleen McKenna appeared to be would undoubtedly face many challenges. Even so, Maxwell suspected that the man fortunate enough to take Miss McKenna for his bride might be wise to consult her before making any major business decisions.

"Miss Kathleen has a point," Carter said, rousing Maxwell

from his reverie. "Your other clippers are bound to need new suits of sails before long if they don't now, and you could have a sufficient supply of sheeting to dress your entire fleet. If that prospect doesn't appeal to you, no doubt you could find a buyer, either here or abroad, for such sturdy fabrics. You supply Steadman Textiles with our raw cotton, and I'm certain you can vouch for the quality of our finished product. What do you say, Maxwell?"

"I say I am amenable to the idea, provided we give first priority to getting the *Steadfast* seaworthy. I must admit, I am rather embarrassed that I didn't come up with this concept myself long ago. We may have just stumbled upon a profitable venture for the both of us, thanks to your Miss McKenna." Maxwell tipped his head to acknowledge the young lady's contributions, and she flushed a delightful shade of crimson.

Music filled the air as the mantel clock in the parlor chimed the hour.

"Oh, my, Kathleen, the time!"

Both Maxwell and their dinner guest jumped at Isabel's exclamation.

"We must get to Kindred Hearts right away, before Miss Amy puts the little ones down for their naps and we miss giving them their gifts."

Chapter 2

While Carter drove the wagon down Croner Hill and over the few short blocks to the Kindred Hearts Orphanage, Maxwell rode in the back amid the lemon crates and Aunt Vivian's last-minute donation of a fifty-pound sack of Georgia cane sugar. All the way, he silently groused about agreeing to accompany Carter as he escorted the two ladies on their little mission of charity. If the mysterious Miss McKenna, with her enchanting eyes, had not been standing behind his cousin when Carter had asked him to come, Maxwell felt certain he would have declined the invitation; but he had not wanted her to presume him a cad.

He had no business tagging along. He couldn't take credit for the gift of citrus they were delivering. If Carter or Isabel had asked his opinion, he would have told them it made much more sense to sell the scarce commodity for top dollar and then make a small cash donation to the orphans from the proceeds. Even if he had thrown his full support behind this idea, he never saw himself as much of a public do-gooder. His younger brother, Lucas, possessed enough sanctimonious piety for the both of them. Unlike Lucas, Maxwell wasn't one to seek recognition for any of his benevolent deeds. He should have pleaded exhaustion from his journey home and headed straight for his rooms on the third floor.

When they pulled up in front of the establishment—the epitome of residential repose—the knot in Maxwell's stomach cinched even tighter. He deplored the prospect of spending his Sunday afternoon perched on the edge of some delicate parlor chair. Beads of sweat dampened the back of his neck at the very thought of making conversation with the house matron, Amy Ross, while surrounded and mauled by a host of giggly little girls.

Amy, a couple years younger than Maxwell, had grown up in Eastead and married Jason Ross, one of his school chums. She was left a widow when Jason died some four years earlier, although Maxwell couldn't recall the circumstances surrounding his death. During one of Aunt Vivian's previous matchmaking campaigns, she had tried to get Maxwell to call on Amy after the young widow had gone through a reasonable mourning period. In the back of his mind, he questioned whether or not today's charitable presentation played a part in a surreptitious conspiracy to throw him and Amy together.

Maxwell had long suspected his aunt Vivian worked hard to surround him with eligible bridal candidates whenever he breezed through town. He cast a suspicious glance toward Kathleen McKenna, who sat beside Isabel on the wagon bench.

Then and there, he vowed to hold Carter's wife to her promise.

Isabel had announced, upon catching a look at the cloudless blue sky and inhaling deep gulps of the rain-swept spring air, that when she and Kathleen were finished, she would see her friend to her boardinghouse and then walk home alone the remaining short distance. "If you so choose," she'd said, "you men are free to leave as soon as you carry the goods inside and allow a moment for proper introductions and salutations to be made." At the time, Maxwell had riled at the idea of her presuming to tell him what he could and could not do, but now he felt more than willing to accept Isabel's offer.

He scrambled off the flatbed and hoisted a crate onto his shoulder while Carter helped the women from the wagon and retrieved Miss McKenna's carpetbag from under the seat. Maxwell nodded for the others to go ahead of him, but Miss McKenna paused at his side, her anticipation palpable.

"I am so glad you agreed to come along." She flashed him a wide smile. "I think you'll find your heart warmed to see the gratitude of the girls when they receive our gifts."

Maxwell stopped and looked at Isabel's friend. He couldn't yet decide whether she was another innocent victim ensnared in one of Aunt Viv's schemes, or if she was a conniving partner in a plot to tame him. Regardless, he marveled at her complexity. If all women behaved like this Kathleen McKenna, he felt certain he would never understand a one. At first meeting, he'd thought the young lady tranquil and sedate. Then, in matters of business, she'd assumed an authoritative and resolute air. Now, she appeared as eager and excited as a six year old surprised with a party on her birthday.

He looked toward the white clapboard residence. "I am not much good with children," he said, swallowing hard. "I've never spent any length of time around little girls."

"You needn't worry. Most won't bite, although little Ruthie may chatter your leg off." She laughed, but if she meant to mock him, her words held no sting.

Miss Kathleen pointed toward the house, her teasing forgotten. "Look, someone is coming. Perhaps one of the girls saw us arrive."

The front door opened wide, and Maxwell expected to see a slip of a young thing, or two or three, racing out to greet them. Instead, the familiar figures of Parson Hull and his wife stepped onto the porch. Each carried a child. Amy Ross followed them outside. She handed the parson a small suitcase before pulling the door closed behind her. At the sight of the foursome coming up the walk, she brightened and waved.

"What perfect timing!" the young widow called out, dabbing at the corner of her eyes with a lace handkerchief. "You all can be the first of our church folk to offer hearty congratulations to the Hull family." She paused, then added, "Maxwell, it is especially nice to see you again after such a long absence."

"Likewise, Amy," he offered in exchange of the greeting, then nodded his hello to the others. "Parson and Mrs. Hull."

"I pray this means what I think it does," Miss McKenna said softly as she clutched her skirts and skittered up ahead of Maxwell so she could address Isabel. "Aren't little Betty and her baby sister the perfect match for the Hulls?" Her question met with a quick hug from Isabel.

Although Maxwell didn't have a clue what the women were talking about, he smiled to himself at the two friends' feminine exchange. While his companions made their way to the stoop, he lagged behind on the walkway, lowering the lemon crate from his shoulder to the ground. He watched while the others clambered up to the porch. The women surrounded Mrs. Hull and the babe in her arms, and Carter moved in next to Parson Hull.

Maxwell paid particular note of the protective way in which Amy Ross squeezed in between Parson and Mrs. Hull and began to pat the blanketed bundle Mrs. Hull held. "Two of my sweet girls are going to have new parents. . . ," Amy managed to say before a catch in her voice rendered her speechless. She kneaded at her lower lip as though desperately trying to keep her emotions at bay.

A slow-in-coming comprehension dawned on Maxwell. The parson and his wife were assuming the raising of these two orphans—and one a cripple, judging by the slightly twisted and misshapen form of the older child's right leg. He felt sorry for the clergy couple, despite the fact that these dear folks showed nary a sign of disappointment at the prospect of rearing someone else's offspring. No two souls could be any more humble and kind and Christian than they. He didn't understand why God had not granted the Hulls' prayers for children of their own.

"These children are truly blessed by your taking them under your wing, Parson, Mrs. Hull," Maxwell said, drawing closer to the group. "As always, you model a higher standard of Christian charity for all of us to emulate." He meant his remarks as a compliment, but a puzzled expression swept across the minister's face.

"The blessing is all ours, not theirs," Parson Hull replied. "God has showered us with more joy than we could ever deserve by bringing these children into our lives to love. We've always wanted to be parents, and now the Lord has answered our prayers."

"Reverend, you will make a wonderful father," Carter said, tousling the chestnut curls of the toddler in the minister's arms. The wee one giggled and squealed, "My papa!" Then she coyly buried her face in the crook of her new father's neck.

Isabel peeked under the covers at the infant Mrs. Hull cradled to her bosom. "Carter's right. No child could ask for better parents than the two of you. And if you ask me, this one looks just like her new mama."

"Do you think so? Really?" Mrs. Hull beamed at Isabel's remark. "Miss Amy said the same thing." The new mother stroked the sleeping baby's cheek, then tipped her head toward the toddler in her husband's arms. "With her big sister Betty's approval, we've decided to name her Dorothy. It means 'a gift from God.' "

While the cluster of adults murmured their endorsement of the name, Amy cleared her throat. "Please forgive me. I do hate to leave this happy celebration, but I left Ginger inside alone to try and console little Ruthie. The poor dear is rather upset over her best friend leaving Kindred Hearts. I'd best be getting back inside." She patted Mrs. Hull's sleeve. "And you'd best be getting these new daughters of yours out of this cool spring air. You wouldn't want them sick your first days together. I'll stop by tomorrow afternoon to see how you four are getting along."

"I am sure, with the Lord's help, we will manage just fine. However, we welcome a visit from you any time," Parson Hull answered. "And if you would, please tell Betty's friend that she'll come back to visit often." He smiled at his wife and moved to take his leave. "Shall we go home, Mama?"

Isabel pulled back and let Mrs. Hull ease past her and down the porch steps. The parson, with Betty still clinging to him, followed close behind his wife. "With your permission, we'll follow you inside," Isabel said to Amy. "We brought along some surprises that might serve to ease the sadness of saying good-bye."

Amy eyed the crate on the ground at Maxwell's feet. "How delightful—and another example of God's perfect timing. Although I suspect we shall have to suspend our weekly sewing circle this afternoon. Our emotions are in such a tizzy, I don't believe any of us could sew a straight seam."

Maxwell heaved the crate back onto his shoulder and had climbed one step when Miss McKenna exclaimed, "Wait. We have to catch the parson's family before they leave. Isabel, we forgot to give Betty and Baby Dorothy their new nighties."

Isabel grabbed the carpetbag from her husband, then the two friends breezed by Maxwell on their way to catch the Hulls. "We'll be right back. You men just wait here," Isabel called over her shoulder. Miss McKenna was already shouting for the parson to stop.

"I will see to the girls and try to corral them into the parlor," Amy said, excusing herself at the door. "You all come right on in when you're ready. Don't bother to knock."

Carter and Maxwell unloaded the wagon and deposited the crates on the porch while they awaited the women's return. Maxwell offered to retrieve the final load and left Carter sitting on the porch step to catch his breath. He had just slung the sack of sugar onto his back when the ladies returned, and he fell into step behind them as they made their way up the walk. The two friends were so engrossed in their conversation, they didn't bother to acknowledge him.

"You know, if Carter and I are unable to have children, I believe I would like to adopt a baby," Isabel announced. She and Miss McKenna had each taken a handle of the carpetbag, and they toted it between them.

"I've decided," Miss McKenna returned, "that if I ever get a husband, I'm going to adopt one of the Kindred Hearts' girls, even *if* we start to build our family the typical way. Of course, I'm thrilled for the Hulls, but all along I secretly harbored a plan in my heart to adopt Betty and her baby sister after the right man came my way." As she spoke, she skipped a step to match her gait to that of her friend. "From here on out, that's one of my requirements for a prospective suitor. He must share my love for the orphans."

"Poor girl," Maxwell muttered under his breath. Even one as pretty as Miss McKenna would be hard-pressed to find a husband who lived up to such expectations. He feared that with her stringent stipulations, his cousin's head weaver might be setting herself up for a life of spinsterhood. Could she really pity the orphans that much? Would her pity last when the child she adopted ran into mischief? Surely she didn't think she could love an orphan like she could love a child born to her.

The clatter and high-pitched voices of children filtered from the parlor as Kathleen led the way inside. She and Isabel had emptied the carpetbag of the remaining flannel nighties by the door, and now she balanced her half of the soft, ribboned parcels under her chin. The Steadman cousins trailed behind, one toting the sack of sugar and the other carrying a crate of lemons.

Unable to see over the top of her stack of flannel gowns, Kathleen fumbled for the handle on the parlor's etched-glass sliding doors; but before she could manage the task, someone on the other side swooshed them wide open. She felt a pair of arms tackle her about the knees, and she teetered before regaining her solid footing.

"Miss Kaf-ween!" Even without seeing her, Kathleen instantly recognized the sweet, childish lisp of three-year-old Ruthie. "They took'd our Betty away—and her widdle baby sistah, too." A gentle sob punctuated the girl's declaration of despair. Kathleen crouched and, sliding the stack of gowns onto the parlor's rug, she scooped Ruthie into her embrace.

"Aye," called Ginger, "'tis me you should blame for Ruthie's assault." The copper-topped Irish lass came slowly toward

Kathleen from across the room. "Aunt Amy set a pot o' tea to boilin' and left me in charge, but Ruthie wiggled off me lap and escaped before I could ensnare her again." The oldest girl under Amy Ross's care, Ginger was of an age when she could be on her own. However, her poor eyesight prevented her from making her way in the world, so she worked to assist Amy in any way she could.

"Ruthie is fine." Kathleen struggled to stand with the youngster who had locked her legs around Kathleen's waist. "Leave her with me. I want to have a word with her."

As the other girls flocked to Isabel and the two men, Kathleen carried little Ruthie over to the parlor's settee and nestled her onto her lap. Kathleen stroked the child's cheek and tried to explain. "I know you will miss Betty, but we must think of our poor, lonely Parson and Mrs. Hull." Ruthie kept her head down, twisting and untwisting the hem of her apron. "They had no little girls to love in their house, no children at all. Yet here at Kindred Hearts, there are more than you have yet learned to count. Besides, Betty's new home is just down the street, and I am quite certain she'll be coming to play with you from time to time."

"Aunt Amy says so, too." Little Ruthie, her dark eyes round as buttons, gazed up at Kathleen. Unspent tears pooled along the child's bottom eyelids, and her nose needed a good wiping. Kathleen pulled out the handkerchief she kept tucked up her sleeve and performed the tasks in a couple quick swipes.

"No more tears now. I have someone I want you to meet, and we brought you surprises."

Ruthie squirmed to get down. "I like surpri—" She stopped midsentence at the sight of an unfamiliar giant of a man filling the parlor doorway. Her mouth dropped open. As fast as she had freed herself of Kathleen's embrace, she scurried back up into her lap. "He's not coming to 'dopt me, is he, Miss Kaf-ween?" But for the fear sparkling in Ruthie's wide eyes, Kathleen might have laughed.

"Dear me, no." Kathleen gave the little one a squeeze. "That man is Mr. Steadman's cousin. His name is Mr. Steadman as well—Mr. Maxwell Steadman—but unlike Miss Isabel's husband, this Mr. Steadman has no wife. He travels to faraway places like Georgia and Florida, and a part of our surprise came all the way from there."

Kathleen glanced at the Shipping Steadman. His pained expression telegraphed his discomfort.

Beside him, the older girls made a grand production of sniffing the handfuls of lemons they had drawn from Carter's opened crate. One had ventured to bite into a lemon's rind, and the others burst into gales of laughter at her resulting sour face.

Isabel had doled out her supply of the gowns, and several of the younger girls held them over the bodices of their pinafores, twirling and pirouetting in circles. In the midst of this cheerful chaos, Maxwell Steadman stood stock-still, his arms folded across his chest like a turtle withdrawing into its shell. Kathleen hardly recognized the bulk of a man who had possessed the power to intimidate her a few hours earlier. Shirking behind Isabel, he no longer cowed Kathleen with his suave mystique. Instead, he presented a living, breathing illustration of such words as *apprehensive. . .uncomfortable. . .vexed. . .helpless. . .distressed.* This mammoth man who sailed the high seas and perhaps had even stood face-to-face with pirates appeared wholly unsettled by a roomful of little girls.

A sly smile tugged at the corners of Kathleen's mouth as she coaxed Ruthie back to her feet. "You see the soft, new nighties Miss Isabel gave to the other girls? Well, I made one especially for you. While I find yours, why don't you go and introduce yourself to the other Mr. Steadman? Tell him I suggested you request that he read a Bible story to you and the other girls."

She knew Ruthie loved being read to more than anything, and whatever hesitation the youngster felt about approaching the stranger would fly away at the prospect of a story. "I wouldn't wonder, if you asked him real nice and polite, but that he'd let you sit on his lap while he reads. He spends all his time around gruff and grouchy men, and I feel certain he would enjoy getting to know a sweet little girl like you."

Ruthie's ringlets bounced like springs as she agreed. She darted in and out among the other girls and planted herself at Maxwell Steadman's side, craning her neck to look up at him. Kathleen couldn't hear with all the other commotion in the room, but she positioned herself to watch Ruthie. After four vigorous yanks at his coattail, Mr. Maxwell glanced Ruthie's way, and the toddler pumped her pudgy finger to indicate for him to lean down. Thin-lipped, he hunched to her level while Ruthie stretched on her tiptoes and cupped her hand to speak into his ear.

As he straightened and Ruthie began to tug him toward the red velvet settee, he shot a steely-eyed stare Kathleen's way. The scene invoked visions of a great bear caught in a honeyed trap, and for an instant she almost felt sorry for the man. She almost regretted preying on his one exposed weakness. She almost rose to rescue him. Almost.

Chapter 3

Kathleen jarred from her sleep, her heart pounding. Perspiration soaked her pillow's casing. The acrid taste of smoke burned her parched throat and dried out her sinuses. She instinctively felt her face to ascertain whether or not she had singed off her lashes and eyebrows.

At the feathery brush of her lashes against her fingertips, she crossed that lissome line from half-awake to fully alert, and she released a sigh of relief as she realized she'd been dreaming.

Staring into the murky blackness of the boardinghouse bedroom Kathleen shared with two roommates, she recognized the slow and heavy breathing of Grace as she slept, accompanied by Pegeen's soft snore. Kathleen punched her pillow and sank back into its goose-down softness.

The more she thought about her dream—no, nightmare—the more absurd it seemed. One of Maxwell Steadman's clipper ships had broken free of its moorings and floated from Boston upriver to Eastead. With Mr. Maxwell standing at the bow and the ship's sails flapping in shreds like strips of burial shroud, the vessel plowed into the side of the textile mill, landing the man right in front of Kathleen's looms. Before he could offer a word of explanation, one of the weave room's whale oil lamps set afire a tattered remnant of sailcloth, which, in turn, touched off an inferno in the wooden building filled with combustible dry goods. While the circle of flame and heat pressed in upon Kathleen, Mr. Maxwell reached out from the ship, coaxing, pleading for her to take his hand and let him draw her to safety. Still, she hesitated. Despite the ever-encroaching danger, she wondered—should she entrust her rescue to the man from whose hand all this chaos sprang? She awoke before deciding.

Kathleen didn't really understand the wellspring of the dream. Maxwell Steadman may have disrupted her life for a short time, but she didn't really think of his rush order for sailcloth as a crisis of life-and-death proportions. Even so, her mind had raced most of the night with the details of what needed to be done in the morning to prepare her weave room for the work at hand. And regardless of how hard she fought the tendency, pleasant recollections of yesterday afternoon with the handsome merchant danced and played in her thoughts.

Rising on one elbow, Kathleen flipped her pillow over and thumped it again, then buried her face. She owned neither a watch nor clock, so she had no way of knowing the time. She measured her hours by the chimes that rang from the mill tower. The carillons signaled the workers' early morning wake-up call, noon meal, and the workday's beginning and end. But for sleepless nights like this one, she had little need for a timepiece.

She kicked her tangled nine-patch quilt away from her feet

and rolled onto her side. Then her back. Then to her other side.

Kathleen's mind refused to rest.

She suspected she had Carter to thank that another roommate had not yet been assigned to assume the vacant spot left by Isabel when she married the mill's owner. Having an entire bed of her own rated as pure luxury, but she was especially grateful at a time such as this. She wouldn't have wanted to inflict a night full of her fidgeting on another poor soul.

After an insufferable length of time, the faint clatter of pots and pans filtered up through the floorboards from the first-floor kitchen, and she knew the boardinghouse matron, Mrs. Cox, had begun breakfast preparations. This meant the time must be around four-thirty. Kathleen threw off her covers and slid out of bed. She felt her way in the dark to the straight-backed bedside chair where she'd laid out her everyday calico and apron before retiring the night before. Trying her best to keep quiet, she began to dress by feel alone.

"Aye! I fear to ask ye." Pegeen's sleepy voice sludged through the darkness. "Did I again slumber through the rise-and-shine call?" In the former days when their workday started at five o'clock, Pegeen had been given to sleeping through the four-forty-five wake-up bell. Grace and Kathleen had been forced to employ all means of torture to roust her from her bed, lest she be put on report and her pay docked. However, since Carter Steadman's decision to institute a ten-hour workday in place of their fourteen-hour schedule, Pegeen had yet to oversleep. Now, they not only slept an hour later, but they also enjoyed a hearty breakfast at the boardinghouse before going to the mill. It was a pleasant change from the old routine of taking a thirty-minute breakfast break two hours into their workday.

"No, no. Go back to sleep," Kathleen urged in a half-whisper. "I am sorry if I wakened you. I thought I would go into work early. You have another hour before the bell rings." Pegeen needed no further coaxing to fall silent, and before Kathleen had tiptoed from the room with her boots in hand, Pegeen's soft snore again rent the air.

The steps creaked with Kathleen's every footfall. When she reached the bottom of the staircase, she paused long enough to don her shoes, then she passed into the kitchen. After she splashed cold water on her face and smoothed her hair into place with her damp hands, she swigged a cup of milk and absconded with a thick slice of sourdough bread to eat on the run. All the while, Mrs. Cox chittered laments about Kathleen not watching after her health. . .and not getting her rest. . .and not eating a proper breakfast.

With Mrs. Cox still tsk-tsking her disapproval, Kathleen grabbed her cape off the row of coat pegs hanging by the door. Then, still wolfing down her bread breakfast, she hastened outside, and by the light of a full moon, she crossed the muddy road to the mill. She made a hurried visit to the outhouse before tramping up the rickety outer stairwell as far as the second-floor weave room, where she spent a major portion of her waking hours.

No hint of daylight yet shone through the floor-to-ceiling windows, which spanned the depth of the room on both sides. Even in broad daylight, however, years' worth of an accumulated mixture of cotton fibers, potato starch, and whale-oil soot coated the windows with an opaque film.

She opened the window nearest the door to allow a bit of fresh air into the stuffy room. Then Kathleen moved down one side of the long, narrow hall and back up the other, raising the flame on the whale-oil lamps and illuminating Weave Room Number One. She paused to survey the one hundred silent looms.

Soon, when the six o'clock bell signaled the call to work and the mill girls all stood at their stations, Agent Woolery would throw the lever to set the pulleys and belts in motion and send power to the machinery. The looms' shuttles would start their clacking. A deafening roar would supplant the stillness, and she would have to strain in order to understand the loudest shout yelled inches from her ear. Still, she found the familiar clamor and its accompanying routine comforting.

As she did every morning, she prayed and asked God not only to watch over the workers and keep them safe, but also to bless the fruits of their labor and use what they produced to meet a special need in the life of its recipient. The thought of Maxwell Steadman being that recipient in the coming days sent a smile playing across Kathleen's lips as she breathed an "amen."

Kathleen moved to the corner of the weave room closest to the door, where the baskets of full bobbins were stored. She knelt down to scrutinize the supply of thread remaining in their reserves, then gauged the time required for her girls to weave it into shirting. By her estimate, the spinners should be able to start supplying them with the heavier thread for sailcloth about the same time the weavers exhausted their current stock of the lighter-weight thread.

Her attention was torn away from her calculations when she heard a man's voice filtering up from the street and through the window she had opened for ventilation just moments before. At first, she attached the voice to the short and squat figure of Agent Woolery, but as soon as she heard her name mentioned, she recognized the distinct speech of Maxwell Steadman. Her pulse raced as she listened to her employer's handsome, seafaring cousin speak of her; and though she knew she should not be privy to Mr. Maxwell's private conversation, the shock of his words kept her frozen where she knelt.

"I'm surprised a maverick like you didn't just give Miss McKenna full run of the mill instead of hiring a new agent. If half of what you tell me about her is true, I don't believe you could find a more capable employee—male or female."

"Quite frankly, the thought did cross my mind," returned the voice of Carter Steadman. "She certainly has the intellect and aptitude for the position, but I figured if I were to promote her from among the ranks of her peers into a position of authority over them, well, as the Scriptures say, 'A prophet is without honor in his own country.' I feared she wouldn't receive the respect and authority that would be due a person of such position. Besides, one with her excellent skills at the loom may very well prove harder to replace than an agent. She has quick hands as well as a quick mind."

Kathleen drew a deep breath. She longed to savor these sweet words of honor from her employer, but his voice trailed off, and she realized they were walking away from the open window and up the stairwell. If she didn't make haste, in a matter of moments, the Steadman cousins would discover she had been eavesdropping.

As noiselessly as she could, she scrambled down the aisle toward her assigned workstation. When the two men stepped into the room, she appeared to be intently examining a shuttle.

"Ah, Miss Kathleen," Carter Steadman exclaimed as he led his cousin through the labyrinth of looms toward the two looms that comprised her workstation. "I should have known we would find you here. We were on our way to my office and noticed the light shining from this weave room. I figured our new man had come in early to get a jump on the day." He ran his hand lightly across the warp threads of one of her looms as though he were playing a harp. "I am glad to have a chance to speak with you, however."

Mr. Maxwell nodded to Kathleen. "Morning," he offered in abbreviated greeting before flashing her a wide smile.

"Good morning, Mr. Steadman." The inside of Kathleen's mouth felt like it had been stuffed with cotton as she returned his smile. She recalled the haste in which she had dressed, and she knew she must surely look a fright. Thankfully, both of the Steadmans seemed preoccupied with business rather than with her appearance. Having completed the customary pleasantries, her employer launched into the topic at hand.

"On our way over, Maxwell and I were discussing his plans to secure fresh crewmen from among the Irish when he travels to Europe. Due to the famine and insufferable conditions in

Ireland of late, my good cousin shall provide stateside passage for the families of the sailors as well, in exchange for their commitment to extended years of service." As Carter Steadman spoke, Kathleen caught a glimpse of his cousin. Deep creases furrowed his brow, and he stood with his arms crossed, rocking his head slowly up and down in agreement.

"He tells me he already has an emissary recruiting men in and around Bray," Carter continued.

Kathleen jerked her focus back to her employer. Her roommate, Pegeen, hailed from a small fishing village near Bray. For all these many months, the Irish girl had been slaving to save enough money to pay for her sister, Francine's, passage from there to the States, but she still needed to set so much more aside. Even though she did not share Kathleen's faith, Pegeen had asked her roommate to pray for God's help in allowing her sister to join her soon.

Even now, Kathleen winged a prayer heavenward. *Precious Savior, if only there were some way Maxwell could be convinced to bring Francine back with him, perhaps such a miracle would nudge Pegeen to a personal relationship with You!* Carter Steadman presented a possible answer to her prayer before she could say a word.

"Maxwell set me to thinking," he said, rubbing his fingers along the watch fob that dangled from his waistcoat. "Our workforce is already somewhat depleted, and with summer coming on, we are sure to lose a few more of our mill girls to marriage and the like. Steadman Textiles could provide jobs for at least a dozen or two of these destitute and starving souls, and Maxwell says he could make room aboard the *Steadfast* for their passage. The way I see it, we all stand to benefit from such a plan."

Tingles raced down Kathleen's spine and gooseflesh erupted on her arms. "Sir, you would be doing me a tremendous personal favor by considering a Miss Francine O'Malley, the sister of my roommate Pegeen, as one of the potential candidates for this program. She still lives at what's left of their family homestead near Bray, and I know Pegeen is anxious to be reunited with her kin. In fact, just last week Pegeen's bunkmate, Grace, announced her decision to return home come summer, so Francine could move right into our room."

She caught Maxwell Steadman studying her as she spoke. A look of bewilderment crinkled his features. "You have an Irish roommate?" he asked. "I thought our local Irish confined themselves to the other side of Old Presser Bridge."

"Most do," Kathleen replied. "But the boardinghouses for the Irish lasses were full when Pegeen arrived in Eastead. Isabel and I first offered to take Pegeen into our room as an act of Christian charity, but I am certain Isabel would agree—Pegeen has blessed our lives much more than we've been a blessing to her. She is a sweet and loyal friend." She lowered her voice almost to a whisper, even though no one but the three of them were in the room. "She certainly helps to temper Grace's sour disposition."

"And I can vouch for her hard work ethic," Carter Steadman interjected. "I've found the vast majority of the Irish to be excellent employees."

Kathleen watched as Maxwell cocked his head to one side and stroked his clean-shaven chin. She could tell the idea of their so freely accepting the Irish as equals puzzled him. Yet, while she still had a good deal to learn about him, she knew one thing for certain. If he possessed even an ounce of the Steadman blood that flowed through Carter Steadman's veins, he would be incapable of taking unscrupulous advantage of the current famine in Ireland by hiring that country's citizens as cheap labor and forcing them into jobs that amounted to slavery.

Maxwell Steadman's intense gaze traveled, first from her, then to Carter. "Do you support Miss McKenna's idea?" His eyebrows spiked in question.

"I do. Wholeheartedly," Carter replied.

At Carter's commendation, Maxwell drew what looked like a small ledger book from the pocket of his topcoat along with a nub of a graphite pencil and began to scribble something down. "When I write my man in Bray about screening mill employee candidates, I'll ask him to get in touch with your friend's sister straight away." He looked up from his writing and glanced at Kathleen.

She drummed her fingers across her lips while she thought about how she might obtain the information Mr. Maxwell needed without letting on to Pegeen about their plans. "I want to keep things a secret until we can surprise Pegeen with her sister's arrival. That way, she won't be disappointed if things don't work out for whatever reason." Kathleen looked toward Maxwell, and his gaze met hers. Suddenly, she knew what to do.

"I have a plan that just might work," she said, squaring her shoulders. "You see, Pegeen only learned to read and write this past year, and she still struggles with some of the bigger words, so I stand ready to assist her. But she needs my aid less and less with each passing day." She didn't try to keep the hint of pride from lacing her words, for after the countless evenings she and Pegeen had worked together by lamplight, Kathleen found great satisfaction in her pupil's success.

"If she follows true to form, during today's noon break, rather than go back to the boardinghouse for dinner, Pegeen will carry her letter to the mill store for posting. Perhaps I can tell her I need to pick something up from the store and offer to mail her letter for her when I go. If I mention the fact that Mrs. Cox is serving shepherd's pie—Pegeen's favorite—I am almost certain to pull off the ruse. Then I shall simply copy down her sister's address from the letter before I post it and deliver the information to Mr. Carter Steadman's office before the bells chime the call to return to work."

Maxwell chuckled. "You seem quite adept at deceptive schemes, Miss Kathleen. However, it would be most helpful if you would drop off the information to my shipping office instead of taking it to Carter. You needn't go much out of your way, and you would save me from having to make another trip to the mill before dispatching a carrier to Boston."

"Yes, Sir. As you wish." She sensed Maxwell's enthusiasm for their newly-hatched scheme was growing with each passing moment.

Mill girls trickled through the weave room door in a steady stream, indicating the fast-approaching hour for the workday to begin. The two Steadmans took their leave and jostled their way toward the exit against the incoming sea of women.

"Top o' the mornin'," Pegeen said in greeting to Kathleen when she took her place at the pair of looms next to Kathleen's. "Although, considerin' me vague recollection as to the wee hour of the morning when ye arose, ye must be thinkin' the day be half-done by now."

"No, quite the contrary. I look forward to seeing what glorious blessings the Lord may bestow on us today." Kathleen picked off a strand of thread that had clung to her sleeve and rolled it between her fingers. "Say, Pegeen, I need to pick up a couple things at the mill store during the noon break. . . ." She struggled to maintain an air of nonchalance in her voice. Dropping her gaze, Kathleen looked at the balled fiber she held before flicking it to the floor. "If you'd like, I could post your letter to your sister when I go."

"Now, such a dear friend you are." Pegeen pulled the sealed packet from her apron pocket and held it out to Kathleen. "When I learned Matron Cox would be serving up the shepherd's pie for the noon meal, I'd nearly decided to wait till tomorrow for the postin'."

Kathleen tried to take the envelope from Pegeen, but rather than releasing her hold, Pegeen yanked it back. "Oh, but 'tis famished ye'll be—missin' both breakfast and dinner besides."

With a gentle tug, Kathleen wrested the letter from Pegeen and buried it into the depths of her pocket before the other girl could change her mind. "I will pick a few crackers from the barrel and buy a wedge of cheese. You needn't worry about me." She took a step back, quite pleased with herself for achieving success in this first part of the plot to reunite Pegeen and Francine. "Pegeen, I have a feeling deep in my bones that we are soon to witness some monumental changes in our lives."

Kathleen inwardly winced at her own words, fearing she might have let her guard down too soon and expressed too much exuberance. Just then, peals rang out from the mill bell tower, proclaiming the start of another workday. She breathed a sigh of relief, knowing that in a matter of seconds the racket of the machinery would render impossible any further discussion.

"This bone-deep feelin' might not be tied to the comely frame of Maxwell Steadman, what passed by me on his way out the door, would it?"

The belts and pulleys overhead rumbled and rattled into earsplitting action. Kathleen answered Pegeen with a smile and a noncommittal shrug before turning away. She jerked the levers on her two looms to set them into motion, and though she could feel Pegeen staring at her, she refused to make eye contact with her friend.

Pegeen's speculation of a second budding Steadman/mill girl romance was wholly absurd. Pure folly. Still, Kathleen knew her friend well enough to know that, with just a shrug, she had turned Pegeen's thoughts to romantic musings—and away from any other suspicions.

Throughout the morning, Kathleen struggled with tasks that, any other day, she performed as naturally as breathing. Time and again, she caught herself staring at the beater bar on one of her looms as it slammed its threads into place, while at her other loom, a shuttle's untended empty quill ruined several inches of cloth. She forgot to move the temple hooks that kept her web snug and found herself tying more weaver's knots than she usually did in the course of a week. Had Carter Steadman happened by and observed her blunderings, he would have withdrawn the glowing recommendation of her that he'd given Mr. Maxwell earlier.

When Agent Woolery passed through the weave room to announce they would be resetting their looms and starting on the sailcloth after the noon break, he had to repeat his request that Kathleen oversee the transition. She had been scratching at a spot on the bodice of her mustard-yellow gingham and wondering if she had time to change into her other work dress before presenting Maxwell Steadman with Francine's address.

Not since her first day at the mill had Kathleen felt so inept. Too many competing thoughts vied for her attention. Her stomach had been growling since ten o'clock. She found it increasingly more difficult to stifle her yawns. She couldn't wait to leave the murky air of the weave room and let the spring breezes clear her head.

At the first clang of the noon bell, Kathleen shut down her looms and rushed to beat the mass exodus toward the door. "Enjoy your meal," she called over her shoulder to Pegeen. "I'll see you back here at half past the hour."

Chapter 4

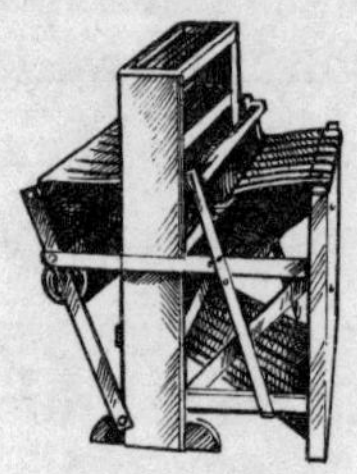

Sorry, Mr. Steadman, but Drake never had me doing anything but accounting and book work. He took care of all the merchant and customer dealings himself." Vern Witherspoon, the droopy-eyed bookkeeper, sat facing Maxwell on the other side of the desk. He held a jumbled stack of invoices and receipts in his broad lap.

Even though the two men had spent the greater part of the morning sifting through the pile of papers, the bundle Witherspoon clutched amounted to a pittance compared to what remained on the desk. Purchase orders, warehouse inventory lists, and yellowed correspondence rose into a mound so thick and deep and wide, not a trace of the wood surface appeared.

Maxwell pushed back in his chair and rose. He raked his fingers through his hair, then began to massage his aching temples.

"You are free to go on back to your books now. I'm not expecting you to fix all the mess left by that rascal Drake. I'll try to get caught up on the backlog in the coming weeks before I sail for Europe, but I need to warn you, Witherspoon. If I can't find a new overseer before then, you may have to help out as best you can in my absence, and my chances of finding a qualified prospect on such short notice are mighty slim."

"Yes, Sir. I'll do whatever I can to help you out, Mr. Steadman." The accountant gathered up his armload of documents. His chair scraped across the wood floor as he stood, and Maxwell watched as his slouching accountant shuffled out of the room.

Maxwell shuddered to think of the business Steadman Shipping might lose if he didn't find a new overseer—and fast. When he and Witherspoon started their work session, he'd held out some hope that he might be able to train the fellow to take over the post vacated by Jedidiah Drake. However, it quickly became apparent that, while the bursar's dull and plodding disposition suited him for a job that required him to keep his nose buried in ledgers day after day, he lacked any aptitude for dealing with people.

Maxwell's head throbbed, and he couldn't yet bring himself to return to the monumental task at hand. He turned to look out the window. A barge bearing the Steadman Shipping insignia and laden with cotton bails floated downriver in the direction of the mill's warehouses. Usually such a sight filled him with a sense of pride and accomplishment. Today, he felt only dread as he realized that the ship's cargo would produce a batch of paperwork that would soon hit his desk.

Cast all your cares upon Him, for He careth for you. The scriptural exhortation, oft recited by his aunt Vivian, popped into his thoughts. In the past, he had always tried to handle his problems on his own. Although he saw himself as a Christian, he wasn't one to spout long and flowery prayers like his brother, Lucas. He didn't want to bother God with his little problems when the Almighty had so many bigger issues needing His attention. Yet Maxwell could no longer stave off this growing feeling of being overwhelmed.

Right where he stood, he closed his eyes and whispered, "Please, God. You know I'm not much of one to ask for help, but I could use some divine wisdom. Point me to the right man for this overseer's job."

Looking up, he scanned the river's far bank. Shanties dotted the hillside. Maxwell grimaced to think that many of the men in his employ lived in such squalor. No one could lay the blame on him. He paid a fair wage to all his workers. Yet many chose to drink their salaries away instead of providing a decent home for their families.

A growing number of Irish immigrants crowded into hovels, claiming the eastern quadrant of the ghetto. They had more honorable reasons for living on the poor side of Eastead. They saved every spare cent they earned to pay the way for family members still in Ireland to cross over to America—Pegeen and Francine's story replayed time and again.

The image of Pegeen's Good Samaritan with celadon green eyes flashed through his mind. His personal observations, albeit brief, added to Carter's praise of his head weaver's good head for business convinced Maxwell that Miss McKenna would make a tremendous overseer. If only she were a man instead of a lowly mill girl.

He pulled his watch from his vest pocket and checked the time. His heartbeat quickened at the thought that she would enter his office within the hour.

Although tempted to amble by the crocuses and savor the warm spring breeze and brilliant blue sky, Kathleen traversed the short distance to the mill store in record time. Even so, a man she recognized as one of the mill's mule spinners had somehow managed to arrive ahead of her.

While the storekeeper waited on him, she availed herself of the pen and inkwell at the end of the long counter. She copied the address, written in Pegeen's amateur cursive, onto a scrap of paper. Just in case anything happened to the paper before she could deliver it to Mr. Maxwell, she tried to set the information to memory. Then she tucked the valuable data in the deepest recesses of her apron pocket and went to help herself to several crackers from the cracker barrel.

By the time she'd sliced a wedge from the grocer's giant cheese wheel, the mule spinner had finished his business, and the storekeeper was waiting to serve her. "How do, Miss," Mr. Mathers greeted her in his slow, backwoods drawl, his beard and mustache further muffling his words.

"I need to post this letter for my friend Pegeen and pay for my food," she said, stretching out both her hands and offering him the items so he could total her bill. "If you will, please add the total to my account."

He thumped Pegeen's letter against his palm. "I seem to

recall I'm holding a letter addressed to you as well. I figured to send it home with Mrs. Cox if you didn't come 'round in a day or two." He turned his back to her to search the various cubbyholes of his desk. "Yup. Here 'tis."

He shoved the well-traveled envelope across the counter toward her. She picked it up and inspected the handwriting. Her mother's unmistakable penmanship revealed the letter's author.

Kathleen couldn't afford to dally more than a minute, two at the most, if she hoped to give Francine's address to Mr. Maxwell and make it back to the mill on time, but she was anxious to learn the latest news of the family. Months had passed since she'd last heard from her folks. Besides, she had to appease her hunger pangs before she headed down River Row toward the Steadman Shipping offices.

She shoved the letter into her apron pocket and gathered up her crackers and cheese. Excusing herself from Mr. Mathers's prying glances, Kathleen went outside and perched on the edge of one of the wooden rockers that lined the store's porch.

A shower of crumbs rained onto her lap when she bit into a cheese-topped biscuit. Between bites, and using her one free hand, Kathleen pulled her mail from out of her pocket and broke the wax seal. When she gave the page a quick shake to open its folds, a silvery daguerreotype fell out.

The photograph bore the images of a stern-faced man and three impish-looking boys—all strangers to Kathleen. The man, who sported mutton-chop whiskers, appeared to be about the age of her father. She guessed the age range of the boys to be between ten and fourteen, the same as her own younger brother and two sisters. Her curiosity piqued, she turned to her mother's letter and began to read:

Dearest Kathleen,

I hope this letter finds you in good health and still enjoying your mill work. We all be fine here in Indiana, but the farm keeps us all too busy to sit down and write. Not much news to report anyway. Our days are pretty much taken up with the same old routines and the usual chores of farming life.

No doubt you wonder why I am sending a stranger's photograph with my letter, so I shall explain forthwith. I think I may have mentioned this man, Amos Grundy, when I wrote you about our last summer's barn-raising. Mr. Grundy is a widower, left to raise his three boys on his own. His wife died soon after we took up homesteading on the property adjacent to his. Well, your pa has been discussing you with Mr. Grundy. He told him of our plan to bring you out here as soon as the crops bear ample harvest to provide for the family without your mill income.

Last time they talked, your pa mentioned that we are setting our sights on bringing you out in the fall. (I had hopes of keeping this a surprise till summer, but considering the circumstances, I thought I'd best let in on our secret now.) Upon hearing this news, Mr. Grundy asked your pa if he thought you might be agreeable to the idea of allowing him to court you whenever you were settled.

He is anxious to find another wife and a mother for his boys. As you can see by the photograph, the gentleman is a good deal older than you. Even so, he is well established and seems like a mighty dependable and hard-working man. Knowing how you love children, I figured you might cotton to the idea of a ready-made family. . . .

Kathleen clinched her fists, crumpling the letter as she lowered it to her lap. She could bear to read no further. A jumble of conflicting thoughts and emotions assailed her. When her folks first moved out west and she went to work for the mill, she had cried herself to sleep, she missed them so. She'd constantly longed for the day when she would receive word that she could join them. However, she had now grown accustomed to living on her own. She liked the independence she had found away from her father's domination, and the thought of being under the authority of the solemn Amos Grundy appealed to her even less.

Kathleen stared back at the four pairs of steely eyes that glared up at her from the daguerreotype. *Dear Father,* she silently prayed, *if this is what You want for my life, please take away this sadness and give me Your peace.* She feared nothing short of a miracle would bring her prayer request to pass.

As much as she loved children, she didn't trust the glint of malice she saw sparking from these boys' eyes. She suspected the trio would seek to make her life miserable with their mischief. Moreover, when the time came for her to marry, she didn't want to wed as the replacement for an old farmer's wife. All her life, she had imagined her husband would be someone closer to her age. Someone with a kind smile, a sharp mind, a gentle strength, and an adventuresome spirit. Someone like. . .

Maxwell Steadman!

Kathleen leaped from her seat, tucking her mother's letter and the Grundy family daguerreotype securely in her apron pocket. She fingered the rest of the pocket's contents to make sure she still carried Francine's address as she hurried down the steps in the direction of Steadman Shipping Company. Her heart pounded harder, faster with each step.

When she entered the outer office, a roly-poly gentleman looked up from his work long enough to point her toward an open door. Before Mr. Maxwell noticed her, she took in the room's disheveled condition and noted his frazzled state. She felt a pang of pity for him at the sight of the chaos he'd come home to face. *The poor man really looks like he could use some help,* she thought. Just then, he glanced up and saw her standing in the doorway. His troubled expression relaxed into a smile.

"Come in and have a seat, Miss McKenna. It won't take me but a moment to shove these papers out of the way." Mr. Maxwell stood as he spoke. He reached for a batch of papers and began tapping them on the desk to square them into a neat bundle.

"Thank you, but I really can't stay or I will be late returning to work." Kathleen felt around in her pocket for the note she'd come to deliver. She tried to ignore the sinking feeling that tugged at her spirit as her hand touched the stiff outline of her mother's letter and its enclosure.

"Here is the name and address of Pegeen's sister." She held it out for him to take. "I want you to know, Sir, how much I appreciate your willingness to go to all this trouble for my friend. Surely such kindness won't go unnoticed or unrewarded by the Lord."

Mr. Maxwell reached out and took the slip of paper from Kathleen's hand. When he did, his fingers brushed lightly against hers, and a warm ripple traveled up her arm.

"I've found reward enough in your appreciation," he replied. "I've always been one to enjoy the planning of a good surprise."

That evening when she returned to the boardinghouse after work, Kathleen read over her mother's letter in its entirety before shoving it in a hatbox under her bed. In a postscript, her mother had suggested Kathleen write a letter of personal introduction to Mr. Grundy, returning to him the valuable daguerreotype he had so graciously sent for her to see. Though she knew she should, Kathleen never quite found the time to pen a reply to her mother nor compose a letter to her unwelcome suitor.

With eye-blinking swiftness, the weeks passed by and the production of the Shipping Steadman's rush order drew near completion. Over the course of the thirty workdays during those five weeks, Mr. Maxwell wandered through the weave room each afternoon to check on the progress of his sailcloth production. Kathleen always knew when he had entered the room. She would look up from her loom in hopes of stealing a quick glimpse of him, and every time, she caught him studying her. Only after they had exchanged surreptitious nods and smiles would he leave the mill; and always after he had gone, Kathleen required several minutes to still her racing heart and dry her perspiring hands.

Each of the five Sundays throughout Mr. Maxwell's stay in town, he squeezed onto the end of the Steadman family pew next to Carter. From her prescribed seat four rows behind the Steadmans, Kathleen inclined her ear toward Maxwell during the singing of the hymns and recitation of the responsive readings. She let herself fall silent and strained to pick out his thundering bass voice from among all the other worshipers, a pleasant warmth washing over her.

During one such time, Pegeen jabbed her in the side. "This is the third Sunday you've done this," she rasped. "Turn to hymn number fifty-one." When Kathleen tried to show her that she'd found the right page, Pegeen just shook her head. "I'm thinkin' your mind is on a certain man, rather than on God."

After Parson Hull pronounced the benediction and the congregation filed out the door past the minister and his family, Kathleen found Vivian Steadman waiting for her on the church steps. Mr. Maxwell stood behind her, sneaking a peppermint to little Betty Hull, and Kathleen spied him giving the toddler an exaggerated wink. Mrs. Steadman looped her arm through her nephew's and insisted upon Kathleen walking with them, claiming she'd sent Carter and Isabel on ahead.

It was on that very Sunday, as they turned onto the lane leading up Croner Hill, that Mrs. Steadman stopped in the middle of the road and exclaimed, "Enough of this stodgy 'Mr. Steadman' and 'Miss McKenna' nonsense. There's no reason why you can't refer to one another by your given names whenever you are away from the confines of work." In order to keep peace with the dear woman, both Kathleen and Maxwell complied.

The following Sunday afternoon, Maxwell offered to escort Kathleen and Isabel to Kindred Hearts for their sewing circle. He stayed just long enough to slip a little green something into Miss Amy's hand and to give Ruthie a quick piggyback ride around the parlor. Still, Kathleen marveled at the difference between the awkwardness he displayed during his first Sunday visit to Kindred Hearts and the ease with which he now joined the girls in outright tomfoolery.

The more comfortable Kathleen grew in Maxwell's presence and the stronger their friendship grew, the greater her dread of that fast-approaching day when the *Steadfast*, replete with a suit of new sails, would carry him off to sea and out of her life.

Maxwell had no way of giving a specific date when he would return. He often discussed the host of reasons why he wanted to cut his trip short, but he had no way of predicting bad weather while at sea or foreseeing the myriad problems that might arise in the process of transporting the Irish immigrants.

Kathleen worried she might never see him again. If she could not convince her parents to let her remain in Eastead instead of joining them in Indiana, she might very well be gone before Maxwell returned.

During one of her many sleepless nights, as she lay groping for any possible solution to her dilemma concerning Amos Grundy and her parents' reunion plans, a crazy notion took seed. *If only Maxwell were to ask for permission to court me, I would have good reason for Ma and Pa to let me stay in Eastead and decline Mr. Grundy's advances.*

The idea no sooner sprouted than she valiantly endeavored to tamp it down with logic and reason. *Just because Maxwell seems to enjoy my company does not mean he has any romantic ideas in mind. He's never made any overtures along such lines.*

Yet when she almost had herself convinced of her fantasy's impossibility, her internal debate roared on. *If a Steadman could fall in love with a mill girl once, why couldn't it happen again?* And so, like the spring blossoms throughout the village, this bud of hope flowered and grew.

The day before Maxwell was slated to sail for Europe, Kathleen set out for Sunday service under weepy gray skies. An occasional raindrop trickled down the brim of her cornette and splattered onto her shawl while she slogged alone through the village streets.

She had dawdled through her morning constitution until all the other boarders had gone. Pegeen must have sensed her dark mood and her need for solitude. She hadn't pressed when Kathleen had urged her to go on ahead with Grace, promising to join them at the church.

As much as Kathleen wanted to savor each remaining moment in Maxwell's presence, she could not shake the feeling of impending heartbreak. Any hope of Maxwell asking to court her had all but withered away. She wondered if things would have been different had she found the courage to confide in him about Amos Grundy. Until the last few days, she'd felt it sufficient to inform Maxwell that, unless some pressing business kept her in Eastead, she would be joining her family in Indiana come fall. Whenever she talked of such things, he would stare at her and nod with a pensive look in his eye. She'd thought for certain he was on the verge of voicing the words she longed to hear, but those words never came.

While he had remained friendly all along, he had made no advances toward pursuing anything other than an amiable relationship. She realized now the full extent of her foolishness in thinking such a fairy tale might come true. Within a day, she would likely say a final fare-thee-well to the one man in her life with whom she never wanted to part company.

Throughout the worship service, Kathleen found her gaze ever wandering to the slumped form of Maxwell in the pew four rows ahead. Normally, he towered above everyone else, with his shoulders squared and his back erect; but on this Sunday, he bent his head low and seemed as deflated and somber as she. For the first time in more than a month, she had not been able to pick out his voice during the hymns. From her vantage point behind him, he didn't appear to be singing at all. She reasoned that his mind was probably racing with the details and preparations for his upcoming voyage.

Kathleen struggled to join in during Pastor Hull's lengthy prayer. She knew in her heart of hearts that God had not turned a deaf ear to her pleas. Even so, she fought an immature urge to pout when He was apparently answering no.

A patch of blue sky peeked through the clouds as Kathleen walked outside after the service. She ambled toward the cemetery to wait for the Steadman clan to exit the church. The girls from Kindred Hearts dashed by her on their way to Sunday dinner, a chorus of "see you laters" trailing after them.

Vivian Steadman was the first of her family to appear. Waving her lace-tatted handkerchief in the air, she trotted in short, wooden steps toward Kathleen.

"I hope you don't mind, Dear—" As she reached Kathleen's side, Vivian had to stop for breath before she could continue. She patted her chest and fanned her face with her hanky. "Carter and Isabel and I have just a very short call to make on Widow Pike. She's laid up in bed after taking a nasty spill, and we rode the buggy over this morning so we could drop her off a few groceries."

From the corner of her eye, Kathleen saw Maxwell leaning against a maple tree in the churchyard, and without warning, she felt a welling of hot tears threatening to spill over their banks. Kathleen hurriedly whisked them away as Vivian motioned for her nephew to join them.

"I know you aren't acquainted with the widow. Maxwell isn't, either. So I didn't think you would object to letting him escort you on to our house. We'll hurry home, full chisel, quick as the delivery's made."

During the past five weeks, Kathleen had never found herself alone in the company of Maxwell. The prospect left her trembling. A trap had been laid, set, and snapped by Vivian Steadman, and Kathleen had been ensnared before she could say a word.

Maxwell stepped in beside Kathleen as Mrs. Steadman

excused herself and headed for the waiting buggy. Cupping his hand under Kathleen's elbow, he guided her in the direction of Croner Hill. "Please don't be upset over Aunt Vivian's blatant matchmaking." Maxwell looked toward the horizon as he spoke. "Actually, this is the one time I solicited her chicanery. You see—"

He stopped alongside the road, and Kathleen followed suit. She watched as he shoved his hands in his trouser pockets and began kicking at a half-buried stone in the soft earth. "Before I leave town, there's a matter I want to discuss with you in private. I have a request I want to make." He looked up at the sky, then back down to his shoes. With a final tap of his boot toe, he sent the stone skittering into the grass.

"I know this may come as quite a surprise to you, so I ask that you hear me out fully before you respond." He darted a glance toward her, and she indicated her agreement with a dip of her head.

"Since Carter has charted the path toward progressive thinking here in Eastead, I talked things over with him, and he assures me he thinks this is a great idea if you are open to it."

He gazed down at Kathleen, and his nervous smile sent fiery meteors blazing through her chest. Her heart began to pound with resurrected hope. She held her breath, afraid even the slightest movement would spoil the moment.

Once he spoke the words, she would breathe again.

Once he spoke the words, she would promise to wait for his return.

Once he spoke the words, she would write her folks with

word of her postponed Indiana travel plans. When next she saw her family, she expected to be Maxwell Steadman's bride. Amos Grundy would have to find himself someone else to serve as his replacement wife and mother to his sons.

Maxwell looked left, then right, before taking a half-step to shorten the distance between them. Kathleen couldn't keep from shivering when he leaned toward her ever so slightly.

"I've pondered the possibilities for several weeks now. . . ." He seemed to delight in her growing tension. The weathered laugh lines around his molasses-brown eyes crinkled in merriment.

"Frankly, Kathleen, I've grown more and more certain of my decision with each passing day. Please excuse my choice of words—but you are the perfect man for the job."

She shot him a puzzled glare and silently mouthed, *What?*

"I want to hire you. You'll be the best overseer Steadman Shipping has ever had!"

Chapter 5

Weeks later, Maxwell stood on the *Steadfast*'s deck at midship and looked out over the choppy waters of the Atlantic. At their present clip, they were on course for making this his fastest journey ever to Europe and back. Even so, it seemed to him that the days since he'd left home had dragged on without end.

The suspense of not knowing Kathleen's decision about her future tormented Maxwell's thoughts night and day. Even if they made the voyage in record time, he had no way of learning before they reached shore whether she'd still be in Eastead or would have already gone to join her family in Indiana as she had been contemplating.

He'd never thought he would tire of the salt air and surf breezes, but at present he would give it all up for the chance to spend time with Kathleen McKenna. Maxwell's vision blurred as he stared down at the swells, which rocked the ship gently from side to side.

The same sea that used to carry him to grand adventures

and distant lands now seemed like a watery prison cell, placing him in solitary confinement away from the one person on earth he wanted to see. The very ocean he once thought he could spend his lifetime sailing upon taunted him by sparkling with the same shimmering green hue he'd seen dancing in Kathleen's eyes.

He recalled that when he'd presented his case for hiring her as overseer, he'd seen those green eyes of hers glisten with tears. He'd wondered from then until now if they were tears of joy or distress.

He had hoped she would accept the position on the spot. Instead, with a controlled voice and staid expression, she had said, "I'll give your proposition due consideration over the course of your absence. You'll have my response when you return."

If Kathleen had decided to reject his offer and had instead continued with her plans to leave in the fall, he simply had to return before she departed to try to change her mind. If she did agree to become Steadman Shipping's overseer, he had already determined to stay in town for as long as it took to see her situated and comfortable in her new post.

Ever since his frustrating encounter with Kathleen on the eve of his departure, Maxwell had been chastising himself for not discussing the job possibility with her earlier. But he had needed until that last day to convince himself he wasn't making a huge mistake. No matter how sharp Kathleen's business acumen, the idea of offering a woman the highest position in his company, second only to him, was not something he had readily come to accept.

Only after carefully weighing the benefits against the liabilities had he decided that hiring Kathleen would be worth the risk. Thanks to Carter, the area merchants with whom Kathleen would have dealings would simply chalk up her hiring as another Steadman idiosyncrasy. After all, if Carter could see his way clear to take a mill girl for a wife, then Maxwell could chance hiring one.

When Carter chose to make Isabel his wife rather than his employee, he made the far better choice. Perhaps you should have done the same. The thought circled round in his mind like a ship caught in a maelstrom. Maxwell tightened his grip on the railing to steady himself. He felt dizzy from imagining what Kathleen's answer might have been had his proposal been one of marriage instead of employment.

"Here now! It's help we're needin'. And fast!"

Maxwell turned to seek out the frantic cry and saw one of the Irish mill girl hirelings coming up the central hatchway from top steerage. When her gaunt form reached the deck and rushed over to him, he recognized her as Pegeen's sister, Francine.

"Oh, Mr. Steadman, Sir, beggin' your pardon, but we've urgent need of a doctor below." Despite her obvious desperation, the lass curtsied before him. "Can you point me to his quarters?"

"Cook Jaggers serves as surgeon in cases of emergency. I'll fetch him straightaway." Maxwell started for the ladder leading down to the galley but stopped and turned back to Francine. "May I tell him the nature of the distress?"

Color flooded the teenager's cheeks. "'Tis Molly, Sir. She's havin' a dreadful time with her birthing. Mrs. Hart's tried to do the midwivin' herself, but there's difficulties beyond her skills, so she sent me to fetch help. The bairn's having an awful struggle trying to enter the world, and Molly appears to be slipping away. We'd best hurry."

"Shall I send down some boiled water and rags?" Maxwell had never witnessed a delivery before, but he vaguely recalled having heard of these items being necessities.

"We're beyond that, Mr. Steadman. A doctor and a miracle are what she's needing now."

The gravity of the situation began to sink in. Maxwell called over his shoulder to the girl on his way down the hatchway leading to the galley. "I'll be back with Jaggers as quick as I can. Tell Mrs. Hart help is on the way."

Three young women, one of them Francine, clustered in the narrow steerage passageway at the base of the steps. "Mrs. Hart says ye both should go on in," Francine said, pointing to a cabin door at the opposite end of the passageway.

Maxwell didn't see how his presence would be much help, but he kept his protests to himself. Staying close on the cook's heels, he squeezed past the ladies and followed Jaggers into the cramped quarters. As soon as Maxwell crossed over the threshold, the stench in the room made his stomach lurch.

A still form lay in the bottom berth along the port side, shrouded with a rag of a blanket. The wife of one of the ship's newly hired sailors stood at the bedside, her apron and skirts stained with blood. She held a small bundle in her arms.

"'Tis grateful I am of your making such haste, but our dear Molly is beyond helping now, God rest her soul." At the midwife's words, a tiny bleat of a cry rose from the bundle in her arms. "I did me best to save the new momma. I'm promising you, I did."

"I've no doubt," Maxwell offered. "You're to be commended for your efforts, Mrs. Hart." Tendrils of hair clung to the woman's perspiring forehead. Distress lined her face.

Cook Jaggers knelt beside the berth and touched the foot of the lifeless figure. "You did better than I could have done, Ma'am. I've never helped with a birthing before, so I doubt I'd have been much aid."

Maxwell stared at the moving blanket the midwife clutched. A feeling of utter despair and helplessness overwhelmed him at the scene he beheld. He thought of his brother, Lucas. Always before, he had ridiculed Lucas for throwing away a promising and lucrative business career to enter medical school. Rather than planning on being a physician to the wealthy, Lucas was determined to care for the poor. Suddenly Maxwell held a newfound appreciation for his younger brother. He finally understood why Lucas had chosen such a calling.

"The child." Maxwell's gaze was transfixed on the tiny bundle. "Will it live?"

"Aye. I'm thinking so. She's whole and hearty, and I'll see to her nursin' myself as my own Erin is nearly weaned."

"What of the woman's husband? Is he not onboard?"

Maxwell didn't recall one of the new sailors having a wife named Molly, but he was still trying to learn all the men's names, much less those of their families.

Mrs. Hart shook her head. "No. Miz Molly said he died of the typhus back in Febr'ary. Said on his deathbed he'd made her promise to get out of Ireland 'fore the fever took her, too. When Miz Molly signed on as a mill girl back in Bray, she kept secret her being with child. None of us knew. She figured she wouldn't be allowed to immigrate if anyone found out, and she was desperate to provide her wee bairn a chance for a decent life." She gazed at the infant in her arms. "Poor thing doesn't stand much hope of that now, bein' orphaned and all. Whatever will become of the dear? I'd be takin' her in, but with five young 'uns, Mr. Hart and me have more stomachs to feed than we can fill now."

Immediately, Maxwell thought of Amy Ross and the Kindred Hearts Orphanage. "I know someone in Eastead who'll give her a home. I'll make the arrangements once we reach shore."

"We've more pressing matters to tend at present." Jaggers rose and stepped back. "Miz Molly's body needs preparing before we can send her to her final resting place in the sea. Mrs. Hart, will you honor the deceased by sewing her final hammock about her?"

"Certainly."

"I'll fetch an extra from the forecastle." Jaggers had one foot over the threshold. "Have you a needle and thread?"

"Aye. A short while afore, during the birthin', I had them

right here at my feet. I fear in all of the panic, they got kicked under the berth." She cast her gaze about the room.

"I'll be fetching the hammock then while you search." The crusty old salt tipped the brim of his hat. "Mr. Steadman, no need for us both to be going." With that he was gone.

"Be a dear—" Before Maxwell knew what had happened, Mrs. Hart thrust the baby in his arms. Ignoring his blubbering protests, she dropped to her knees in search of the missing items.

"What am I to do with you?" Maxwell asked the teeny babe, frowning. "I've never held a baby before." Just then, the infant flung her miniature arms wildly about and managed to grab hold of Maxwell's shirt at the spot just over his heart. He broke out into a wide grin. Now he knew the meaning of the phrase "tugging at one's heartstrings." He marveled at the intricacy of God's handiwork as he studied the baby girl's delicate features and diminutive fingers. If she hadn't been too tightly wrapped, he would have counted her toes.

"Has she a name, Mrs. Hart?" Although Maxwell couldn't bear to take his eyes off the infant to see if the woman had found what she was looking for, he could still hear her rousting about on the floor.

"Alas, no," came a muffled response. "Before we could ask, her momma's soul had departed."

"What would you think of naming her 'Molly' then—in memory of the deceased?"

"I think ye have a fine idea, Sir." Mrs. Hart rose from the floor and shook the dust from her skirts. "Look-a here, but what the wee bairn hasn't taken to you!" the midwife exclaimed, stroking the fuzz of chestnut brown hair on the baby's crown. "Seeing as how she's sleeping snug in your arms, would you mind holdin' her awhile longer as I tend to her mother's final needs?"

When the ship's bell signaled the first dogwatch, the off-duty crew and passengers gathered on deck for a brief committal service before releasing the body of Molly O'Fallon into the sea. The ship's captain, Gable Putney, read Scripture and said a few words before turning to Maxwell to pray. Though no one on board had known the deceased particularly well, all the women wept aloud. Maxwell, too, fought to keep tears at bay.

As the assembly disbursed, Maxwell saw Mrs. Hart and her children waiting for their turn to descend through the hatch leading to steerage. In her arms, she held the infant Molly.

"Might I have a word with you, Ma'am?" Maxwell called out to Mrs. Hart after excusing himself momentarily from his conversation with the captain. She sent her young crew of five down below and crossed the deck to stand before Maxwell and the ship's captain.

"I've been discussing with Captain Putney, here, the issue of the orphan's care. We both appreciate what you're prepared to do in looking after her. However, I feel we owe it to her departed mother not to expose the newborn to the unsanitary conditions of steerage until she's gained some strength." Maxwell wanted to catch a glimpse of little Molly, but Mrs. Hart held her close to her bosom and bundled up against the cool sea breeze.

"I offered the captain to give you my cabin, but he insists on being the one to move off the quarterdeck. We argued about this matter until he pulled rank and ordered me to comply with his command." Maxwell clicked his heels and jerked his right hand away from his brow in mock salute. "Cap'n Putney's bunking with his first mate so you can use his quarters until we reach America. He said he'd never be able to sleep with a crying babe in the cabin next to his anyway."

With ever-increasing frequency, Maxwell found himself offering to look after little Molly so Mrs. Hart could tend to her own family's needs. He had plenty of time on his hands aboard ship, and he saw this as good experience. He planned to amaze everyone with his child-tending skills when he'd go to visit Molly at Kindred Hearts. He could just imagine Kathleen's shocked expression.

Often Maxwell carried the sleeping newborn from the captain's cabin next door to his own and tucked her into an open chest he'd converted into a makeshift crib. He spent his days caressing her delicate skin and memorizing Molly's tiny features, laughing when she puckered her rosebud lips. He marveled that the soft down of her hair matched the chestnut brown shade of Kathleen's. He swore they shared the same celadon green eyes as well, but Mrs. Hart assured him a baby's eye color would change.

By the time they sailed into Boston Harbor three weeks later, Maxwell had taken full charge of Molly's care. He relinquished his ward to Mrs. Hart only at feeding times and during the night's midwatch between midnight and four o'clock. He even mastered the art of nappy changing, though occasionally the odor made him gag. Still, he didn't mind suffering through the unpleasantries for the chance to watch this living, breathing miracle.

When the awe of holding the tiny infant overwhelmed him, he remembered back to the day he met Kathleen. Her words echoed in his heart and mind. He couldn't fathom then how she might ever think it possible to love a child born to another with the same devotion a parent had for a child of his own flesh and blood.

He had thought it most peculiar to consider the caring for an orphan anything other than an act of Christian charity. Now he was beginning to understand what Parson Hull had meant when he'd said he had received a greater joy and blessing from his newly adopted daughters than he could ever hope to give.

This tiny human being held the power to make Maxwell smile even while she slept. And each time Molly latched onto his index finger with the strength of a Lilliputian Goliath, he could feel his heartstrings cinch another notch tighter.

He hated to think of this special time coming to an end. Only his hope of seeing Kathleen spurred him toward home.

When the bell tolled the end of another workweek at the mill, Kathleen, in symphony with the other weavers, yanked the metal levers to the right of her loom. With a collective shudder, the machines ground to a halt. A deafening stillness ensued.

Kathleen came alongside Pegeen, and together they joined in the push for the door. Although they stepped into the full sun of a late summer day, the air felt cooler to Kathleen after leaving the stifling heat of the steam-powered mill.

"Grace ought to have arrived back home in Vermont 'bout now, given her stage met no delays," Pegeen said as they crossed the dirt road and headed for their boardinghouse.

"I expect you're right," Kathleen agreed. "And I also expect the next time we hear from her, she will have the title 'Mrs.' in front of her name." The fragrance of roses scented the air as they dashed up the stoop and passed Mrs. Cox's prized bushes on their way through the front door.

"I wonder who might take her place in our room." Pegeen climbed three stairs, then paused in midstride and looked back at Kathleen. She lowered her voice to a whisper. "I know I be awful for e'er even thinkin' such things, but I hope whoever joins us possesses a mite sweeter disposition."

Kathleen kneaded her bottom lip to keep from breaking into a wide smile. Her whisper matched Pegeen's. "I have to admit, I've wished for the same myself." So far, she had managed to keep from leaking even the slightest hint of the surprise she hoped would greet Pegeen one day soon. However, with Grace now gone and Pegeen's speculations growing, Kathleen feared that the secret would be increasingly hard to keep.

Abruptly Pegeen stopped moving when she opened their bedroom door, and Kathleen plowed into the Irish girl's back. A squeal split the air. Kathleen worried she'd injured her friend, but before she could express her concern, Pegeen screamed out, "Francine!"

A teenaged version of Kathleen's roommate, dressed in a threadbare gown, leaped up from the edge of the bed and ran toward Pegeen. The two sisters shared hugs and kisses, tears and laughter. Then they stood back, looked at each other, and started the celebration all over again. Kathleen tried to observe the reunion from the hallway but could hardly see for her own happy tears.

"Ooch! Ye have to be tellin' me now." Pegeen pinched Francine's cheek playfully, followed by a gentle love pat. "Who? I mean, what? How can it be that you're here?" In her sister's presence, Pegeen's brogue was thicker than Kathleen had ever remembered hearing before.

"From what I'm understandin', your roommate played more than a wee part in the idea." Francine tipped her head in greeting toward Kathleen, while Pegeen just stared with her mouth agape. "Might'n you be the fair Kathleen I've been hearing so much about? If so, I'll be forever beholden for your kindness."

Kathleen tried to dismiss the embarrassing accolades with a wave. "I did nothing but suggest your name to the two Mr. Steadmans when I heard of their plans to hire new workers from Bray."

"Mercy! Your mention of the Steadman name is re-mindin' me, I made Mr. Steadman a promise to give ye this note first thing upon our meeting." Francine reached into her pocket and withdrew an embossed note card bearing the

Steadman Shipping crest on its wax seal.

As Kathleen accepted the note, heat flooded her cheeks. She felt her knees starting to give way, so she moved to sit down on her bed.

"I'll be going to introduce Francine around to the other girls and giving you a private moment to read." Pegeen offered Kathleen an understanding smile as she tugged her sister toward the door.

Maxwell is home. The realization brought an instant smile.

During the first month after Maxwell's departure, Kathleen had been so heartbroken and embarrassed by her misinterpretation of his feelings for her, she'd set her mind to heading for Indiana before he returned. She had even penned a letter to her parents in which she said she would be willing to consider the courtship of Mr. Grundy when she arrived. Yet, that letter—like all the others—never got mailed.

The longer Maxwell's absence dragged on, the more Kathleen's heart yearned to see him again, until her longing to be in his presence eventually overcame her embarrassment. She determined to accept the overseer's position after all. She must be near him, even if it meant as one in his employ rather than as the one he loved.

She had sealed her decision by finally posting a response to the letter she'd received from her mother more than two months earlier. Kathleen wrote her parents of the rare opportunity she'd been given to serve as the Steadman Shipping overseer. She begged for their understanding of her being unable to join them in Indiana in the fall. Then she asked that they express to Mr. Grundy the honor she felt at his asking to court her—and to please pass along her sincere apologies at having to decline. With one last look at the daguerreotype, she had slipped it in the envelope and breathed a sigh of relief when she handed it over to Mr. Mathers at the mill store to be mailed.

Now, she was ready for a new chapter of her life to begin.

Kathleen traced over the wax imprint on Maxwell's note before breaking the seal. A quiver raced through her as she began to read the bold script written by Maxwell's hand.

Dear Miss Kathleen:

If you find it convenient, I should like to meet with you this evening prior to the supper hour. Aunt Vivian and Isabel asked me to mention that they will have a place set for you at the table. They hope you can stay and dine with the family after we conclude our business.

Best Regards,
Maxwell Steadman

She knew he had only business in mind. No doubt he wanted to learn her response to his offer of the overseer's job. Still, the thought of seeing Maxwell again after all this time left her trembling.

Kathleen quickly changed into the mint-julep green gown she'd sewn from her new allotment of material. Then she made her excuses to Mrs. Cox as to why she'd be missing supper and headed out the door. Above the chatter of the other boarders,

Kathleen could hear the laughter of Pegeen and Francine floating through the sitting room's open window as she passed by.

Kathleen expected a servant to answer when a short while later she pounded the brass knocker on the door of the Steadman mansion. Instead, the appearance of Maxwell sent her pulse racing and left her mouth dry. She had forgotten just how small she felt when standing this close to him.

"Welcome home, Mr. Steadman," she said. After the tension of their last meeting and their lengthy separation, Kathleen no longer felt comfortable calling him by his first name. Suddenly she couldn't think of what else to say. In the looming presence of Maxwell, Kathleen found herself unable to think at all.

"Thank you. I'm happy to be back in Eastead." Maxwell motioned for her to come inside and pushed the door shut behind her. "I'm glad to see you. It was so good of you to come on such short notice."

They stood alone in the expansive marble foyer, although Kathleen could hear noises coming from the library. She thought sure she must be imagining it, but Maxwell seemed as nervous as she. He kept glancing toward the library, then down the hall. He ran his finger around the inside of his collar and tugged.

He cleared his throat before he spoke again. "When last we talked, we left some business unfinished."

Finally, he let his gaze rest on Kathleen, and her insides withered under his scrutiny. Determined not to let her tumultuous emotions show, she put on her most serious expression and gave him a quick nod.

"Let's step into the parlor, shall we?" Maxwell motioned for her to lead the way.

Kathleen poised herself on the edge of the divan, while Maxwell began to pace back and forth on the marble hearth of the cold fireplace. He paused and drew a deep breath.

"I would like to re-address the matter of the position at Steadman Shipping, which we discussed prior to my departure."

As he spoke, Kathleen thought through her response. Her mouth felt so dry, she only hoped her voice wouldn't crack when she accepted the job. She wanted him to think she could be the epitome of professionalism.

"A situation has arisen."

Kathleen jerked her full attention to Maxwell. He was staring at her with a strange look in his eye.

"I have reconsidered my previous offer."

What is he saying? Would he dare deny me the overseer position now? She felt her jaw clinch as a flash of anger shot through her, followed by a heart-piercing pain. She dropped her gaze to her lap so he wouldn't notice her welling tears.

"I have another proposal. . . . What I believe to be a more suitable arrangement for us both. . ."

He lifted an armless chair and positioned it opposite her, then took his seat and scooted forward so close, his face was within inches of hers. His intent stare forced her to meet his gaze. She felt certain he could hear her heart pounding. Or was she hearing his?

"For weeks I thought about asking you to be my wife when

I returned. I had decided if you said yes, I would curtail my travels as much as possible and stay right here in Eastead so I might be near you—and eventually a house full of children. . . ." Maxwell's voice trailed off, and he gave her a slight smile.

"I thought you needed to know these were my thoughts before a sweet Irish lass named Molly came into my life."

At Maxwell's mention of another woman, Kathleen felt the color drain from her face. To her horror, he didn't stop there.

"Please wait here for a moment. There's someone I want you to meet." Maxwell stood abruptly and walked out of the room.

A crushing heaviness filled her being. She feared she might faint. She could not imagine how any man could be so cruel. First, to tell her he'd considered speaking the very words she so longed to hear, only to crush her hopes and shatter her heart—and then to insist on introducing her to the woman who had won his affections away from her. She longed to run before he returned, but her absolute shock kept her frozen in place.

Only a few moments had passed when Kathleen heard Maxwell's heavy footfall on the foyer's marble tile outside the parlor door. *This Molly must have been waiting in the library,* she thought, *eager to swoop in and gloat over her conquest of Maxwell.* The vengeful thought no sooner flashed through Kathleen's consciousness than a pang of guilt ensued.

"God, grant me the ability to be gracious, though I feel anything but," she whispered in prayer. "In my hurt, don't let me lash out at this innocent woman—or Maxwell, either, for that matter."

Determined not to let her emotional state add to her humiliation, she squared her shoulders, drew a deep breath, then rose to meet the woman Maxwell loved.

Maxwell hurried across the foyer and into the library, where Isabel stood waiting for him to take Molly from her arms. He grimaced to think how badly he had bungled his attempt to explain things to Kathleen.

He'd thought it necessary to express what his intentions had been before Molly entered his life because he never wanted Kathleen to think he proposed marriage to her just to give his Molly a mother. Still, he knew he'd left her totally befuddled in the parlor just now. He only hoped she'd forgive him once she fully understood.

"Miss McKenna, I would like to introduce you to Miss Molly O'Fallon—soon to be Molly Steadman, if I have my way."

Kathleen appeared to be studying her hands. At his words, she slowly lifted her gaze to look at him. Her composed demeanor gave way to a look of shock.

"Why, it's a baby!"

"Yes. Didn't I make that clear? During our ocean crossing, little Molly here was orphaned minutes after her birth." Maxwell made shushing sounds to soothe the baby's mewings as he moved to close the distance between Kathleen and him.

Reaching to pull the blanket away from Molly's face, Kathleen leaned in to get a closer look. "But my, she is beautiful.

Poor, sweet dear. What's to become of her? Will you turn her over to the care of Miss Amy at Kindred Hearts?"

"Perhaps you didn't understand me a moment ago. I plan to make Molly my daughter and spoil her royally." Maxwell laughed, and the baby started in reaction to the sound, then stilled. "You'll hear all the details in due time. I've decided to reopen my parents' old place on the east side of Croner Hill and make a home for us there. Arrangements have already been made with the woman who served as the baby's nursemaid aboard ship to continue in that capacity." The serious gaze Molly transfixed on him reminded him so much of Kathleen, he laughed again.

He offered the precious bundle for Kathleen to receive. With tendermost care, she took the baby from his arms.

"Kathleen, about that job we discussed—" Maxwell paused, and Kathleen looked up from Molly to gaze into his eyes. He swallowed hard against the lump forming in his throat. Here, right in front of him, were the two most cherished ladies in his life.

"About the job?" Kathleen urged him on with a lift of her eyebrows and a nod.

"Right. About the overseer's position." He took a deep breath and began again. "I've decided there must be a man somewhere out there who can fill that vacancy. But, Kathleen, I could never find another person on earth who can fill the role I'm proposing to you now."

Maxwell stroked Molly's chestnut hair. As he did, his hand brushed against Kathleen's. "From the first day I met you, I admired your good business sense. I've always appreciated your intelligence. Yet as much as I value those qualities in you, I've come to realize in these past months away from you, my feelings go much, much deeper than that."

A tear trickled down each of Kathleen's cheeks, but Maxwell knew by her radiant countenance, they were tears of joy.

"You are a woman of immense heart, Kathleen, always giving yourself freely to everyone you meet." He brushed her tears away with his thumb.

"I've seen how you care for those in need. Just by watching you, I've learned what a genuine Christian should be. You've taught me the true meaning of love."

He patted the blanket around Molly's chest. "You are the one who planted the idea in my mind that a man can love an adopted child with the genuine love of a father. If I hadn't met you, I am quite certain I never would have ventured to let this little girl twist my heart into knots."

The baby chose that moment to let out a squeak, but Maxwell kept his gaze fixed on Kathleen.

"I love you, Kathleen. I can't imagine living my life without you by my side. Please, would you marry me? Be my wife and the mother to whatever children God brings into our lives." He searched her celadon green eyes and found his answer before she spoke the word.

"Yes," she whispered. "It's the only Steadman position I ever really wanted to hold."

Maxwell tenderly encompassed Kathleen and Molly in

his arms. "Good, because you are the only woman I ever want to hold." He leaned over the sleeping infant and brushed Kathleen's lips with a kiss.

SUSAN DOWNS

Susan resides in Canton, Ohio. She and her minister husband are the parents of three grown sons and two teenage daughters. Three of their five children joined the Downs family by way of adoption, and Susan readily testifies to the fact that, no matter how they were added to the family, she loves them all the same.

A Second Glance

by Kathleen Paul

Dedication

To Case Tompkins and Evangeline Denmark.
Your encouragement reminds me
who is our Lord and King.

Chapter 1

Ginger Finnegan ignored the noise she heard coming from behind the chicken coop. She tilted her head and a lock of straight hair fell out of the bun at her nape. It draped over her cheek like a copper curtain against the afternoon sun. With her fingers she felt the damp material in her hands, systematically exploring the folds and seams until she came to the collar. Satisfied, she snapped the wet nightgown in front of her and reached up to grasp the laundry line. She secured the garment with wooden peg pins and felt inside the basket to pull out another piece.

Just before she shoved the half-filled laundry basket, she heard the noise again, this time from behind the shed. Her foot nudged the basket across the trampled grass. She followed the line with her hand and hung the next gown.

Those rascals are getting closer, Lord. What mischief be in their conniving little hearts? Well now, perhaps me an' Your sweet Holy Spirit can convince them of the error of their ways. For it is sure I am, they're up to no good.

As she hung the next wee nightgown on the line, Ginger first hummed and then began to sing an Irish blessing song she'd learned at her granny's knee:

Ah Father, Your goodness to me
exceeds all that could be
expected to come to some
who bow to Your majesty.

I thank Ye for home and hearth,
for family and friends
who add to the warmth
of living me life for Thee.

Ginger had a fair idea of who would be most likely to plot a prank against her. She cheerfully entered the little girls' names into her song:

For Patty and Opal, me dears,
who lighten me day
with joy and a cheerful way,
I ask more blessings
from Your giving heart
to strengthen them while they play.

And Aunt Amy, Lord, Your kind servant,
sharing Your love so rare,
may I never cause this good lady
a minute of shame or despair.

Having planted the seeds she intended, Ginger trilled over the notes of a chorus and went on to the other verses with words her granny had actually sung. At the end of the laundry line, Ginger carefully took a step back and reached up to find the second line.

"You knew we were here, didn't you, Ginger?" Patty called from behind the shed.

"Yes, I did." Ginger repositioned the basket so she could scoot it ahead of her in the opposite direction as she continued hanging the clothes.

A coppery-red head popped out from behind the shed. Although Ginger only saw an outline, she imagined the tight curls glistening in the sunlight and the disgruntled look on her eight-year-old sister's face. Another form emerged beside her sister.

"How do you do that?" asked Opal. Dark hair, dark eyes, skin tanned by the sun, she always shadowed Patty wherever she went each day. Ginger grinned as she saw with her limited vision that Opal at this distance literally appeared as her sister's shadow. At seven years of age, Opal followed Patty as the older girl's willing slave and accomplice.

"Oh, the Lord's been generous with me hearing because me eyesight's so poor."

"We were extra awfully quiet," said Patty with a sigh.

"And do I dare ask what dire deed ye were going to do once ye'd snuck up on me?" Ginger hung another gown.

The two little girls giggled.

"I have a snake," said Patty. "Wanna see?" Ginger suppressed a shudder and nodded. She left the laundry and moved to the back porch steps. Sunshine drenched the area, and Ginger could see the gray mass before she reached out a hand in a habitual gesture of affirmation. She hated to appear awkward just as much as she hated to appear squeamish.

The girls followed her to the stoop. As soon as Ginger sat with her hands held out, Patty placed their captive in her palms. Patty and Opal plopped down on the step to watch her.

Ginger slid her fingers along the warm, dry scales of the foot-long snake.

"Ye've had him awhile, have ye not? He's too dry to be good for him."

"We caught him after breakfast," said Patty.

"And where did ye have him during our midday meal?"

Both girls giggled.

"Well then, maybe ye better not tell me."

The girls giggled even harder.

Ginger held the snake close to her face and turned him in the light.

"Can you see the stripes, Ginger?" asked Patty. "He's got thin yellow stripes. One on his back and two on his sides. I named him Homer."

"Mostly I see the black," said Ginger. "But up close I can see his stripes. I'm thinking he's a ribbon snake, and one we will call a dead snake if ye don't put him back where he belongs."

"How do you know he's a boy snake, Ginger?" asked Opal.

"You're the one who said 'he' when you gave him to me."

Patty sat up straighter, ready to impart her superior knowledge. "All snakes are boys."

Ginger raised her eyebrows and turned her face to her little sister. "How is it that God made only boy snakes, Patty?"

Patty sighed her exasperation. "He wouldn't make anything that ugly and make it a girl. He just wouldn't. God is very nice."

"But God is nice to everyone, Patty, no matter what they look like. It wouldn't be nice for all the boy snakes if God hadn't made them girl snakes for company."

"How come you don't keep company, Ginger?" asked Opal. "Mary's younger than you, and Jeff Miller comes over to sit in the parlor and keep her company. How come nobody keeps you company? Is it 'cause you're blind?"

"Not blind," interrupted Patty, indignantly. "Just near-blind. And no, men don't want wives that are near-blind 'cause of all the things they can't do. Ginger's the only old girl not working in the factory. That shows you she's not gonna be able to keep a house and raise kids. She and me are going to live with Auntie Amy forever and take care of orphans forever and ever."

"I'm perfectly happy to take care of orphans forever and ever, Patty," said Ginger, giving her sister's shoulders a hug with one arm while roughing up her curly red locks with the other. The snake lay in a coil on her apron. "But I'm thinking some handsome young man will charm ye into becoming his wife someday."

"Nope," said Patty with confidence. "If I don't stay and take care of orphans, I'm gonna go out west and see that Mississippi River."

A skittering racket came from above and behind them.

"What's that noise?" Ginger stood abruptly and turned to peer up at the house. The girls bounced to attention beside her.

"Uh-oh," said Opal.

"Alys, you climb right back in that window!" ordered Patty.

"Alys," called Ginger, unable to see more than a dark shape against the white of the clapboards. "What are you doing?"

"She's climbing down the porch roof, Ginger," said Patty, used to being her sister's eyes. "She's gonna break her fool neck."

"Laura and Rissy barred the door so I couldn't get out," called Alys, her angry voice cracked with emotion. "They said they was gonna starve me 'til I let 'em play with my Pennydoll."

"Alys, go back," urged Ginger. "We'll come up and unbar the door."

"She's got Pennydoll under her arm, Ginger. She can't hold on good," announced Patty.

"Oh dear! I'm gonna go get Auntie Amy," cried Opal, and she bolted into the house.

Ginger squinted, trying to see if the little girl was going back to the window. The dark upright form suddenly fell flat against the slanted roof of the porch.

"She's sliding!" screamed Patty.

Ginger quickly sidestepped until she stood directly below the falling girl. With a clatter and whoosh, Alys flew off the edge of the roof and landed on Ginger, knocking her down.

Ginger remembered raising her arms in a dual effort to catch little Alys and protect her face. Apparently she had not been successful at either endeavor. With her head swimming and a cacophony of voices clamoring about her, she tried to sit up.

"No, stay down," ordered the familiar voice of Aunt Amy.

Ginger gratefully leaned back on the grass. She tasted blood and felt nauseated.

"Hold this under her nose, but don't smother her," Aunt Amy said.

Immediately a cloth covered Ginger's mouth and nose. She instinctively knocked the arm away that held it.

"Ginger, you're bleeding all over," complained Patty. "I gotta hold this under your nose."

Shadows shifted above Ginger, and a competent hand reapplied the cloth. "Like this, Patty."

"What happened, Auntie Amy?" Ginger reverted to calling the woman the name the little girls called their guardian.

"Alys has broken her arm and your nose. Jess ran to get the doctor."

Ginger groaned. "Not Dr. Morris," she muttered, but Amy Ross had left her side, presumably to attend the younger victim of the accident.

"I'll protect you, Ginger," whispered Patty. "He's a grubby old man, and I hate him!"

"Ye shouldn't hate, Patty. Granny taught us better. Aunt Amy's taught us better. And Jesus, Himself, tells us to love our enemies."

"I'm still gonna sit right with you and not leave even for a minute. Even if Dr. Morris tells me the house is afire, I'm gonna sit right there with you."

Patty's free hand clutched Ginger's sleeve. Ginger lightly clasped the tight fist. "Ye know the man would never do me harm, Patty. He's just a gruff soul with no feeling left in his heart. May the Lord bless him and give him kindness."

"He made you cry." Patty sobbed and laid her head on her big sister's shoulder.

Ginger put an arm around her thin frame and squeezed gently. "'Twas me own stubborn heart that caused the grief, Little Patty. I refused the grace God had given me for the moment and stormed against His will."

"Dr. Morris said you weren't worth his time to look at your eyes."

"That was his ignorance speaking, me girl. If I weren't worth much, God's own Son wouldn't have bothered to die for me sins, now would He?"

Ginger heard Aunt Amy's approach. Her skirts rustled and a smell of lavender water announced her presence.

"Can you stand, Ginger?" she asked, placing her hand soothingly on the girl's shoulder. "We've taken Alys inside to wait for the doctor. You'll be more comfortable in the parlor, too."

Ginger sat up with the help of both Aunt Amy and Patty.

"I know the blood is alarming," Aunt Amy acknowledged to the younger girl, "but your sister's going to be all right. She isn't fatally injured."

"She tried to catch Alys, Auntie Amy."

Aunt Amy took the blood-soaked cloth as she helped Ginger to her feet.

"I know, and Alys might have broken more than her arm

if your sister hadn't broken her fall."

"Auntie Amy, Dr. Morris is mean." Patty's voice trembled. "You won't let him hurt Ginger, will you?"

"Patty," protested Ginger, but dizziness and a wave of nausea prevented her from saying more.

Patty persisted, "You won't let him touch her eyes, will you?"

"He'll examine her, Patty. Ginger looks like she's going to have two black eyes. Why ever are you so upset?"

"Last time he hurt her. He poked and pulled her eyelids and told her she was blind as a bat and should have been drowned when she was born."

The horrified gasp from her guardian roused Ginger to respond. She hugged the form gone rigid beside her.

"It's all right, Aunt Amy. It was a long time ago."

"It most certainly is not all right," said her mentor, returning the hug. "He shall not be allowed to say such outrageous, hurtful things during this visit."

The back door swung open and Rissy's strident voice rent the air. "Hurry, Auntie Amy. The doc's coming in the front door with Jess."

Chapter 2

Aunt Amy guided Ginger to the sofa by the window, ordering her to lie down with her feet up.

"Patty, run and get your sister a fresh cloth." Aunt Amy walked across the room and greeted someone at the door. Ginger listened for the taciturn doctor's nasal tones.

"I'm Dr. Steadman."

The pleasant voice surprised Ginger. A new doctor? She longed to see what he looked like, but moving her head made her nose throb. She closed her eyes. As soon as Patty returned, she'd ask for a description.

Meanwhile, Ginger breathed a sigh of relief. She always tried to alleviate Patty's worries and hide her reaction to the old doctor, but in truth, her stomach turned to stone just at the mention of his name.

"Dr. Morris said he wouldn't come, Aunt Amy," Jess explained. "I passed Mrs. Miller in the lane, and she said this Dr. Steadman had set up shop by the apothecary. And he come right away."

"Came right away," Amy corrected. "I see he did, and we're grateful." She turned to the girls hovering inside the doorway. "Shoo, now. You can wait in the hall or on the porch. We'll tell you as soon as we can how Ginger and Alys are faring. Don't worry now. The good Lord is caring for them."

"I brought Alys her Pennydoll," said Laura. "She dropped her in the hall."

"Thank you, Dear," said Aunt Amy.

All but Patty reluctantly left. Aunt Amy nodded her approval. "You can stay with your sister."

Ginger lay still, listening intently to the doctor's every word. In between the soothing flow of Amy's comforting patter, the doctor interjected a bare minimum of instructions and comments. He uttered each sober phrase with the same lack of warmth. Alys whimpered and then cried out as the doctor straightened the arm. Amy's voice droned on, distracting the young patient with nonsense about her special doll and the dessert Auntie Amy planned for the evening meal. But the doctor offered no sympathy.

Ginger set her jaw. This man's voice sounded younger than old Dr. Morris. And his steps across the room had been firm and steady, unlike the old doctor's shuffle. But his heart beat without the compassion of the Divine Healer.

Ginger imagined Jesus, the Great Physician, taking Alys into his arms, holding her on his lap, and cuddling away the fear and pain.

Pulling Patty closer, Ginger asked, "What does he look like?"

"He's young, and he looks like Maxwell Steadman, only

shorter. He looks strong and he doesn't smile at all. Do you suppose he thinks Alys is gonna die?"

"Surely not! She hasn't had time to sicken. Perhaps he is a man who never smiles a'tall."

"He's too young to be so gloomy," objected Patty.

"Well, he hasn't said anything mean like old Dr. Morris." Ginger would give him that.

"That may be because our auntie Amy's standing right beside him."

"And it may be because he says hardly a word a'tall."

"Sh!" warned Patty. "I think he's done."

"This is to help the child sleep." His voice had a pleasant timbre even if the words were spoken with no enthusiasm. "Drink it all," he instructed.

"It's nasty," complained Alys.

"You've had a nasty fall, so you have to drink the nasty medicine."

Was that supposed to be encouraging? Ginger sighed loudly. *Oh, merciful Father, send Your comforting Spirit to this man, and put a tad of compassion in his voice when dealing with Your precious little ones.*

She saw Dr. Steadman and Aunt Amy walk away from the patient.

Patty patted Ginger's arm. "I'll be right back." She moved over to the other sofa where her friend Alys lay quietly.

"Pennydoll's going to like staying in bed for awhile." Patty kneeled on the hard wooden floor. "She doesn't like adventure very much."

Alys sniffed. "We can do spelling words. Pennydoll's good at spelling."

Patty nodded. "And Auntie Amy will let me bring tea up to you tomorrow when you feel better. We can have a tea party in your room."

"Patty, you aren't mad at me, are you?"

"No, Alys. Why would I be mad at you?"

The voices faded into secretive whispers.

In a minute, the doctor carried Alys up to her bedroom, with Aunt Amy showing the way.

Well, that would be a point in his favor over Doc Morris, thought Ginger. *The old doc wouldna' have gone out of his way to help our aunt Amy.* A new idea occurred to her. *Oh now, Lord, that would be an interesting thing. Suppose the young doctor took notice of our charming widow. Perhaps he would court her. 'Tisn't right that someone so kind and generous not have a man to love and cherish her.* Ginger sighed and pushed aside the ugly loneliness that swelled in her breast. *None of that, Ginger Finnegan. 'Tis your lot to love the children, and 'tis a good life the Lord has provided.*

Patty came back to her big sister.

"Why did Alys think you would be mad at her?" asked Ginger as soon as they were alone.

"She thought she near killed you 'cause you been so still." Patty shoved Ginger with her hip to gain more room as she sat on the edge of the sofa. "She says she nearly cried when she heard you make a noise 'cause before that she thought you were laid out like her mama was when she died."

"Poor thing. Maybe I can help Aunt Amy bake her a berry

tart for your tea party tomorrow."

"One for me, too?"

Ginger could hear the grin in her sister's voice.

"Sure, and I'll be making one very wee tart for me own sister when I make one for her friend."

"How wee?" asked Patty.

"So wee, I'll be cutting a blackberry in two in order to fit it in the crust."

Patty giggled and then became very quiet as the heavy footsteps of a lone man descended the stairs. The sisters reached to hold hands as they faced the doctor without Aunt Amy's fortifying presence.

He entered the room without a word and went to gather his things into his bag at the other sofa. As he straightened, the sunlight from the window behind him outlined his form plainly for Ginger. Dark hair topped a short and stocky build. Without being able to see clearly, Ginger knew the bulk of him was muscle, not flab, for he moved gracefully for a man. He walked over and set his bag on the floor beside Ginger.

"You'll have to move." He addressed Patty and turned to move a straight-backed chair to sit in while he examined his next patient.

Patty's hand tightened around Ginger's.

The chair dropped with a thud beside the sofa.

"Move aside." His deep voice held no patience.

"No," said Patty.

"What's this?" The doctor's voice dropped into a heavy growl.

"I won't let you hurt my sister."

"I'm not here to hurt your sister. I'm in the business of healing." He sat in the chair.

"No, you can't touch her until Auntie Amy comes. I'll defend her to the death. I'll bite you and scratch you and kick you."

"Patty!" Ginger tried to sit up, but Patty lay across her midsection and had successfully wedged Ginger into the crack between the seat cushion and the back of the settee. Ginger floundered briefly and gave up. With the pain in her face and her awkward position, sitting up to reprimand her sister was out of the question.

Patty sobbed. "She's my sister and all I have left in the world. We're nothing but lowly orphans, but we have each other."

"Cease this melodramatic drivel this minute," the doctor ordered. "Who's filled your head with such nonsense?"

"I read extensively to my children, Dr. Steadman. Patty particularly likes the poets." Amy entered the room and came to place her hand on Patty's back. "It's all right to allow Dr. Steadman to examine Ginger now, Patty. Your loyalty does you credit. Your dramatics do not. Please compose yourself."

Patty slipped off the couch and stood beside her guardian. Auntie Amy put an arm around her.

"Well, then." The doctor cleared his throat. He reached for the cloth and removed the shield Ginger had unconsciously held tighter to her face.

"Here's the bowl of warm water you requested," said Mary.

She'd entered the room with the smooth, quiet glide that characterized her. Dr. Steadman took the bowl from the older girl, and Ginger saw his nod without seeing his expression.

Can the man not utter a simple thank-you?

He turned back to his patient, and Ginger had to acknowledge his soothing touch did much to offset his reserved manner. He carefully wiped the dried blood from around her nose and cheeks and set the soiled cloth aside. Gentle fingers probed the swollen flesh below her eyes.

The doctor came into focus as he leaned close. Just inches from her face, his hazel eyes peered into her own. Ginger held still, wondering at the intensity of his gaze. Rarely did she have the opportunity to behold a stranger's countenance.

His warm breath against her cheek smelled of peppermint. She could see the tawny brown of his eyebrows and lashes and the darker stubble on his chin. Mesmerized by his nearness, Ginger studied the clean, strong lines of his face.

Then he spoke. "I see no damage to her eyes. There will be swelling, of course, and bruising. There's a heel print along this cheekbone. I think the girl's boot actually missed her nose."

His callous clinical tone stirred coals of anger in Ginger's breast. *He's got the chance to do Your good, Lord, and he's wrapped it up so tight it can't come out.*

"And are ye thinking I'm deaf as well as blind, Doctor?" she sputtered. "Ye talk as if I'm not lying here listening to every word. 'Her eyes, this cheekbone, her nose!' Well, it be me eyes, me cheekbone, and me nose. There be a person lying beneath the face ye be looking at, and the person would like the courtesy of being addressed in a polite manner, regardless of me being a meek and humble, poor, blind orphan."

Dr. Steadman recoiled against the verbal blast. "If you're meek and humble, I'd fear meeting your aggressive kinsmen," he said. A note of amusement lightened his tone for the first time. "And poor? None of you fortunate young ladies taken into Kindred Hearts are truly poor. I became a doctor to help the families of seafaring fathers and those who work in the mills. You're not blind, so the only veracity in your diatribe is that you're an orphan. I assume you told the truth there."

"Doctor," Amy interrupted. "Both Patty and Ginger are well acquainted with poverty. They were the first to come to me almost four years ago. Their father died in an accident, loading textile goods on a shipping dock. Their mother worked in the mills and wore her strong body down to a frail piece of humanity. A simple congestion carried her away. The little girls managed a living with their grandmother until that dear lady's passing." Amy paused to take a deep breath. "And as for being blind, Dr. Morris informed me the disease in Ginger's eyes was beyond anything medical science could treat."

"Bah!" said the young doctor as he snapped his bag shut. "Bring her to my office next week after the swelling has gone down, and I'll have a good look into her eyes. I suspect that she will benefit from strong lenses in otherwise ordinary spectacles."

Ginger held her breath. Could it be true? Surely not, not for someone like her.

She squinted, waiting for her guardian's response, straining to see the expression on Aunt Amy's face. She saw the rigid posture and wondered at the lady's outrage. She raised a hand to touch her mentor.

Aunt Amy let out a horrified gasp. "Be still, Ginger." Her voice quavered. "Don't move an inch. Doctor, take care."

"What is it, Mrs. Ross?" The doctor lost his arrogant tone as puzzlement invaded his speech.

"There's something moving in Ginger's pocket, the pocket of her apron. There! It moved again."

Ginger stiffened.

"What is it?" she hissed in a terrified whisper.

Patty giggled. She reached into the deep pocket and pulled out the ribbon snake.

"It's Homer, Ginger. You had him on your lap when Alys came out the window."

Ginger relaxed, but Auntie Amy stepped back.

"Kindly return. . .Homer to his home, Patty. And I don't mean a drawer in your room. Take him outside where you found him."

"Yes'm." Patty scooted to the door.

"Homer?" The doctor sounded incredulous.

"I believe I mentioned that I read to the children."

"Yes, you did, Mrs. Ross. But I hardly thought *The Odyssey* would be one of your choices."

"My girls may come from unfortunate circumstances, but they each possess a fine mind."

The doctor rose. "I'm sure they do, Mrs. Ross. Now if you'll excuse me."

"Yes, of course, Dr. Steadman. I'll see you to the door."

Ginger grinned to herself as she watched the dark-suited form of the doctor follow Aunt Amy in her mauve day dress out of the room.

"Now, Lord, they be a wee bit prickly with one another, but they are of about the same age, and both easy on the eye." Ginger paused in her prayer to remember the doctor's fine hazel eyes and his stubborn chin. No doubt a'tall. To Ginger's way of thinking, he was a fine-looking man. "Aunt Amy could help him see the joy of Ye, Lord, and he could lighten her load, share the responsibilities, don't Ye know. Iffen it be Your will, Lord, a wee bit of romance wouldna' do them no harm."

Chapter 3

Sprinkles of rain dotted the dusty road in front of Dr. Lucas Steadman as he made his way up the lane toward the apothecary. In a few minutes he'd be in his office. He'd been fortunate to find rooms on a busy street, one where his shingle attracted attention. Nonetheless, it wasn't likely any patient would be waiting for him.

Eastead residents didn't necessarily respect old Dr. Morris, but they went to him out of habit. And perhaps they didn't trust a Steadman to be concerned for their welfare.

Lucas had too much time between patients. But with an office on a main street, his accessibility was beginning to be noticed. Most often business came to him secondhand. When old Doc wasn't available, the injured or sick came to him.

Lucas looked up at the clouds swelling in the sky. The invisible hand of the wind pushed them into banks of gray. For a moment he wondered if his prime location had been good fortune or the manipulation of family patriarch Maxwell.

Ah well, my goal is to help the people of Eastead. Does it really matter if Big Brother puts his oar in? If more of the poor people receive aid, that should be uppermost in my mind.

Lucas stopped beside the road, hunching his shoulders against the quickening rain. *But it isn't, is it, Lord? Your Scriptures say that we all sin and fall short of the glory of God. And I'm proving it. I certainly don't have Your forgiving nature. I don't like having my formerly wayward brother showering me with kindness.*

Just like the older brother in the parable of the prodigal son, I resent Maxwell. I see it, Lord. I know it's wrong, and instead of repenting, I grind my teeth over his generosity.

"Lucas! Lucas Steadman."

The sound of the friendly voice halted him at the corner of North Elm and Congress. He looked over his shoulder and lifted a hand to wave at his old schoolteacher, Mrs. Keller.

"You going to the square?" she asked as she hurried to catch up to him. Her black umbrella bobbed over her head, keeping time with her lively step.

"Yes, Mrs. Keller, and I'm hoping you'll walk with me." Lucas shifted his black bag to his other hand and offered to hold the umbrella for her.

She nodded, smiled with genuine friendship, and resumed her quick trot down the street. Caught off guard, Lucas snapped into motion to fall in beside her.

"Going back to your office?" she asked.

Lucas nodded, wiping the few raindrops off his face.

"I saw that fancy shingle." She turned her head stiffly and gave him a quick wink before focusing again on the street before them. "I always said you'd reach the goals you aimed for.

"Now your brother, Maxwell, I have to admit, has surprised me. You were the brother with all the sense. He was the brother with all the high spirits. Each of you had too much of a good thing. He needed some sense. You needed some humor. Now he's settled down and is showing some responsibility. What about you, Dr. Lucas Steadman? Have you discovered a smile or two in your heart?"

Lucas set his jaw. Getting into a conversation with a woman who'd known him since the first day he walked into the schoolroom had been a mistake. "Mrs. Keller, you know I never did see Maxwell's 'high spirits' as a good thing. He caused my parents grief. He caused the township grief. His pranks were destructive. I was embarrassed to be his brother."

"Ah, so you haven't changed."

Lucas didn't answer. Anything he said would spur Mrs. Keller on to make another unwelcome comment. Yet he couldn't be rude to her, either. This woman had listened for hours when in first grade he had grand schemes to travel the world. The next year, before and after school, he'd yammered on and on about being a journalist for the Boston paper. He'd report all the things he would see and share with people through the printed word. Third grade had toppled his ivory tower. In third grade Timothy O'Rourke stopped coming to school and started working to help support his family.

One afternoon, Lucas went looking for his friend Tim. He crossed the river for the first time. The wooden boards of Old Presser Bridge clapped like the footsteps of the Billy Goats Gruff. He hung over the rail and peered at the dark swirling waters. Throwing sticks into the current, he chuckled as he wondered what troll lived underneath, waiting to eat those passing over.

On the return trip he knew who the troll was. His father was the troll. Or maybe it was just the Steadman Shipping Line and not really his father who hammered hope out of the poor people in the shacks across the river. Surely his father didn't know the miserable conditions the families lived in.

In the middle of the dilapidated bridge, so different from the whitewashed bridge uptown, Lucas dropped his clean linen handkerchief in the water.

He did it on purpose.

His mother always made him carry the crisp white square of linen.

It floated for only a second on the turbulent river. First it took on the dingy brown color of the water around it. Then the current twisted it, tugged it under, and swept it away. Lucas couldn't have rescued it even if he'd tried. One puny scrap of cloth had no chance against the river. And Lucas was just a child watching.

Lucas thought about the tattered clothing, the ragged children in the houses behind him. He'd found Tim's home, but Tim was not there. His mother held a sick baby in her arms. Although the cloth wrapping the baby had been clean, the stains of years marked poverty as Lucas had never seen it before.

"I'm Tim's friend," he told the sad woman.

"Are you?" The words must have been hard to say. They sounded strangled.

"I miss him at school."

"Do you?"

Lucas looked at the limp child.

"Is that Maggie?"

"It is."

"Tim told me about her when she was born in the spring."

"He did?"

"Is she sick?"

"She's dying."

The breath stopped in his throat. He swallowed and breathed again.

"I'll get help."

She gave a lethargic nod and closed the door.

Lucas did try to get help. He went to the next shack and listened to an old woman's diatribe: no money for doctors, no medicine for sick children, no help for the needy. He didn't believe the crone's cynical words and ran to the next home. This man, with rheumy eyes and a toothless snarl, brought curses down on the Steadman name. He ranted at the unknown lad on his doorstep.

"Them two brothers are the devil's own. Misers! They got money for big, fancy houses, but look where we're living. We's the ones who break our backs."

Lucas hurried away, never saying he was the son of this horrible monster everyone hated. He kept pounding on doors and found no one to help.

"Go home to wherever you belong," said the last woman, not unkindly. "We know Lydia's Maggie will die tonight. She asked to be left to rock her child until her babe passes over. We won't disturb her as she says good-bye to little Maggie. Tomorrow we'll stand beside her in her sorrow."

Lucas made one last protest. "But she's alone."

"No, Lad, that she's not. The Lord is with her as she walks through the valley of the shadow of death." She gave his shoulder a gentle shove. "Go on home, now. Back where you belong. This is no place for the likes of you."

On the bridge Lucas watched the waters that carried away the handkerchief. A tangled clump of brush bumped against the bridge supports in the water. The dense, dark mass reminded Lucas of a troll. He watched it float downstream.

The troll was make-believe. His father was not a troll. His father didn't know, couldn't know, about Tim's mother and sister.

Lucas ran to tell him. He ran with all his might, even up Croner Hill. He ran all the way.

He burst in the front door and heard his mother's voice. Her friends laughed in the parlor. He ran past the open door, across the parquet floor, and up the polished stairs.

Lucas barreled into the library without knocking. His father sat at his desk. Before he opened his mouth with a ready reprimand, Lucas poured out the story of his search for his friend, the dying sister, the sad mother, the angry neighbors—no doctor, no medicine, rags and tattered clothes, no heat, little food.

"And they say it is all your fault, Father. That you and Uncle keep all the money and don't give them any."

His father's face grew red. "You will not associate with such riffraff, Lucas. What was this boy doing at a school on our side of the river?"

"Father, Tim's my friend. Mrs. Keller likes him. He's smart as me."

"Nonsense."

Lucas didn't understand. Just what was nonsense? His friendship with Tim? Or was it that his teacher liked the poor boy? Maybe his father didn't believe that Timothy O'Rourke could be as smart as a Steadman. But the baffling "nonsense" word didn't drive his purpose from Lucas's mind.

"Father, you have to help. Send the doctor."

"Now calm down, Lucas, and listen to me. They wouldn't appreciate my interfering with their ways. Those people are different from us, Son. They have their own medicines—plants and roots and things." Father gestured vaguely with his hand. A fierce frown chased away the uneasy look on his face. "See here. They earn their wages, and I give them what's due without fail. This is preposterous—expecting me to give my money to them. I earn my money and have the right to spend it or save it or invest it as I see fit. They earn their money and spend it however they choose. No doubt much of it is spent on whiskey and dice."

His disapproving glare fell on his young son. "Go now, Lucas, and prepare yourself for supper. I don't want to hear another word of this. And you are forbidden to cross the river again until you are much older and have a realistic grasp of these things. Close the door with more decorum as you leave than you used opening it."

Grasp of what things? Lucas asked himself as he pulled the door shut.

He couldn't ask his mother. Soft laughter still rose from the first-floor parlor. He found his older brother.

Twelve-year-old Maxwell stopped what he was doing and actually sat down to explain the situation. "You've got it wrong, Lucas. They're the lucky ones. Oh, I don't mean not having any money. I wouldn't like that. But they don't have to wear ties and tight jackets and sit without squirming in the front pew of church. They don't have to go to school all day, every day, and they aren't expected to bring honor to their family name. Their mothers don't cringe when they belch. They don't have to be polite to a herd of old ladies. You just got a bad look at things. Don't worry."

"The people said the children die all the time, Maxwell. Lots of children."

"Well, I suppose they were exaggerating some. You know, embellishing a tale to make it more impressive."

Lucas nodded his head. Maxwell certainly got into trouble often enough for "embellishing" a tale.

Lucas left Maxwell and went to his own room. He tried to talk to his mother about it after supper, but she focused on how annoyed she'd been when he clattered into the house.

"I had company, Dear, and you entered just like a ruffian. You didn't acknowledge our guests, and you barged through the house. I know you wouldn't disgrace Mother on purpose. You must be more mindful of your manners."

"Tim's little sister was dying, Mother."

"I'm sure Tim's mother has lots of children, Lucas. She will find comfort in all the others. I don't see how you came to know this Tim. They have so many children, dozens. He shouldn't have been at our school. She may even feel relief that the poor girl is in heaven and she has one less to look after. I don't see why they want so many. I'll have to speak to Mrs. Keller about that boy. She'll know why he came over the river to school. It is most irregular. Of course that was last year, you say, and this year he is gone. Perhaps I won't pursue it. After all, if he is already not attending, it is neither here nor there."

Lucas couldn't press the real issue. His father came in, having smoked his evening cigar as he strolled through the gardens. He took his place in front of the fireplace, an elbow on the mantle, his foot on the andiron. He told an amusing anecdote from his day, and Lucas's mother and brother laughed. The evening progressed in a normal pattern.

To Lucas the stark difference between his comfortable, warm parlor and the desolate shanties across the river etched a line in his heart between right and wrong. His cheerful, unconcerned family stood on the wrong side of that line.

Chapter 4

Lucas smiled as he secured the bandage around Mrs. Miller's arm. She was the third patient he'd seen that day, and he'd just heard the front door open and close again.

"Change the dressing daily, Mrs. Miller. Use this salve." He handed her a squat brown glass jar containing a mixture he'd had the apothecary, Mr. Kranz, mix up to his specifications. Lucas felt good about showing him something new, and he was gratified that the older man had welcomed new ideas fresh from the University of Pennsylvania School of Medicine.

Lucas almost patted his patient on the shoulder but remembered his greatest hurdle establishing a medical practice in his hometown was familiarity. Too many of his prospective patients had watched him run through the streets chasing a hoop, or slide down the snowy hills, or limp home after falling into the canal.

Stiffly courteous, he put his hand under old Mrs. Miller's elbow and helped her to stand. "If you see any sign of infection, come back to me immediately."

"Oh, Mr. Lucas, I mean Dr. Lucas, it feels so much better." She opened her cloth reticule, extracted a large coin, and placed it in his hand. "I'm so glad you've come back to us."

Lucas tucked the half dollar into his vest pocket. His last payment he'd put in the shed behind the building. What was he going to do with two laying hens? Impatient to see who awaited him in the outer office, he edged Mrs. Miller out of the examining room.

At the end of a short hall a curtain of dark calico covered the doorway into the sitting room. Lucas pushed the cloth aside, allowing his patient to move through. Side by side on two straight-backed chairs sat the redheaded sisters from Kindred Hearts Orphanage.

He heard the little one whisper, "Mrs. Miller." The older nodded and stood to face his departing patient.

Lucas needed to straighten his only examining room before the Irish sisters came back. "I'll be with you in just one moment," he said.

The older girl's eyes shifted to him. He noticed their startling green color, much brighter than his own hazel eyes. Her unfocused gaze disturbed him. He should be able to do something about that, and the thought made him glad. Letting the curtain drop, he started back down the hall. He grinned as he heard Mrs. Miller's shrill voice.

"Oh, I burned myself, Dearie, rendering lard and just plain careless. You'd think at my age I'd know not to take my eyes off what I'm doing."

A murmured response didn't make it through the curtain. Lucas strained to hear the words as he gathered up the linen scraps he'd used to clean Mrs. Miller's wound.

Mrs. Miller's voice came clear into the back room. She evidently knew the girls from somewhere. In no hurry to leave, she continued in her usual friendly manner. "You know I used to work some at the big house when I was younger. Came in as an extra maid when Mrs. Steadman, the doctor's mother, had parties or houseguests. Oh my, she gave some mighty fine parties. It was a pleasure just to go and look at the fine clothes and pretty rooms. And to think her son chose to do something like doctoring."

Lucas carried the bowl of water to the window and hurled its contents out into the backyard. He rushed, wanting to get to his next patients before Mrs. Miller told them his entire personal history.

"And he's a good doctor, too. Not like old Arnold Morris."

Now that's good to hear.

"But it's odd, isn't it? A son of a wealthy family choosing to leave his family's business and mingle with the townspeople rather than stay in his own circles. His mother certainly had a busy social life. But he always was different. He was neat as a pin. His parents and brother, careless with their things. He always looked serious. His mother and brother, delighted with life, and his father looked angry."

Yes, that's true, but I've really got to interrupt this. He grabbed a rag and wiped away a smear of ointment from the examining table. *Everyone in this town knows too much about my background, and nobody understands why being their doctor is important to me.*

"All those years I tidied up after them, I never thought I'd be paying a Steadman for services rendered. Makes me feel odd."

Oh, no! Another reason why the townspeople find me hard to accept as a doctor.

"Now his dear mother doted on him even as serious as he was and her being such an important hostess and a little flighty, if you know what I mean. People came from all over the East Coast to her parties, you know."

One of the girls spoke in a low murmur. A pause followed, and Lucas stopped what he was doing, hoping to hear the front door open and shut. Relieved that Mrs. Miller might finally be done spilling his family secrets, Lucas opened a cabinet and stored the last remaining bottles cluttering the countertop. His hand patted the wood above the drawer containing his collection of spectacles with lenses of various strengths.

Lord, I pray that it be Your will to give this young woman the gift of sight. Last summer, I thought I had been a fool to buy Barker's entire stock of spectacles. Now I see Your hand in my friend Barker's decision to dash off to Georgia mere months after he opened his shop in Philadelphia. I trust we have the right pair for the Irish orphan. Won't she be surprised?

"Some of the entertaining I'm sure had to do with business." Mrs. Miller's strident voice broke into his thoughts, and his sense of peace evaporated.

"The Steadman Shipping Line is very important," she continued. "But some of those people were political, straight from Washington, D.C.

"She was a debutante from New York City before she was Mrs. Steadman and had money from her family. And they say when she passed, she gave it all to her second-born son, Lucas, now our doctor. It was in her will. Imagine a woman having enough to call her own to do something like write out a will."

Lucas juggled the wet rag in his hand, frantically looking in the corners of the room for the basket he used to hold laundry. "Where is it?" he muttered.

"I remember when Lucas Steadman wrote to the Boston newspaper, addressed the letter right to the editor. Imagine a boy doing a thing like that! He offered to write articles about the happenings in Eastead—as though anyone would want to read about our little town."

Lucas flung the wet rag out the open window and hurried down the short hallway to the waiting room. He stopped short of the curtain, took a deep breath, and calmly pushed the fabric aside to enter the outer room.

"I'm ready for you, Miss," he said. He didn't like the grin on the older girl's face. Had she heard him rushing? Did she know how anxious he was to cut off Mrs. Miller?

"Good day, Doctor," said the irrepressible gossip.

"Good day, Madame." He turned to the two Irish girls. "If you'll come this way."

Ginger followed with her hand planted firmly on Patty's thin shoulder. She could almost sympathize with the young doctor. Mrs. Miller knew too much about every family in town. She'd been a maid in each of the big houses. And she worked from time to time, helping out in the more modest homes, usually when there was a birth or an illness or houseguests. Besides being a hard worker, she was a good listener, whether she was part of the conversation or eavesdropping. Next to her love of listening came her love of chattering. Pastor Hull's admonishments against gossip went right over the woman's head. Ginger doubted Mrs. Miller knew her passing on this little bit of knowledge and that little bit of history qualified as gossip.

Patty stopped and effectively blocked her sister's way in the narrow passage. She reached up and took hold of Ginger's hand. The doctor's footsteps continued down the hallway.

Patty pulled her sister down and spoke in her ear. "I think we ought to come back when Auntie Amy can come, too. That doctor's not likely to be in a good mood after hearing Mrs. Miller talk about him."

Ginger stooped down even farther to whisper back, "If we aren't feeling brave, Patty me girl, then we'll just have to pretend."

"You're scared, too, aren't you, Ginger?"

Ginger puzzled over the question a moment. The doctor's vulnerability under the good-natured attack of Mrs. Miller's gossip had changed Ginger's perception of him. The sounds of his frantic haste from behind the curtain triggered a response. Often one of the girls alerted Aunt Amy that Mother Ross was coming down the street.

That cantankerous woman interfered at every opportunity. As Amy Ross's mother-in-law, she held the title to the house they lived in. Periodically, she surprised the orphanage with a visit and scowled at all she met there. Her inspections caused havoc. Amy Ross dealt with it well, but her devoted girls tried to protect their beloved guardian.

When the elder Mrs. Ross came charging down the street, the orphans scrambled to straighten the house before the tyrant's shadow touched the front door.

Ginger's mind dwelt on the mystery of young Dr. Steadman. Perhaps the doctor's curt utterances reflected something other than callousness. Perhaps he was insecure in his new position. And didn't she, herself, often speak with more bravado than she possessed to hide her own insecurity? If she was guilty of such prevarication, perhaps the young doctor was as well.

Ginger smiled at her sister and answered the question.

"Only a wee bit nervous. I'm thinking the doctor has a human heart after all."

Patty squeezed Ginger's hand, and the two hurried to catch up.

"Sit here," said Dr. Steadman, who continued talking while Patty guided Ginger to the chair he indicated.

Ginger chafed under the blunt order. *Well, Lord, only a second ago I thought I could like this man, and now I'm wishing I were home. I take back me suggestion that Ye push our aunt Amy and this man together. It wouldna' do. Give me patience. That's what I be needing, or I'll be telling this oaf to sweeten his words with a please and a thank-you just like he was one of the younger girls.*

Dr. Steadman surveyed her face, touching the bruises gently. As he leaned closer, Ginger again smelled peppermint on his breath. She could see the frown in his expression and wondered if he saw something in her injuries to concern him.

"You're healing well," he said.

Ginger let out a sigh with the breath she had been unconsciously holding.

He leaned back so she could no longer see his features. His voice continued in his coldly professional manner.

"Has your sight always been limited?"

"Aye."

"Any injuries or illnesses as a child which further impaired your vision?"

"Nary a one."

"Do you have any trouble distinguishing colors?"

"No, Doctor, I know me colors." *What? He thinks because I'm weak-sighted, I'm weak-minded as well?*

He came closer, placed his fingertips gently below each eye, and pulled down.

"Look up," he ordered.

Ginger did.

"Down."

She followed his instructions but felt a rage growing within. Was he wasting her time? Did he enjoy these arbitrary commands. What good was it to look up and down with eyes that barely saw?

"To the right, slowly, and then, in one steady movement, all the way to the left."

Once she had complied, he crossed his arms over his chest.

"Certain structural defects can result in blurring of vision. These, we know, are errors of refraction. Your extraocular muscles are performing well. We know that the inside of the eye can be damaged or hold irregularities that affect sight, but it is difficult to see."

Now he be lecturing me. Ginger leaned forward and squinted, trying to get a better look at the instrument he'd picked up off the table. *Lord, Ye wouldna' let this doctor stick part of that thing in me eye? In addition to the patience, I'll be asking Ye for courage.*

Dr. Steadman lit two lanterns and put his hands on Ginger's shoulders to push her back into the position he required. Ginger felt her body tense. What was he going to do?

"At this point in medical advancement, I can only examine the front of the eye, the cornea, and the general condition of the conjunctiva."

"What have ye got in yer hand, Doctor?" Ginger interrupted the flow of unneeded information to get to the thing that troubled her.

"This?"

Ginger saw him hold up a blurred round shape and nodded.

"Just a magnifying glass," he said.

Ginger clenched her hands into fists by her side. She'd tried to avoid this visit to the doctor, but Aunt Amy had gently insisted.

My nerves are twisting, Lord, all over me body. Me lungs don't work. I can't breathe. Me stomach don't work. I'm afraid I'm going to be sick. This doctor's going to poke and prod and find nothing whatever to do for me. So why did Ye have me come here?

Ginger looked straight ahead when Dr. Steadman told her

to, and she tried not to think of anything at all. She tried to relax her hands and shifted them to lie in her lap. Aunt Amy had said that assuming a pose of gentility aided a woman's composure.

"Aha, just as I thought. I see no evidence of disease. No injury or scarring to the cornea, no clouding, no pigmented cells on the white surface. Miss. . .uh?" The doctor lowered the magnifying glass.

And why did I think he knew me name? "Finnegan, Ginger Finnegan."

"Miss Finnegan, I have spectacles that will aid you." He crossed the room, pulled a shallow drawer completely out, and strode back to her side.

Ginger's stomach cramped, and again she squeezed together the hands clasped in her lap. *Oh, Lord, could it be?* She closed her eyes and continued to pray, barely aware of the voices and movements around her.

Patty gasped. "Oh, Ginger, there are dozens and dozens of spectacles just like Mrs. Keller wears. Dr. Steadman, where'd you get them all?"

"I trained at the University of Pennsylvania. I grew very interested in the study of ophthalmology. Our School of Medicine has the most progressive programs in the United States. We are to our continent what the University of Edinburgh is to Europe. Many of our faculty trained in Scotland. John McAllister of Philadelphia is famous for his manufacturing of spectacles. Let's try one of these stronger lenses for you, Miss Finnegan."

He placed the drawer on a table. Gently he perched spectacles on the bridge of her nose and guided the wire temple frames under her hair and over her ears. He stepped back.

"Miss Finnegan, you must open your eyes. Only you can tell me if the lenses improve your sight."

Chapter 5

The Finnegan sisters walked hand in hand down the street toward Kindred Hearts.

"Look, Patty, there be leaves on the ground."

Patty giggled. "Of course there are. It's fall."

"No, I mean there be individual leaves, not all blurred together." Ginger took a deep breath as if she could pull the wonder of this day right into her lungs and keep it. She sighed. "Ah, such beauty."

"I don't get it. You could always see color. Why are you so happy?"

Ginger stopped and stared at the ground where the wind had pushed oak and maple leaves against a white picket fence. Autumn had splashed vibrant red, orange, and gold hues along the dirt path. "I can't tell you what it's like, Patty. Everything has sharp edges. The colors are richer. I want to just look and look and look. . .at everything." She quickly raised her face to the trees in the yard.

"Ooo." Swaying, Ginger dropped Patty's hand and put her

palms on her cheeks.

"What's wrong?" Patty grabbed her sister's arm.

"The world tilted there for a moment. Dr. Steadman did say it would take awhile to get used to me spectacles." She slowly opened her eyes, then shut them again. "I think the excitement is getting to me, Patty. Me stomach has gone wobbly."

"You're sick?"

"Dizzy, Patty, like you wound me up on the swing hanging from the backyard tree and then let me spin."

"Maybe you should take those spectacles off."

"No!" She opened her eyes and looked straight ahead. A kitten sat on the porch of the house behind the fence. Ginger watched it slowly lick its paw, then methodically stroke its head in a feline bathing ritual.

"There's so much to be seeing," Ginger whispered. With a stronger voice and a smile, she added, "Besides, Patty me dear, how could me stomach be connected to me eyes? I was more nervous, I'm figuring, than I wanted to admit. That's what's set me stomach to whirling about inside me."

"You almost fell off the step of the doctor's office," Patty pointed out.

"Well now, that's what Dr. Steadman was talking about when he said it would take awhile to get used to seeing." Ginger grinned at the view before her. She thanked God for pouring blessings into her with so many lovely sights.

"It's a good thing, being a doctor, helping people," she said. "Did you notice how Dr. Steadman fairly hummed with joy when he found the right spectacles for me eyes?"

"He grinned," said Patty, taking her sister's hand and giving it a pull. "Let's go. I want all the girls to see you. Won't they be flabbergasted? Aunt Amy will be pleased beyond measure."

"Aye, she will be." With careful steps, Ginger walked beside her sister. "He grinned, all right. Had you ever seen the doctor smile before?"

"Dr. Steadman?"

"Now were we talking about old Doc Morris who smells of camphor and sweat, or young Dr. Steadman who just placed a miracle upon me nose and gave ye a peppermint as we left?"

Patty giggled. "Dr. Steadman."

"So did ye ever see him smile before?"

"I seen him make a tight little sorry smile that didn't mean he was happy. Just something polite to put on his face when he was saying good day to Aunt Amy."

"I'm thinking he has a grand smile. One that makes you feel special."

Patty stopped. "Ginger?"

Ginger looked down quickly and felt again the strange tilting and loss of balance. She grabbed Patty to keep from falling.

"Ginger!" Patty screeched.

"Oh, just a minute. Be still, Patty. The world is moving under me feet, and me stomach is flitting about."

"Should I run to the house? Should I get Aunt Amy? We're almost home, Ginger. Are you going to make it?"

"Aye, just give me a minute. Just a minute."

"You should take off those spectacles, Ginger."

"No! Never. I'm going to wear 'em 'til I go to bed. It can't be the spectacles, don't ye know, Patty? The spectacles are a miracle, a gift from God, Himself. I can see every freckle on yer face, every lash upon yer eyelid, every wrinkle in yer frown. Quit frettin'. I'll be fine."

As the day went on, Ginger began to doubt that she would be fine. If she remained still and focused on one thing, her stomach didn't lurch. Sudden movements, however, made her surroundings pitch and reel. She reached for things and knocked them over, misjudging their positions. Nausea plagued her, and by the time she prepared supper that night, her head ached. As she peeled a carrot, tears streamed down her cheeks. How could her miracle be ruined by this illness?

Aunt Amy bustled into the kitchen and, seeing Ginger's distress, quickly enveloped the young woman in a warm embrace. "Ginger, what's wrong?"

Ginger dropped her knife and carrot on the table and turned to bury her head on her mentor's shoulder. She sobbed, feeling too miserable to try to explain. Her joy had been sabotaged by an awful sickness.

"I'm putting you to bed." Aunt Amy guided her toward the stairs.

"The supper," Ginger objected.

"There are plenty of girls to make our meal. Hush now, and let me take care of you. You've always been a godsend to me, Ginger—helping with the little ones, singing them to sleep, knitting their mittens and scarves, rocking them when they're sick. You always coddle the other children. This time, we will take care of you."

They reached the stairs and started up.

"I'm never sick, Aunt Amy, never." Ginger held her eyes closed against the constant shifting of the world around her. She feared she'd never make it to the second floor.

She heard an anxious voice from above. "Something's wrong with Ginger."

Many hard shoes tapped out an urgent scramble in the hall. As she and Aunt Amy came to the top step, small hands reached to support Ginger. The little girls surrounded her, and with hugs that encumbered her movements, they assisted her to the bedroom she shared with Patty, Susannah, and Alys.

"Mary, Amanda," said Aunt Amy, "will you go down and finish supper? Jess, please fetch Dr. Steadman."

"Oh, no," said Ginger through her weeping, "I don't need the doctor."

"I'll be the judge of that," answered Aunt Amy. "Go, Jess. Patty, turn down the cover on your bed. Ginger, sit down. Susannah, fetch her nightgown."

Within minutes, Ginger lay cocooned in a colorful quilt, her head resting on her feather pillow and her eyes closed tight against the confusion of the room around her.

"Girls, I think Ginger needs some privacy now. I know you all want to help her, but what she needs most is quiet. So let's leave her in peace. Go finish your chores before we eat. If a worry crosses your mind, girls, turn it into a prayer. Patty and Alys, you may stay here."

"Yes, Auntie Amy," said Opal. "Get better, Ginger."

"Get better," echoed Marissa.

"I'll help in the kitchen," said Melody.

A shuffling of feet told Ginger that most of girls had left the room.

"I could read her a story," offered Alys.

"That's a good idea, Alys," said Aunt Amy, "but why don't you wait until after Dr. Steadman has looked at her?"

Ginger felt a small hand on her shoulder. "Do you want to hold Pennydoll? She's good to whisper to."

Ginger felt tears sting her eyes. Alys rarely let Pennydoll out of her arms. Afraid to open her eyes and again feel the room rock and undulate around her, Ginger held out a hand and received the treasured doll into her keeping.

"Rest, Ginger," said Aunt Amy. "Patty and Alys, I trust you to look after her. Call me if you need anything."

With a soft swish of woolen skirts, Aunt Amy left the room, softly closing the door behind her.

Chapter 6

The door creaked open. Ginger stirred from her light doze and listened. A step sounded upon the bare floor, and she knew it wasn't one of the girls nor Aunt Amy.

"Dr. Steadman?"

"Yes, how are you feeling?"

"I think I've been asleep."

A damp cloth rested across her eyes. She peeled it off and tried to sit.

"No, stay still."

"I feel better."

"Stay still."

She heard the scrape of the wooden chair across the floor. He sat next to her and reached out to put his hand on her forehead.

"Where are Patty and Alys?" she asked as his hand withdrew.

"Eating their supper."

"Where are my spectacles?"

He looked around, then reached to the dresser.

"Here."

"Thank you." Ginger fitted them onto her face, tucking the wire loops around each ear.

She watched Lucas Steadman bend to pick up something from the floor. His eyes looked forlorn, but he gave her a feeble smile. Holding up Pennydoll, he asked, "Yours?"

Ginger started to shake her head but remembered the nausea that overwhelmed her when she moved. "No," she whispered.

"I believe the last time I was here, the little girl who fell off the roof clutched this doll in a desperate grip."

"Ye remember?"

"I pay close attention to my patients, Miss Finnegan. It's important to me that I do everything within my power to make them well, and if I can't make them well, to help them be comfortable."

"Ye pay close attention?" Ginger gave an unladylike snort. "Ye didn't even know me name after ye tended me bruises. And ye don't know the name of the little girl who loves that poor doll."

Dr. Steadman's mouth twitched in annoyance. "A patient's name has nothing to do with the treatment of illness."

He rested his elbows on his knees. Holding the doll in both hands, he gently moved it back and forth as he stared at the cloth face.

"Ye seem sad," said Ginger.

"Ira Blake died this afternoon."

"Ah, I see. But he was old, Dr. Steadman, and he's been ailing a long time."

Dr. Steadman nodded.

"Ye not be blaming yerself?"

"No. . .and yes, Miss Finnegan. I did all I could, but the human body is still very much a mystery. It's true we know more than we did a hundred years ago, but so little compared to all we should know. Patients die every day because their doctors just don't know enough." He sighed. "And Miss Finnegan, it is probably due to my ignorance that you have been sick half the day."

"Why is it ye be takin' the blame?" Ginger's hand tightened on the counterpane, her fingers digging into the colored swatches. "Ye haven't even looked at me. I coulda' eaten something bad at breakfast. I might be low with an illness that'll take itself off in a day or two. Ye're makin' judgments too fast, I'm thinking, on very little evidence."

He shook his head, still watching the doll in his hands. "I've talked with Patty and Mrs. Ross. The timing's not right for ingestion of tainted food, and you have no fever. Plus, you ate what the others ate, and no one else is ill.

"No, I think I should have been more cautious in giving you the spectacles. I should have given you some guidelines—wear them only for a few minutes at a time; gradually increase the length of time; avoid excessive motion until you become accustomed to viewing the world with new vision."

Ginger giggled.

"What's funny? I've caused you a great deal of pain today."

"I'm laughing because me sister, Patty, had the good sense to tell me to take off the spectacles. And do you think I listened?

Oh no, Ginger Finnegan had her mind made up to see the whole world all at once and all in one day. I was too stubborn to heed her wee, wise voice."

"But if I had—"

"Aye, but ye did, don't ye know? Ye told me that it would be an adjustment, and I was too greedy to mind yer words."

"You're very generous, Miss Finnegan. . .and very forgiving."

"And yer generous and unforgiving, aren't ye, Doctor?"

He shifted his gaze to rest upon her face for the first time. "What do you mean?"

"Ye're generous with yer time and yer talent. And with the things ye possess like yer learning from that fancy School of Medicine in Philadelphia."

"I told you the Steadman Mill—my cousin Carter—takes care of the medical expenses for Kindred Hearts."

"Ye woulda given me the spectacles on yer own, Dr. Steadman. Ye don't fool me. When ye put them onto me face, I could feel the zest of ye rising up and spilling over."

"Zest?"

"Me granny called it the zest of a person, the thing that stirs the blood. For some it's singing a song, or rocking a baby, or watching a planted field pop up with seedlings. Everyone has something that causes that zing. Granny said it happens when ye put yer hand to the right plow."

"I'm sorry, I don't follow your meaning, or rather, your granny's meaning."

Ginger reached out and touched his hand that still cradled Pennydoll. "Everyone has a job to do that God designed just for him or her. When ye're in the midst of doing that job, ye're as close to God as standing by His side. Ye're in partnership with the Almighty. And the satisfaction that rushes through ye is as good as hearing Him say, 'Well done, thou good and faithful servant.' It's yer zest in life."

He sat quietly for a moment, then shrugged. Pulling his hand away from her touch, he pushed the doll into her grasp. Tapping his fingertips on his knees, he looked away.

"You said I was unforgiving."

"Aye, that shows in the way ye talk to people and the stiffness of yer neck and spine. Yer whole body's rigid. Even yer voice is cold and hard. Ye don't give of yerself, and that can only be because ye lack trust. Ye don't trust those around ye. And the reason a person has no trust is because that person has not forgiven someone who betrayed a trust."

"And you are what? Nineteen, twenty years old?"

"Twenty, but I'm quoting me granny who was sixty-nine when she died. And she pulled her wisdom from the Bible, a book from God, who is beyond the counting of years."

He stood.

"You'll wear the spectacles with moderation tomorrow."

"Yes, Dr. Steadman."

"You'll wear them when sitting until you feel comfortable, then try standing and walking."

"Yes."

"You'll take the spectacles off and rest your eyes."

"Yes."

He walked to the door and opened it. Just before leaving,

he turned and looked directly into her eyes.

"Miss Finnegan, I can't forgive someone who never recognized he did wrong, who died without giving me the opportunity to make peace with him. It's too late."

The door closed firmly.

"No," whispered Ginger. "I don't know the answer to yer pain, Dr. Lucas Steadman, but I do know it's not too late."

Chapter 7

Lucas shifted the weight of the basket under his arm, and two hens inside cackled their protest once more.

"I'm taking you to a good home, not a stewpot, so just be quiet," he told them.

As he approached the orphanage, he heard laughter from the backyard. Carrying his burden around the side of the house, he came across a half dozen little girls doing a very disorderly raking job. Their piles of autumn leaves varied in size from mountainous to minuscule. Ginger sat on the stoop, bundled up against the cold, her spectacles in her mittened hands.

Two of the girls abandoned their rakes when they saw Dr. Steadman and his basket. Lucas looked down into identical faces and knew he'd never met these two before.

"What have you got?" asked one.

The other squealed. "The basket is moving. Is it a puppy? We need a puppy."

"Chickens," said Lucas. He almost laughed as their eager expressions fell to total disgust in a second. They turned as one and ran to Ginger.

"The doctor has chickens in a basket," said the first to reach her.

"Live chickens," said the other. She didn't quite make her stop in time and fell into Ginger's lap.

A moment of confusion followed as Ginger tried to move the girl off her lap without damaging her spectacles. As soon as possible, she put them on and stood to greet the doctor.

The twins ran back to their game in the piles of leaves, and Lucas came to stand in front of Ginger.

"Chickens?" she asked, tilting her head as she looked up at him.

He nodded. Auburn tendrils escaped her knitted hat, and the wind played with them, making them dance across her cheek. The heavy lenses magnified her green eyes, and he marveled not only at the lovely verdant color but the essence of wonder in them.

"Doctor?"

He realized he was staring as a smile broke across her face. Her joy dazzled him, and he took in a quick breath. He must say something.

"Laying hens. I don't cook. There's no kitchen." He stopped blathering and deliberately breathed, slow and steady, in and out. She was just a woman, an obstreperous lass with an undeniable natural beauty, but nonetheless outspoken and irrepressible. "Yesterday, when I was here, I saw you have a chicken coop."

"The hens are for us?"

"Yes."

She smiled again, and Lucas looked quickly away.

"Faith," she called. "Dr. Steadman brought us two more hens. Will ye please me by putting them in the coop?"

A girl came running to take the basket. She wore too many layers of clothing for him to determine if he'd seen her before. She said a hasty thank-you before darting off to the coop's door.

"Have a seat," said Ginger, moving to one side of the step.

Lucas glanced down and saw her invitation to sit beside her. Panic rose up inside him. He again averted his gaze, watching intently as the eager girls dragged their rakes with little effect through the crisp leaves.

This is ridiculous. What is happening? When have women ever interfered with my plans? His thoughts only had a moment's pause before the answer came tumbling through his well-ordered mind.

This is the first time in my life I haven't had my all-encompassing goal in front of me. I've finished school. I've set up my practice. Patients are beginning to knock on my door. I've relaxed. And now a pretty girl with a winsome smile has turned my head.

Oh, Lord, what is my goal now that my seventeen-year ambition has been attained?

He looked at Ginger's charming face and decided he was too confused to deal with the issue. He cleared his throat, knowing it was a nervous habit and that he gave away his unsettled state of mind each time he did it.

"I think," he said, "I'll help the girls with their chore."

"Aye now, that would be a good thing. They're supposed to be putting those leaves on the garden. Mostly, they're just stirring 'em round the yard like a big batch of porridge. Aunt Amy said I could only supervise today after my illness yesterday. And how do ye tell a child how to rake? Ye have to show 'em, or it's no good a'tall."

Charging into the girls' activity, Lucas confiscated a rake from a more-than-willing child. Enthusiastic cheers and peels of laughter met his action. With long, strong sweeps he began to move the smaller piles past the chicken coop. He raked vigorously, trying to rid his system of an unsettling frustration. The children danced around him, sometimes even managing to help.

Overhead, sullen clouds glowered in the sky. Cold breezes picked up momentum and swished at the leaves, trying to swirl them into the air and scatter them back across the yard. The air smelled of the tart fragrance of crunching leaves. Down the street, a faint trail of smoke from leaves being burned made its way toward the orphanage, adding a whiff of another pleasant odor.

With a suggestion here and a command there, Lucas eventually had his crew organized and the project nearing completion. Every time he looked to the house, he saw Ginger still sitting on the cold step, watching their progress. He ignored the distraction she presented.

Once he yelled, "You should go in out of the cold."

She just waved and flashed him a beguiling smile.

He returned to the work at hand, glaring at the area before

him still strewn with festive oak leaves.

"Hot tea!" called Aunt Amy as she put a tray down next to Ginger, then quickly retreated from the cold wind.

The girls sent up a whoop and threw down their rakes. Lucas followed them to the back porch and accepted a mug of strong brew. Honey and milk softened the bitter tea, and he gratefully sipped until he caught Ginger watching him. The warmth stealing through his veins had nothing to do with his drink.

"Tea on the porch?" he asked Ginger as she poured another mug and handed it to Opal.

"Aunt Amy's heart is too big to be leaving the girls out here in the cold for long without giving them something to warm their insides. However, the time it takes to unbundle them, allow them to drink a cup of something warmin', and then bundle them up again and scoot them out the door. . . Well now, ye can see that they wouldna' be getting much work done a'tall. And then there's the sweeping up of leaves and mud the wee girls track in on their shoes." She smiled up at him. "Will ye sit with me now?"

He nodded but had to wait for six little girls to shuffle around on the step before he had a space of his own.

"Thank ye for helping us," Ginger said.

A chorus of thank-yous followed from the girls.

"My pleasure."

A ruckus emanated from the chicken coop.

Ginger chuckled. "It sounds like the old lady hens have decided their wee house has no room for two more biddies."

At the next series of thumps and loud chicken screeches, the girls on the steps rose to their feet and stared anxiously at the shuddering building.

"Will they hurt each other?" asked Opal.

Before either adult could answer, the door banged open and nine irate hens poured out. They scattered across the yard, with one poor fowl harassed by two dominant hens. The others lost interest and slowed to a stop, picking a spot to scratch and peck the ground.

The rooster strutted out of the coop last, conveying a sense of overwhelming dignity. It was clear the fiasco was none of his doing. With a final cacophony of squawks, the two belligerent hens turned their backs on their victim and took up the occupation of the others, a thorough investigation of the newly swept yard.

"I'm thinking we'll be leaving 'em out for a bit," said Ginger. "Maybe without being elbow to elbow in the coop, they can get to know each other."

"Do chickens have elbows?" asked Opal.

"Well now, I know they have toes, and I'm thinking they have knees and elbows, too. What think ye, Dr. Steadman?"

Lucas felt a bubble of mirth rising to his throat. He managed to choke out, "Chicken anatomy was not part of my course of instruction, Miss Finnegan," before collapsing into undignified guffaws.

The children joined him, and when the hilarity settled, one of the twins challenged him to a game of tag. Of course the girls nominated him "it," but his longer legs gave him an advantage.

Ginger watched, and then, defying Aunt Amy's instructions to stay quiet, she pushed her spectacles deep into her pocket and joined the game.

The children loved playing with her. When she was "it," a new set of rules came into play, obviously developed to accommodate her poor vision. Instead of running, they hid. She walked slowly around the yard. Often, just as she passed a hidden child, she'd turn and reach into a bush and grab the player. When Lucas was "it" again, he noticed the girls tried to run interference and keep him from tagging Ginger.

In the end he got her. Grasping her hands, he dragged her back to the "jail."

"Snow! First snow!" yelled the children.

"It's snowing?" asked Ginger. "Let me go. I need to see."

Lucas released her. She dug into her pocket and jerked out the spectacles.

"Here, look," said Lucas, almost as excited as Ginger.

He held out the dark sleeve of his coat. The wool material caught the floating flakes.

"Oh!" She clasped his arm with two hands and brought it close to her eyes. "Oh, dear Lord, another miracle."

She looked up at Lucas. Her face glowed with awe, and he thought what a blessing it would be to share her joy each day of the year. The feeling clutched at his heart, and he struggled to banish it. He must not become involved with this woman before he had time to think logically about his future and establish new goals.

"We'd better put the hens back in the coop," he said.

She nodded, apparently unfazed that he did not share her exultation over a snowflake. She moved slowly to gather the children and tell them to shoo the chickens back in their shelter.

"And this time, me dears, be sure the latch is put on tight."

"Dr. Steadman?"

Lucas turned to see Amy Ross standing in the open kitchen doorway.

"We're about to have supper. Would you join us?"

"Thank you, Mrs. Ross, but I've made arrangements for supper."

"You'll be going up Croner Hill to eat with Mr. and Mrs. Steadman," said Ginger.

Lucas jumped. He hadn't heard her return to his side. The light of day was fading rapidly. He could no longer make out the freckles on her pert nose. He could still see her smile, and that smile made him nervous. He cleared his throat before speaking.

"No, I eat at Mrs. Stanberry's Boardinghouse."

"Ginger," said Aunt Amy, "see that he stays." She turned and went back into the house, closing the door behind her.

"You're telling me you eat at a boardinghouse when you have family who would welcome you to their table?" Ginger's eyes grew large, brimming with disapproval.

"We've never been close," he explained.

"I'm thinking the ones ye need to forgive are not all dead, Dr. Steadman. I'm thinking yer excuse for the way ye be won't matter much when ye stand before God Almighty."

"And I'm thinking, Miss Finnegan, that it's none of your

business with whom I eat my meals."

A twitch at the corner of Ginger's mouth grew into a smile, clearing the stormy scowl on her face like the sun breaking through after a rain.

She chuckled. "Aye, yer right, of course. I shouldna' be nattering on about the speck in yer eye when there's a plank in me own."

Lucas crossed his arms over his chest and gave her a nod. He didn't want to venture a statement lest she somehow find a way to continue badgering him.

A twinkle in her eye forewarned him.

"So," she said in a voice that was almost a purr. "That clench in yer jaw and that miserly nod is yer way of admitting ye do have a speck, is it?" She laughed at him when he refused to answer.

"Well," she continued, "we'll send one of the girls down to Mrs. Stanberry's to say ye'll be dining with us. Aunt Amy particularly told me to keep ye, and I'll be in trouble if ye don't stay. Ye wouldna' want me to be in trouble, now would ye?"

The trouble is, thought Lucas as he rigidly kept the smile from stealing onto his face, *I don't want Ginger Finnegan to have any more trouble in her life. Now why should I care, Lord, and what do You want me to do about it?*

The back door creaked open, shedding a ribbon of light across the small porch.

"Coming, Dr. Steadman?" asked Amy Ross.

Lucas kept his eyes on the smiling pixie face before him. "Yes, Mrs. Ross. I believe I am."

Chapter 8

How did you learn to flirt?" asked Susannah. She set the pan of scrubbed potatoes on the table in front of Ginger.

Startled, Ginger looked up from dicing an onion for the evening stew.

"I can't tell ye how, 'cause I don't know. I've never flirted, not once, in all me days. How could I know how to learn such a thing?"

"Mary says you do. With Dr. Steadman. All the time. He comes here almost every day. For all sorts of reasons, she says, but mostly to see you."

Ginger dropped the onion pieces into a kettle of water and said nothing.

"Are you mad because Mary said that?" asked Susannah.

"No," said Ginger. "I'm thinking about what she said."

She reached for a potato to peel.

"Don't be mad." Susannah sat down and picked up another paring knife. "Mary thinks it's grand. So do I. So do all the girls. We like Dr. Steadman. He's handsome when he smiles."

"Well, there it is, Susannah. I like teasing a smile out of him. I never thought of it as flirting."

"He's been coming here every day for weeks. He's been coming since first snow in September, and now it's December. That's a long time, Ginger."

"No, me girl, ye can't be saying it's every day."

"Almost. He comes to see you, so he must be feeling something for you. What would you say if he asked you to marry him?"

"Susannah!" Ginger stopped what she was doing long enough to glare at her young helper. "He comes to bring us the things he can't use, things traded to him for doctoring. Then he stays to eat with us because. . .well, because he likes our food."

"Mrs. Stanberry is one of the best cooks in the county. She wins ribbons every summer at the fair. They have dessert every night at the boardinghouse. He doesn't stay because our food is better."

"Well, I'm not a candidate for a doctor's wife."

"Why not?" asked Susannah. "Before you had your spectacles, Mary said no man wanted a blind wife to tend his garden, cook his meals, raise his children. But now you can see almost as good as anybody. Why can't you be a doctor's wife?"

"Lucas Steadman would be wanting a wife with more than me pitiful schooling."

"He likes you."

"But think of how some people feel about the Irish."

"Dr. Steadman has more sense than to hold the opinion that all Irish are bad."

"Well, maybe so, but I'm thinking the man wouldna' look twice at the likes of me."

"Ginger! You're not very observant. He's already given you more than a second glance."

Ginger shook her head. "He'd also be needing a fine lady. Remember, he comes from the houses on the hill."

"Isabel and Kathleen Steadman don't come from grand houses, and you read plenty good. And you always help the little girls with their schoolwork, especially their sums. You'd make a good doctor's wife. You're always the one who takes care of any of us when we're sick."

"Aunt Amy takes care of ye."

"You help. Lots."

"This is a foolish discussion we're having. There's no sense nattering on about me and the doctor. Ye're seeing things that cannot be and wasting the time of day doing it. Tell me how ye're doing with memorizing yer poem for Christmas Eve."

"My hands are busy while we talk, Ginger, so I'm not wasting the time of day. You know I get stuck in the last stanza, and you're just trying to change the subject." A knock sounded at the door. Susannah sprang up from her chair to answer.

Ginger turned at the sound of delighted laughter. Susannah threw an impudent grin over her shoulder and stepped back. Dr. Steadman stamped snow off his boots before entering.

Susannah giggled as she took his coat and hat to hang on a hook beside the stove. She giggled more as she poured hot tea in a mug and placed it before him where he sat at the table with Ginger. She giggled every time Ginger sent her a glare.

"Miss Susannah," said Dr. Steadman. "Excessive giggling is a sign of a nervous disorder. Should I prescribe a tonic?"

That set the poor girl off again, and Ginger ordered her from the kitchen.

Dr. Steadman watched her go with his eyebrows raised, then he turned to Ginger.

"You're flushed. Are you feeling all right?"

"I'm fine, Doctor. It's the heat from the stove, perhaps."

He narrowed his eyes and studied her a moment.

"Perhaps," he finally agreed.

Ginger sighed her relief when he didn't inquire further into the cause of Susannah's giggles or her own blushes.

"I've brought you something," he said, pushing a book across the table.

Ginger wiped her hands on her apron and picked it up.

"*A Christmas Carol* by Charles Dickens," she read. "Did someone barter this? It's not like yer usual payments. It doesna' cluck nor squeal. Ye canna' eat it, nor wear it, nor use it in some practical manner."

"I got it from Maxwell."

Ginger gasped. "Ye've been to the house?"

He nodded. "After all your nagging to reconcile with my family, I went up there last night."

"Nagging? Me nagging? I never, Dr. Steadman. It's bad of ye to say such a thing."

He laughed. "So you don't nag me, Miss Finnegan? You just

mention every time Isabel Steadman or Kathleen Steadman happens to stop by Kindred Hearts. You point out Carter's charitable project with the children in the church. You draw my attention to Maxwell's offer to host the church Christmas party. You just remind me you're praying for my heart to soften. No, you never nag, Miss Finnegan."

Ginger clamped her lips down against an answering smile. "Ye've just described me granny's method of making us see her way of doing things. At times, I wanted to run from her constant nattering."

"But at all times you knew she loved you."

"Aye, that's right, to the point I'd wish she didn't love me quite so much."

"Well, your nattering at me has convinced me you are the best friend I've ever had."

The statement surprised Ginger. She looked directly into his eyes and tried not to be too thrilled by the affectionate warmth she saw there. *So, it's a friend I am. I'm glad to be a friend. . . . I am! Ah, but because of Susannah's silly chatter, for a wee little bit, I let meself hope for more.*

"Tell me how Mr. Maxwell came to give ye this book."

"They, Kathleen and Maxwell, were surprised to see me. I hadn't warned them I was coming."

"Ye don't warn yer family," objected Ginger.

"Well, you might if you've been a curmudgeon forever and barely spoken a civil word to them."

"Aye."

"But as I was saying, they didn't expect me and were in

the middle of unpacking crates that had come in on one of Maxwell's ships."

"Why are they Maxwell's ships and not yer ships, too?"

"Father left the business to Maxwell. He said I was too soft. Mother left me all her money, which I used to go to school and set up my practice."

"Was she agreeing for ye to be a doctor?"

"No, she just didn't want her son to starve or wear shabby clothing."

"She loved ye."

He grunted. "To be fair, I know she did. But she didn't understand me. And it distressed her that I associated with lower classes."

"I'm thinking she feared for ye."

"Feared for me?"

"Sure and don't ye know, she'd been tole all her life these people ye befriended were dirty and rough. She probably thought ye'd come home with some strange disease or be killed in a brawl. Her mother's heart couldna' stand the thought of losing ye."

He studied his hands folded on the table.

Ginger sighed. "Am I nagging ye again?"

He nodded and looked up at Ginger. A slow smile moved his lips and spread to his eyes.

"You want me to forgive her."

"Aye, Doctor, and yer father, too."

"All right, Miss Finnegan, you've won. Actually, as I walked home last night under the starry sky, I couldn't help but hear

God's voice in my heart. And oddly, He was saying much the same things you've been saying. . .only without the Irish brogue."

"Oh, I'm that glad, Doctor." Ginger picked up her paring knife and another potato. "Now, would ye mind explaining to me just why ye have the same bitterness toward yer brother, Maxwell, and yer cousin Carter?"

"Pride."

"Well, I'm not denying I'm a brilliant person, but one word is not going to clear me confusion on the matter."

"For years, Miss Finnegan, I was the 'Christian' in the family. We all went to church, but I was the one who believed and acted upon that belief."

Ginger tried not to look appalled at the smugness of his words. Apparently she did not succeed.

"You're right," said the doctor. "I was a self-righteous snob. I had this great plan to become a doctor and serve the poor and thus make amends to society for my family's sins. It was an immature attitude that I latched on to as a child, and unfortunately as I grew up, I never relinquished it."

"But why hold yer grudge against the two young Mr. Steadmans?"

"You're going to laugh at me, Ginger. And I don't blame you. I think God must have laughed at my foolishness when He wasn't thoroughly exasperated by my stubbornness."

It took her a minute to answer. He'd called her by her first name. Feelings she knew she had no right to encourage tingled in her chest. *Oh, Susannah and yer foolish talk, what have ye done to me heart?*

"I won't laugh."

"When I came back from medical school and found my brother and cousin reconciled with God, doing good works, and married to godly women, I was disgusted. They'd stolen the march on me. They were doing the generous, kind acts out of the purest of motives. That had been my destiny since I'd started plotting my future when I was eight years old. I was as mad as a hornet that I wasn't the one and only grand benefactor Steadman."

He stopped his tirade and looked at her. "You're smiling."

"But I'm not laughing."

"Your eyes are laughing."

"Well, so is me heart, but ye'll have to be satisfied I'm not rolling on the floor and holding me sides. Will ye let me tell ye why I'm so filled with joy?"

"All right."

"The doctor I first met when Alys slid off the roof and kicked me in the face was stiff and stodgy. God wanted to work through ye to help the people of this town, but ye clogged up yer vessel with yer own self. Now yer letting all that go, and God's going to work mightily through ye, Dr. Steadman. I know He is."

Aunt Amy entered the kitchen. "Susannah said you were here, Doctor. Will you be able to stay for supper?"

"Yes, Mrs. Ross, and I have a book I'd like to read to the girls afterward while they work on their sewing projects." He held up the Dickens novel. "This came in a shipment of books from England. Kathleen thought you and the girls would enjoy it."

"*A Christmas Carol.* I've heard it's good. Pastor Hull recommended it. We'd be delighted for you to join us in the parlor after supper. Wouldn't we, Ginger?"

"Aye, that we would." Ginger smiled at the doctor, and this time she knew she was flirting. But would it do her any good? Now that was the question.

Chapter 9

A lantern dimly lit the space just inside the front door of the orphanage. Already wearing a heavy coat and boots, Ginger pulled on a knitted cap, wrapped a scarf around her neck, and reached for mittens.

Aunt Amy draped a woolen shawl over her charge's shoulders. She patted Ginger's arms and tucked a stray lock of coppery hair under the rim of her cap.

"I should not send you, but I truly fear for Patty, Ruthie, and Opal." Her raspy voice held the lingering effects of a powerful infection in the lungs.

"I'll be all right," assured Ginger.

A chorus of coughing from the bedrooms upstairs echoed down the wood staircase. Ginger and Amy both turned anxious faces upward.

Fear clutched Ginger's heart. It seemed that each girl who became ill had a worse case than the child before. Starting the day after Christmas, the children had taken colds, one after the other. Even Aunt Amy fell to the epidemic, but her convalescence had been cut short by the need to get up and see to the small children. Ginger alone had not succumbed, but days of tending the others showed in circles under her eyes and sagging shoulders.

There must be a turn for the better soon, Lord.

Ginger gathered what strength she had left and squared her shoulders. "Well, I be doing no good with me feet planted here."

"Wait," said Aunt Amy. "Let me pray first."

She put her arms around Ginger and murmured a blessing. Ginger stood mutely, too tired to do much more than soak in the comforting words.

Dr. Steadman had said to send for him if matters got worse. At two in the morning, the condition of three little girls had gone beyond what Amy and Ginger could handle. For hours that night they had watched the girls' breathing become more labored. A hollow, deep cough shook their little frames, and their fevers climbed no matter how many times the women wiped away the perspiration with cold rags. Aunt Amy and Ginger prayed with every breath, then decided to send for the doctor.

"The moon is shining brightly," observed Ginger as Aunt Amy released her. "I'll not lose me way."

Just five months ago, she would never have dared to walk through town by herself. But with the urgency of the girls' illness prodding her, she fought irritation at Aunt Amy's concern. "Now ye go back upstairs to the wee ones, and I'll be back with the doctor as soon as can be."

Once out in the piercing night cold, Ginger bent her head

against the biting wind and trudged through a foot of recent snow. Her breath puffed out before her in clouds. Without the gravity of her mission weighing on her, she would have been tempted to stop and marvel at the sparkling scene in the moonlight.

She soon turned off the side street onto a more traveled road in the center of town. There she found wagon-wheel ruts of hard-packed snow. The snow squeaked under her boots. Icy patches threatened to fell her. She carefully chose where to place each step.

Dear Lord, let the doctor be at home, not out with someone else who be ailing. I know many people, in town and around, have been sick with this awful coughing, but we need him, Lord.

Aye, now, I'm not forgetting we need Ye as well. Please send comfort to Aunt Amy, ease the little girls' breathing, Lord, so it isn't so hard for them. Protect them all.

Ginger caught a sob before it rose in her throat. By batting her eyes, she fought tears.

"They'd only freeze on me face, Lord," she muttered. The cold air drawn in when she spoke aloud hurt her lungs.

Straightaway, her mind turned back from her own discomfort to the distress of those at home. *Please, Lord, place yer healing hand on me Patty. I love the little girl, and it would be a blight on me very existence to have to go on without her.*

She broke into a run when she rounded the corner of North Elm and spotted the apothecary with Dr. Steadman's sign hanging just beyond. In order to wake him, she ducked down the alley to the back entrance. He'd said on several occasions patients had roused him by banging on the door closer to the little room in which he slept.

She knocked loudly. Then, too impatient to wait for a response, she began to pound with the side of her closed fist.

"I'm coming! I'm coming!" The doctor opened the door and blinked at her. "Ginger!"

"They're worse," she cried. "Patty and Opal and Ruthie. Ye must come, Doctor."

"I will. Step in out of the cold while I get dressed." He took hold of her arm and pulled her into the dark examining room. The door closed, and she heard him scratching around. Soon a flame leaped up from the end of a matchstick, and he lit a lantern. In the haze of light she saw her cold spectacles had fogged over in the warm air. She stood numbly, looking at the blur.

"Oh," Dr. Steadman exclaimed. He quickly removed her spectacles, blowing on the lenses, then polishing them with the material of his robe.

"Here." He put them back on her face and then placed the lantern in her mittened hand. "Take this through to the sitting room. I'll be ready in just a minute."

Ginger collapsed in the same chair she had sat on when she first came to Dr. Steadman's office. *Thank Ye, Lord, that he's here. Please give him wisdom. Use him to heal our little ones. Give us all the strength to do Yer will. Help the wee ones.*

Her head nodded until her chin rested on the thick knitted scarf around her neck. It had been such a long, hard week. Now Dr. Steadman and the Lord could take over. She dozed.

"Come on, Ginger. I'm ready."

She stood and started toward his voice even before she fully awoke.

"No, we're going out the front."

She ran right into him. His arms came around her to keep them from falling. A moment passed before his hand under her chin forced her to look up. He examined her face.

"Are you all right?" he asked. "When was the last time you slept more than a snatch of a nap?"

She shook her head, unable to answer.

He gently guided her head back down to his shoulder. Pulling a deep breath, he rested his cheek on the top of her knitted cap. His arms tightened, and she enjoyed the warmth of his embrace.

"My dear Ginger, we can't let you get sick as well."

Suddenly he released her, and with hands on her shoulders, turned her around. "Let's go take care of those girls."

She opened the door while he blew out the lantern. As soon as he locked the door behind him, he put his arm around her waist. He left it there, steadying her balance on the icy patches, lending her strength and warmth as they trudged back to the orphanage.

It feels good, thought Ginger. *Oh, Lord, what a privilege 'twould be to have this man by me side forever and a day. I'm asking for miracles tonight. And I know Ye give abundantly. So when Ye've finished healing our wee girls, Ye might touch this man with a love for me whether I deserve it or not. Aye, Lord, I wouldna' mind that miracle a'tall.*

Chapter 10

January twelfth. Three weeks of coughing and fever. Five days since the doctor had come in the middle of the night. He'd practically lived at the orphanage, sitting beside the girls' beds during the night watch, supporting one sick child after another while Ginger or Aunt Amy spooned broth into their little mouths. He also insisted the women get some rest.

During the day he made his rounds and saw a few patients in his office. Every evening he came back to help with the worst cases at the orphanage.

In spite of the dire circumstances, Ginger had stolen some precious memories. One night she knelt beside Opal's bed, holding the sick girl's hand. Dr. Steadman prayed in soothing tones while the tonic he'd given the child took effect. Opal's breathing became less ragged, more steady. Ginger pulled off her spectacles, rested her head on the mattress, and closed her eyes, reveling in the peaceful moment. Dr. Steadman's prayer ended. The hush over the room was too blessed to disturb, so

Ginger allowed herself the luxury of not moving, just resting. Then came the miracle she'd asked for.

The doctor bent forward from the chair he sat upon. That sweet smell of peppermint reached her nose, and then she felt the soft touch of his lips brush her forehead.

She opened her eyes and looked at his face. It was close enough that she didn't need her spectacles to see the embarrassment register as he realized she was awake.

"Stealing kisses?" she asked.

He smiled.

"There's no need to steal what would be freely given." The boldness of her words shocked her. Out they'd come with no thought of propriety. She felt her face burn with shame and turned away in confusion.

"No, you don't," said Dr. Steadman. "I like what you just said. I shouldn't have stolen the kiss, Ginger, but there are times when you seem to be the only answer to my loneliness. I'm feeling more comfortable with my family. And bless them, they've taken me back without a word of reproach." He reached to take her two hands in his. "Remember you accused me of being stiff and stodgy."

"Aye, I do."

"I'm better now."

"Aye, much."

"I've quit worrying so much about whether or not I have an image—like 'respected doctor' or 'benefactor.' I just do my job. I actually enjoy people now. I'm so grateful for your pointing me in the right direction." He squeezed her hands. "I need you.

When I feel my muscles getting tight, tense, stiff, I remind myself of your laughing eyes."

His thumb slid gently across the back of one hand. "Be my friend, always?"

"Aye, I will."

Ruthie in the next bed began to cough. She cried as the spasms wracked the sore muscles in her chest.

As the doctor moved to take care of his patient, Ginger gave up resisting falling in love. She treasured each moment she worked by his side. Still, she wasn't sure he loved her the way she did him. With so much to do to make the girls comfortable and with the weariness of working long hours with little sleep, she had little time for romancing.

Sometimes she felt surely Dr. Steadman loved her, too. Then she'd think of how unworthy she was to be his wife and tell herself she was spinning fairy tales. She sought wisdom from the Lord.

Here I am again, Lord, lying in me bed with me bones so tired, I canna' turn over. But am I asleep? No, I am not! And why is that? Because me heart is troubled, full of joy, full of woe.

Does he love me? Why is it Ye're not answering me? Sometimes I think the answer is yes and Ye're showing me he cares. He strokes me cheek so tenderly. He holds me hand while we pray.

Why can't the tiresome man just say, "Ginger, me love, I canna' live a day without ye?"

Are the words too big?

Aye, I know I'm whining, Lord, when I should be praising Ye for the returning health of the girls.

Aye, I know I'm an impatient one with no respect for Yer timing of things.

Ye know I love praying with him when he's finished his doctoring and the results of his efforts are in Ye hands. But if he ends one more time with, "And thank You, Lord, for Ginger. Amen," I'm going to kick his shin.

All right, so I won't resort to violence.

Is it because I'm so tired, Lord, that me feelings just won't settle down? Is all this turmoil because I'm not trusting Ye the way I should? Why can't Ye just put it in that aggravating man's head to either kiss me proper or tell me to go soak me head?

Am I grumbling again? Well, I beg Yer forgiveness and ask humbly that Ye remove the source of me griping. Amen.

Even after the girls were allowed out of bed, some still labored for each breath. It had been a hard illness on many of the people in Massachusetts and the surrounding states. Dr. Steadman brought in a newspaper that reported many had died of the congestion, but officials said the epidemic was easing off.

Each day brought hope as one after another of the girls threw off the illness and began to regain strength. Only the littlest tyke in the orphanage still gave them grave concern. Dr. Steadman sat vigil over her bed, or rather he dozed.

Ginger came into the sickroom at first light. She crossed to the window and pushed the curtains aside, hoping to see pink clouds reflecting the promise of a new day. Ice covered most of the inside of the glass pane. Outside a stiff north wind jerked the black bare limbs of the oak in an endless motion that had lasted all night. Pulling the heavy material back across the window, Ginger blocked out the dismal winter scene. She heard the doctor stir behind her and turned.

"How's little Ruthie, Doctor?" she asked.

He heaved a sigh and rose from the chair he'd been in all night. Stretching his arms way above his head, he smiled at his capable nurse.

"At last she's taken her upward turn. She's going to make it, Ginger."

He took Ginger's hands in his as he'd done a dozen times in the past few days. She bowed her head and listened once again as he prayed, this time thanking God for Ruthie's broken fever and restful sleep.

He closed the prayer with, "And thank You, Lord, for Ginger. Amen."

A twitch of annoyance pulled down the corners of Ginger's mouth. *Oh, Lord, another pound of patience, please,* she prayed before she looked up into the doctor's face.

How could she scold, even in her heart, one who had given so much to the children? He looked tired. Lines of weariness across his brow only made him dearer to her. At this moment her fairy tale seemed real. She had to break the spell or perhaps say some foolish thing.

"I'll be getting the well ones up now. Why don't you lay down for a wee bit on the cot in the next room?"

"Yes, I could use a little bit of sleep."

Ginger left him and quietly roused the healthier sleepyheads.

In an hour, only three girls remained in bed. She started down the hall with an apron in her hand. Mary and Amanda had gone off to the mill. Jessica would be helping Aunt Amy serve breakfast to the younger children. Ginger searched her tired brain for ways to keep the children happily occupied. Still too weak to go back to school, they became easily bored and crotchety.

"Are you going down to eat?" asked Dr. Steadman behind her.

She turned and smiled. Carrying his jacket over a bent arm, he buttoned his vest as he walked toward her. His normally neat hair needed a combing, and his eyes still looked sleepy.

"Aye."

"I smell Mrs. Ross's pancakes. Mind if I join you?"

"Not a'tall."

The wind rattled the windows, the front door banged open, causing a commotion. A child's light footsteps raced through the house to the foyer. The door slammed shut.

Ginger and Dr. Steadman continued down the stairs. He worked a cufflink into his sleeve. She tied the apron behind her back as she walked.

"It's true, then." The outraged voice came from the elder Mrs. Ross. She stood rigid in the foyer, her expression as glacial as the cold morning outside the door. The harshness of the winter's day had swept right into the house with the disagreeable old woman. She cast a withering glare at the couple descending the stairs.

"Mother Ross," Amy said as she came into the small entranceway from the kitchen. "What's wrong?"

The older woman's head swiveled to pin the young widow with her accusing gaze. "You and your orphans haven't been to church in two weeks. That's one thing wrong. Don't think I didn't notice.

"Then I hear rumors that this man is living in your home. I, of course, did not believe such a vile thing of my son's widow. But here is the proof, seen with my own eyes." She nodded toward the stairs where Lucas and Ginger stood frozen in place. "Can you deny he's been here all night? He's coming down from your bedrooms, and he isn't even fully dressed yet."

"You know this is the doctor, Mother Ross," Amy explained. "He's been here for the girls. I think we would have lost Patty and Ruthie without his skill."

"Excuses! Lies! I will not have you turn my house into a brothel. I will not have this immoral woman living under this roof."

Ginger heard a growl from Dr. Steadman. He left her on the steps and stood before the elder Mrs. Ross. His profile showed his anger, hard and cold. Ginger watched the muscle in his jaw work before he spoke.

"Mrs. Ross, you are speaking out of ignorance. Nothing has gone on here that would cause shame to come upon anyone. That is until you walked through that door with your unfounded and ugly suspicions."

He turned and spoke to Ginger.

"Ginger, pack your belongings and Patty's as well."

"Where are we going?" she croaked.

"To my brother's house. I'll go borrow a closed carriage from him. I don't want Patty out in the cold."

Ginger retreated up the stairs at full speed.

He then addressed Amy. "I'll hire Mrs. Miller to come help you until the other children are fully recovered. I thank you now for the good care you've taken of Ginger and Patty, but with your permission, I'll take over their charge."

"Don't you say yes to that," ordered Mother Ross. "It's indecent."

Lucas turned back to her. She recoiled, taking a step away from his righteous wrath.

"There's nothing indecent about it, Mrs. Ross. Ginger will be my bride. She'll be married out of my brother's house instead of this one."

"I'll say what your mother, God rest her soul, would say, young man. A Steadman does not pick his wife from the Irish rabble. I don't know how your parents could stand the heartache. It is a blessing they have already departed this earth. First your cousin and brother marry mill workers, and now you choose an Irish wench."

"The Irish lady has a pure heart with the glory of our Lord lifting her above the rabble of this earth." Lucas allowed his accusing glare to rest on the well-dressed matron before him. He wanted to be sure she understood that he considered her behavior reprehensible. At the moment he found it hard to believe God loved Mrs. Ross. With difficulty, he restrained his tongue. "I want to marry Ginger Finnegan, and the Irish in her makes her dearer than you could possibly understand."

Behind him something clattered and banged as it bumped

down the stairs. They all turned to see a basket at the bottom of the steps with clothing strewn behind it. At the top of the staircase stood Ginger with her palms pressed to either side of her face.

"Dr. Steadman!" she said in a horrified whisper.

He grinned at her. "What?"

For a moment she didn't answer. Then she lowered her hands to her sides and walked down, stopping just two steps from the bottom.

She smiled at him, and a twinkle lightened her eyes. "I love ye," she said.

He stepped forward and put his hands around her waist.

"Well, now," he said in a heavy imitation of her Irish brogue. "I'm thinking that be the best news of the morning. And if ye be willing, I wouldna' mind a kiss a'tall."

She leaned into his embrace and he kissed her.

"Well, I never!" The words were followed by the opening of the front door, a draft of sweet cold air, and the resounding clap of wood against wood as the elder Mrs. Ross departed, slamming the door.

Maxwell had not only sent a closed carriage, but a man to drive it. Inside, Patty marveled at the rich leather upholstered seats and the pockets lining the walls on either side of the door.

Ginger curled up under a carriage rug with her Dr. Steadman, contentedly snuggled against his side. "Ye never told me ye love me," she said with a mock pout.

"Sure I did."

"Ye did, now? And when was this? I know the last few weeks have been a strain, but I'm thinking a girl would remember when the man she loves tells her those special words."

"It was the night I asked you to marry me."

"Ye asked me to marry?"

"Sure."

"When?"

"When Opal passed her crisis." He cleared his throat, and Ginger knew he was nervous.

"I don't remember a thing about marriage and love," she told him. "I remember something about friends and needing."

"I said forever," he explained.

"Ah, Lucas me love, ye do need me."

"I do, Ginger, forever. I love you. Will you marry me?"

Patty turned from her examination of a bolster built into the seatback. The armrest moved up to be hidden in the upright cushioned back or extended down for use. She interrupted her scrutiny to frown at her sister. "I thought that was all settled," she said.

"Shh!" said Ginger.

"I thought that's why we're going to the big house," insisted Patty.

"Shh!" said Lucas. "I'm waiting for the answer."

"Aye, Lucas, I will marry you and be your friend forever."

KATHLEEN PAUL

Kate lives in Colorado Springs with her eighty-six-year-old mom and a college-age son. Her married daughter also lives in town and recently gave Kathleen her first grandbaby! "Everyone in our family reads voraciously. I already have two bookcases filled with children's books to read to that precious grandson."

In the house, two small dogs, Gertie and Gimli, provide entertainment with their outlandish antics. Kate's hobbies include oral storytelling, mentoring new writers, and knitting.

A recent **Heartsong Presents** novel, *To See His Way,* won second place in the national Romance Writers of America/Faith Hope and Love Historical Short Fiction contest.

The Caretaker

by Kelly Eileen Hake

Dedication

To the two unstoppable forces in my life:
God and my mother!

Chapter 1

Amy Ross hurried out to the water pump for what must have been the fifth time that morning. She didn't have long to get the little ones washed for church, or they'd be late again. Last week Pastor Hull told her that although he didn't mind seeing her girls scamper down the aisle just before prayer, some of his other parishioners were not as understanding about the disturbance.

Lost in her musings, Amy didn't notice the goose slipping through the fence and making a beeline for her until it was too late. At the impact, Amy shrieked and clutched the cold water pump handle. That move only compounded the problem when the handle broke and the pump doused her with water. Struggling to free her skirts from the determined goose, she slipped in the slick mud and landed with a dismaying splat. Amy glared at the creature now settling contentedly in her lap. Then she heard it: a deep-throated chuckle from the other side of the fence.

"I believe the culprit belongs to me." The caretaker next

door didn't bother to hide his entertainment over the spectacle.

She turned the full force of her glare upon him, picked herself up off the ground, and stalked over to the fence. She tried to ignore the squish of mud in her half-boots.

"I wish you joy of her," she gritted from behind clenched teeth, then thrust the noisy, menacing bird into his arms

He was about to respond when all sixteen of her girls poured from the house and pushed their way around her. Their cacophony was deafening.

"Auntie Amy! Auntie Amy!"

"What happened? You're all wet!"

"Ducky, Ducky!" three-year-old Ruthie crowed with glee, stretching out to stroke the goose.

"Oh, your best church dress—are we late again?"

"It's not a duck, it's a swan!" Alys caught hold of Ruthie's pudgy hand before it reached the bird.

Amy's anger evaporated as she surveyed her troops, then glanced at their new neighbor. He looked amused and a bit puzzled—not that she could blame him. Her foster family was a bit much to take in all at once. She felt the corners of her mouth quirk upward. Ducky, indeed.

"Children! It's a goose, and we can't be late. Everybody back inside, and make sure you don't leave anything behind!"

As the girls rushed off, Amy turned to face her neighbor. . . or rather, her neighbor's goose, she corrected. Since she came nose-to-bill with the misbehaving bird, Amy realized that its owner must be at least a foot taller than she. She opened her mouth to speak but thought better of it when Jessica began calling from within their small home. "Aunt Aaaammmyyy! We've only got five more minutes 'til we have to go!"

"I'll be by later to fix your pump since it's Gussie's fault it's broken." The assertive baritone voice commanded her attention. "After church."

"Thank you." Amy noticed his rough cambric workman's shirt and broadcloth pants with relief. He must be the new caretaker, so at least she hadn't made a fool of herself before the owner. Still, his offer to fix the pump was a kind one. She favored him with a smile and turned to go back to the house, dragging her sodden skirts with as much dignity as she could muster. She might be coated with mud, but she was still a lady.

Once inside, she hurried up the stairs toward her room. The last caretaker of the adjoining property had been completely irascible. That one frequently voiced his unwelcome opinions: Not only should children be seen and not heard, they really shouldn't be seen! Especially not on his property.

Amy grimaced. How glad she'd been to discover he was only the caretaker! Gladder still when he'd moved away. She prayed this one would be an improvement. He hadn't introduced himself, but he was responsible enough to fix the pump. He looked younger, too, with his broad shoulders and laughing green eyes.

She hastily changed clothes, then tucked one last pin into her wet brown hair. There. That should hold it. Her second-best cotton gray dress would have to do for today. Hearing Jessica call again, she snatched her chip-straw bonnet off the peg near the door and headed out.

The girls milled around outside, skirting mud puddles. As Amy reached the road, all sixteen fell into step around her, whispering and giggling until they reached the church and settled into their usual places. There was even enough time to hug Ginger and whisper last-minute congratulations on her recent marriage. Amy sat in the front row with Mary and the youngest girls, while Susannah and Amanda sat behind, monitoring the older ones. Seventeen people made for a tight fit, but the townspeople generously paid for these two pews.

Accounting columns and lesson plans meandered through Amy's mind while they waited for Pastor Hull to begin. She lifted her hand in greeting to Isabel, Kathleen, and their husbands when they waved from the row across. Kathleen bounced little Molly on her knee as the child began to fuss.

Finally, Parson Hull walked to the pulpit and gave the opening prayer. Afterward, Amy smiled as he nodded at her in approval. The pastor always had a soft spot for them, even more so since he'd adopted Betty and her baby sister. Amy and her girls had made it on time today—water pump fiasco notwithstanding.

After the hymns, about halfway through the sermon, Amy became aware that some of the women in the congregation kept sneaking horrified glances her way. Considering her rather sizeable entourage, being stared at was nothing new, but this seemed different.

What was everyone gawking at? Afraid everyone was noticing the state of her hair, Amy cautiously raised one hand to check, then frowned. Surely her new bonnet concealed her wet hair. She fingered the delicate mauve ribbons tied jauntily beneath her chin. Jason gave the bonnet to her during their betrothal. The girls "borrowed" it for her birthday and refurbished it using bits from the ragbag. They'd used her favorite color, and several ladies in the congregation complimented her about the charming result.

She lowered her hand into her lap and thought over the past few years. Some people wondered why she gathered orphans instead of getting remarried after Jason's death. Most folks just didn't understand that she knew true love with her husband and could never settle for anything less.

Precious gifts from God, the girls filled her days with purpose and her heart with joy. They were her family now.

Amy rose and blended her voice with those of the other parishioners in the benediction. As she placed a hand upon Ruthie's back to guide her into the aisle, Amy noticed a stain covered her much-mended glove. It was almost the exact shade of mauve she favored.

Recognition hit, and Amy gasped as she touched her face. She drew her fingers away to find a fresh smearing of mauve dye. The water in her hair had made her ribbons run. No wonder all the womenfolk had been staring! And still were. Several women shook their heads, and a few actually pointed at her, as though she were the one lacking in decorum.

Only one option presented itself. Seizing a girl with each hand, she hurried toward the door and tried to ignore the whispers that followed her. As she purposefully strode up the aisle, someone snagged her elbow.

Amy turned to face the disapproving scrutiny of her late husband's mother. She pasted a smile on her mauve-stained face. "Mother Ross, what can I do for you?"

"I'll be over tomorrow to check up on the girls and discuss your wont of conduct," the woman hissed. "Your behavior is scandalous." With that parting shot, she grandly sailed toward the door, leaving Amy and the now wide-eyed girls in her wake.

A small hand tugged on Amy's sleeve. "Do we have to see her again?" a pleading voice whispered. "We just saw her on Wednesday." Several heads bobbed in solemn agreement.

Amy closed her eyes. She wasn't the only one who dreaded Mother Ross's visits.

Since she and Jason married young, he had not thought to draw up a will. It was typical of Jason, who loved life and reveled in each day, to not think of tomorrow. He'd made each day of their single year of marriage a joy.

As a wedding gift, Jason's parents gave them the charming little two-story residence, but Jason never received the deed. Upon his death, Amy's mother-in-law claimed ownership, blaming Amy for the untimely demise of their beloved only child. Although she allowed Amy to use the home as an orphanage, Hortense Ross ensured that the entire town knew of her "generosity" and, although they never parted with money for its upkeep, used it as leverage to "keep an eye on the dear girls" and monitor Amy's behavior. A visit from Mother Ross inevitably meant a thorough inspection of the premises, a stern lecture on decorum, and a large basket of mending to complete before the week was out.

Sighing, Amy pulled herself, mauve stains and all, back to the present. "Yes, I suppose we will see her tomorrow, ladies, so we must make sure the house is neat." She led them home amid protestations that working on the Sabbath was wrong.

"Even Jesus worked on the Sabbath by healing the unfortunate. We just have to make sure we give Mother Ross no reason for disapproval. The Lord understands that we're serving the greater good."

When they reached the house, Amy faced her charges. "Now, girls, I'll hear no more complaining." She ushered them through the mud patch her front yard had become and into the house. "Let's get going."

Amy took off her hat and caught sight of herself in the small hall mirror. "I really am quite a sight," she admitted aloud. The dye from the ribbons stained her light brown hair and left streaks on her cheeks and chin.

"Miss Amy," Susannah asked. "The little ones are changing now, but how are we supposed to clean this morning's dishes without any water?"

Noting Susannah's appalled look, Amy wondered how she could possibly clean her face. She walked out to the yard, praying for a miracle. It was answered. The caretaker came through the gate, holding a bucket of water.

"Hello. I saw you in church and thought you might be needing this." Her gaze slipped from green eyes framed by shining black hair, to trace the line of his broad shoulders and strong arms, and then to the bucket he hefted with one hand.

Amy quickly stifled her embarrassment. "Thank you. We

have a lot to do today." She noticed his face cloud over as he stiffened.

"I'll just fix your pump, then I'll be on my way."

"Again, thank you. I've told most of the girls to keep out of the yard because I don't want them to slip in the mud, so they won't bother you." She accepted the pail and lugged it toward the house. The pump would be fixed, and they had water for the day to wash up and clean the house. It seemed all her troubles were solved. *So,* Amy puzzled, *why am I wondering whether I will ever face this man while looking presentable?*

Chapter 2

Tyler Samuels watched his neighbor as she walked away. This one seemed all right—she'd even smiled at the "ducky" misinterpretation—but appearances could be deceiving. He'd thought she'd want the water to wash her face, but she seemed more interested in making the children work—even on Sunday, just like another headmistress he'd known—and she wouldn't let the girls out because she didn't want them to dirty their clothes.

He knew how it could be with orphanages. He'd stick around for a few months to make sure she treated the girls kindly and cared for them properly. His resolution strengthened at the memory of his sister, Emma. She'd been so weak toward the end. . . . His hands curled into fists at the image of another orphanage—another woman entrusted with the care of children. Only that woman hadn't cared for her charges, instead stealing from the orphanage while the children suffered. . .his sister included. He wouldn't let it happen again. No, with the Lord's help, he'd see to it that this was not the case at Kindred Hearts.

"Whatcha doin'?" A small voice piped up behind him, startling Tyler.

He looked over his shoulder to find a small blond girl regarding him with curious hazel eyes—eyes like Emma's. He forced himself to smile. "I'm fixing the water pump."

"Was it your ducky, uh, goose that broke it?"

This time his smile was genuine. "Yes, Gussie's mine." The girl must be about eight years old.

"Can I see it?"

"Anytime. Just climb through that hole over there with some of your friends, and you can see her whenever you want."

"Really?" She visibly brightened.

"What's your name?"

"Prudence." She grimaced. "But don't call me that. Everyone calls me Prudie."

"All right, Prudie it is. I'm Tyler Samuels, but you may call me Mr. Sam."

"Oh. Auntie Amy says you're the new caretaker. I'm glad, 'cuz I didn't like the old one. He was mean when I asked him what he took care of."

The caretaker? In an odd sort of way, he was. He'd really only bought the large house so he could look after the orphanage. He felt protective of the children, and this engaging little minx proved no exception.

"I take care of the house, the plants. . .and even you, if you ever need something."

She backed away. "No. Auntie Amy takes care of me." With all the wisdom of a child, she added, "You can take care of your goose. Oops, I gotta go now."

Tyler watched as she scampered toward the house where Amy stood in the doorway, waiting. He didn't know what to make of this woman. At times she seemed unduly strict, meting out a load of chores on a hot day and not allowing the girls a bit of time for fun, presumably because she didn't want more dirty clothes. Still, tiny Prudie appeared alarmed at the thought of being separated from her.

That didn't matter. If anything, the two aspects of Amy's conduct alarmed him that much more. Many years ago, Mistress Lowland charmed the townsfolk while abusing her charges.

Shrugging his shoulders, Tyler set to work again, ignoring the hot sun as he repaired the water pump. The work went slowly since the parts were so old and badly worn. He smiled. He'd gladly repair half a dozen water pumps to watch Amy's losing battle with a goose.

A shadow fell across him as he labored, and he looked up. No stray cloud overhead blocked the sun as he'd expected. Instead, a shapely figure in gray calico leaned above him, holding out a glass of lemonade. Suddenly realizing how thirsty his work left him, he licked his lips.

"Mr. Sam?" Amy's voice sounded hesitant.

He straightened from his work. "Samuels, Tyler Samuels, Ma'am. The kids may call me Mr. Sam."

"Would you like some lemonade, Mr. Samuels? Maxwell Steadman was kind enough to bring several lemons back for us from his last trip."

"Thank you, Amy." He gratefully accepted the glass.

"The kids call me Auntie Amy." Her voice stopped him before he took a sip. "You, Mr. Samuels," she stressed the syllables of his name, "may call me Mrs. Ross."

She was married? No. He hadn't seen a husband around the house or at church. He eyed her speculatively, recalling he'd only seen her wear gray or mauve—the colors a woman wore after heavy mourning. On the other hand, the colors suited her light honey-brown hair and clear gray eyes. "I'm sorry for your loss." His words rang with undeniable sincerity.

"Thank you."

Anticipating cold refreshment, he raised the glass to his parched lips. Her desperate, "Wait!" didn't register until too late. Tyler took a large sip and promptly began spluttering. The woman was trying to kill him!

"Oh dear." She sighed. "I tried to warn you; the appeal of Prudie's lemonade comes more from her generous heart than the taste of the brew. She asked me to give it to you so she could finish her chores."

A likely story. She probably wouldn't let the child stop working long enough to bring it to him. That—or she merely wanted to see him sample the vile concoction. Did he see a smile hovering on her lips?

"And Prudie. . .found, er, happened upon this while she visited with you." She pulled his pocket watch from her apron pocket.

"That must have fallen out while I worked, but it escaped my notice." He cleared his throat. "I appreciate your returning it. You called her away rather quickly, so she must have forgotten to give it back. Thank her for me, and tell Prudie I'll have a little reward for her the next time I see her."

Amy gasped. "That's not necessary!"

Did she enjoy being so heartless she wouldn't let him give the child a small token of his gratitude? "Neither was the lemonade she so thoughtfully made for me. Sometimes we do things because they are kind, not because they are necessary. Many children would take this for themselves rather than return it." He curled his fingers around the treasured watch. She looked as if she were about to choke but quickly collected herself.

"However, like the lemonade, sometimes the sentiment doesn't quite carry through with the action." She straightened at the look on his face. "All right then. I'm sure she'll be very surprised by your unexpected generosity." Her strangled voice died off as she surveyed the mess around him. "I brought out an empty glass. It looked as though you were almost finished." She held it out, and he traded away the horrid lemonade.

An odd need to justify his continued presence in her yard surfaced. "Almost. These repairs are only temporary. I'll have to purchase some new parts tomorrow." He waited to catch her reaction. She looked uncomfortable, but determined.

"No. Once you've repaired the pump, you've finished your part."

"As near as I can tell, this pump worked just fine for several years and probably would have lasted a long while yet if my goose hadn't come along." Tyler issued a quick prayer for forgiveness for that little exaggeration. He intended to make sure the girls had water, regardless of this opinionated woman's stiff-necked pride.

He noted the play of emotions across her flushed face with interest. Apparently she had some sense because practicality defeated pride and she answered, "Then I have no choice but to again thank you for your generosity, Mr. Samuels."

He nodded and resumed working but watched out of the corner of his eye as she glanced surreptitiously toward the window and hastily poured out the lemonade before going inside.

He still didn't know what to make of Mrs. Ross. She seemed excessively prim for one so young. Lovely to look at, too, he admitted to himself. She was more than presentable when dry and free of mauve dye. Still, he wouldn't let a pretty woman turn his head. There were danger signs.

Mrs. Ross. He couldn't believe he'd called her Amy—it just suited her so much better. Oh, well. It was too late to erase the social gaffe.

After he finished this water pump, he would do his level best to avoid her. Tyler continued working until a stray thought struck him. If she'd been married, could one of those little girls actually be her own daughter?

Chapter 3

Amy straightened the kitchen after breakfast the next day while Jessica and Susannah did the dishes. Mary and Veronica already reported to the mill for their day's work, and the little ones were cleaning their rooms when Mr. Samuels knocked on the kitchen door.

"Hello, Mrs. Ross. I've brought the parts for the water pump. I wanted to let you know so you could get a few bucketfuls of water while it's available."

"Certainly, Mr. Samuels." She spoke quietly, uncertain how to express her gratitude to this enigmatic man filling her doorway. "I hope you didn't go through too much trouble for us. It's working just fine."

"It's no trouble at all. I need to replace a few parts, or it won't work much longer. I saw one of your girls gathering eggs, so I figured you were all done with your breakfast. . .and I wanted to give this to Prudie." Amy followed his gaze to the blue leather-bound book in one of his large, capable-looking hands.

The memory of his flashing green eyes and the determined

set of his jaw when she'd tried to talk him out of this course of action the day before made her cautious. "I wish you'd take my word for it, Mr. Samuels. You really don't need to reward her."

His jaw tightened. "As I told you before, Mrs. Ross, I think I should."

Stubborn man! Still, he didn't know Prudie was a reformed—make that reforming—pickpocket. A recent arrival, she'd resorted to thievery to survive and hadn't quite broken the bad habit. If Amy had her way, he would never know. She sighed and sent Jessica to fetch Prudie.

"Hello, Mr. Sam!" Prudie smiled when she saw him.

"Hello, Prudie. I've brought you something as a thank-you for finding my pocket watch."

Amy gave Prudie a meaningful look, and Prudie flushed. The child's words came in a rush. "Thank you, Mr. Sam, but it was really nothing. I mean, you fixed our water pump and all."

He smiled and bent down to be at eye level with her. "Nonsense. This is my reward to you." He held the book out to her. "I got it at the mercantile when I went shopping this morning. My sister had one like it, and I thought you might enjoy one, too."

Prudie looked pleadingly at Amy. Amy gave up and nodded her assent. Prudie accepted the beautiful little book of fairy tales with a wide smile. "Oh, thank you. It's so pretty!"

He grinned, apparently pleased. "Mrs. Ross, my apple trees are full of apples. Why don't you send the girls over to pick some? I'll fill extra buckets with water and finish the pump."

Amy smiled. "How nice. Apples would be welcome." She

shut the door as he left and looked down at Prudie, who clutched her book, staring at it with something akin to awe.

"Prudie, look at me." She captured the girl's attention with her firmest tone. "This must never happen again. Promise this is the last time."

Prudie's lower lip quivered, and she looked down. "I know, Auntie Amy, but sometimes I just do it without thinking. I'll try harder—honest I will."

"See that you do." Amy smiled and gave her a hug. "Now go ask Jessica to take you and the others to pick apples." She'd barely finished speaking before Prudie set off, clasping the book to her chest. "Wait a minute. Leave the book with me. We'll read it together after Bible study tonight."

When Prudie skipped off, Amy took a moment to study the book. A truly lovely volume, its delightful illustrations filled nearly every page. She carefully set the book on the hall table, then slipped off to her room to tidy herself. After tucking a few wayward tendrils back into her simple bun, Amy turned her thoughts toward a less pleasant subject. Mother Ross planned to visit again today. The very notion set Amy to pacing about her room. Even this room had become a source of disagreement between them.

Mother Ross had been less than pleased when Amy retained the master bedroom. Although she tried to pass off her bitterness as concern that the children should occupy the largest room by urging Amy to use the small attic as her sanctuary, Amy knew the woman only wanted to make her pay for Jason's death. Still, Amy held firm. A woman needed something to call her own, and she found comfort in the memories this room held.

Amy stopped pacing. She'd lost so much. First, her beloved husband, then their son. His son. . . *And it's all my fault.* Amy shook her head, refusing to indulge in tears. She wouldn't think of it today. She simply had too much to do. She shoved the painful thoughts aside and left the room.

As Amy walked through the hall, she reassured herself all was in readiness for Mother Ross's visit, although the woman would undoubtedly find something out of place. Amy peeked into all the rooms, thanking the Lord once again that the house met their needs.

When she and Jason first moved in, she thought the house perfect for the family they planned. Now her girls filled the two guest rooms and the nursery, and she'd converted the study into yet another bedroom. Each room held one of the older girls and three of the younger. The oldest girls were "in charge" of their own girls, and this small, family-like system proved most effective.

Someone knocked on the door just as Amy reached the bottom of the stairs.

"Isabel! Kathleen! Come in. I'm so glad you're here!" As she took them into the parlor, she whispered under her breath, "Mother Ross is coming today."

The two women exchanged a telling glance and asked in unison, "What can we do?"

Amy bit her lip and stared at the baskets of fabric they held. "I'm thankful for the quilting scraps, but where can I put them?"

"Right here," Kathleen exclaimed as she set her basket in a clearly visible place by the doorway, "and let her see it. When I think of all the hardship that dour old woman has caused you. . ."

Amy grabbed Isabel's basket, chiding her friend for carrying heavy burdens in her delicate condition. Isabel had other ideas.

"Piffle. I'm not even starting to show yet. It's when I can't carry things that you should worry about me. What time do you expect Hortense to arrive?"

Just then the front door whooshed open. Mother Ross never bothered to knock.

Amy took a deep breath and retraced her steps to the front hall. "Good day, Mother Ross, I—"

"What is this?" Her mother-in-law's outraged voice cut short the greeting. "What is this heathenish novel doing in my house?" She swiped the fairy-tale book from the side table and thrust it under Amy's nose.

"It's mine!" Prudie piped up as she took the book.

Mother Ross made an attempt to snatch it back. "I won't allow nonsense penned by the devil himself to remain in my house!"

"I'm sure Parson Hull would be appalled to hear you say so, Mrs. Ross. He gave Betty one exactly like it." Isabel's calming voice halted the woman's tirade as she stepped into the entryway.

Mother Ross's lips stretched painfully into some semblance of a smile. "Really? Well then, the child may keep the book."

At first, the unprecedented capitulation surprised Amy, but she quickly realized her mother-in-law would never offend one of the richest women in Eastead. She cleared her throat.

"Why don't we all go to the parlor, and I'll have one of the girls fix us some tea." Her relief at her friends' presence escalated. Perhaps she would be spared the coming lecture, after all.

"Yes, that will be satisfactory, but first I'd like a word with you, Amy. In private." Steel lay beneath the sugared tone.

Perhaps not. Amy suppressed a sigh. Susannah would be in the kitchen, Isabel and Kathleen waited in the parlor, and she'd set the other girls to stripping beds before they went to pick apples. As much as it rankled, she would be forced to take her mother-in-law to her bedroom, her sanctuary.

They passed every other room in the house, and nothing escaped Mother Ross's attention. She stopped in every doorway and peered into each room as Amy led her down the hallway. When they reached the modest room decorated in shades of blue and cream, Mother Ross picked up the small portrait of Jason from where it sat on Amy's bedside table. She gazed at it longingly, momentarily clasped it to her breast, and reluctantly set it down.

Amy's heart ached right along with the older woman's, and she wished for the ten thousandth time she'd never sent Jason out into that storm. For a moment, the two women silently grieved for him. When Mother Ross lifted her chin, Amy took a deep breath in preparation for the imminent scolding. It wasn't long in coming.

"I know I told you I planned to visit today. Did you really think to avoid my displeasure by inviting the Steadmans' new wives? Really, I am surprised they continue to visit you at all, considering their recently elevated position in society, but then blood will always tell, won't it?"

Anger rose within Amy's heart, but she firmly tamped it down. "I'm blessed in my wonderful friends."

"Indeed, but even their support cannot save your reputation if you continue to comport yourself in such a harum-scarum manner. Few church members will countenance a connection to such a poorly bred woman and her ragtag group of hoydens if you indulge in such unseemly displays. Your actions have been suspect from the moment you engaged the affections of my son. . . ." Her voice wavered, then strengthened with resolve. "Again you justified all of my suspicions by sullying the family name with your latest antics. And in church! Need I remind you of your dependence upon my good graces?"

Amy knew she must choose her words with care, but she would not allow Mother Ross to walk all over her. She whispered a quick prayer before responding. "You've made that abundantly clear, Mother Ross. However, this scandal was caused by nothing more than a broken water pump and could be silenced by a few judiciously chosen words. I trust that your place in society will allow you several avenues to dispel such vicious gossip."

The woman appeared slightly mollified. "I will do what I can, of course."

"You have my appreciation for all you do. Now, I am sure the tea is ready, and my guests are waiting." With that, Amy walked out the door and headed for the stairs, certain Mother Ross wouldn't miss the opportunity to chat with some of

Eastead's most influential hostesses.

After they had taken tea and visited a short while, Amy's guests rose to leave. As she walked toward the parlor door, Mother Ross spotted the baskets of material and stopped. "Another quilt? I do hope you intend to donate it to the upcoming bazaar." She added pointedly, "Positively everyone is giving something to help the less fortunate."

Isabel spared Amy when she spoke up. "Yes, it's a little project we're working on, but the quilts we make are intended for the girls, as, I hope, are some of the proceeds from the bazaar. I do, however, admire your efforts to give the girls some employment."

Evangeline hesitantly stepped into the room and tugged on Amy's skirts, wanting to know where they should put the apples.

Mother Ross looked confused. "Of course, but I'm not really sure what you mean."

Isabel smiled. "Why, I'm referring to your wonderful idea of hiring the girls to do your mending." She indicated the basket Mother Ross had brought with her.

Evangeline, probably remembering pricked fingers and crooked stitches, piped up, "Oh, we don't get paid."

Mother Ross flushed. "I hold the conviction that the girls should be industrious." She turned to address Amy, trying to change the subject. "But surely you plan to give something appropriate to the bazaar?"

Kathleen stepped in, picked up the basket of mending, and handed it to Mother Ross. "Why, that's a wonderful idea.

Since you understand the girls will be occupied making something for the church bazaar, I'm sure your servants are anxious to resume their duties. Oh, look at the time. We really must be going now."

Taking Kathleen's suggestion, Mother Ross hurried toward the door. Isabel and Kathleen winked conspiratorially at Amy as they followed.

Chapter 4

Tyler glared at the woman who huffed across the lawn, carrying what looked to be a basket of shirts. He and a gaggle of girls had come to the front door to ask Amy where she wanted the apples just in time to overhear the last bit of that exchange. Since the pump sat beneath an open window, he also hadn't missed the dressing-down Amy had withstood from her mother-in-law. Her skillful handling of the situation impressed him.

Mrs. Ross, the elder, displayed all the charm and manners of a shrew. The woman, he decided unequivocally, was a menace; the kind from whom he hoped to shield the girls. She reminded him forcibly of Mistress Lowland. No one deserved the kind of treatment those two women seemed determined to mete out to those less fortunate. He shook his head.

"Mother Ross is always like that," Marissa informed him gravely.

He nodded and looked up to find Amy, as well as two other women, doing the same. "That's right, 'Rissa," Amy exclaimed, scooping the child into her arms. "Mother Ross is difficult, but we each handle grief differently."

The child wriggled to be let down, and Amy hastened to make introductions. "Isabel, Kathleen, this is Mr. Samuels, the caretaker next door who's been kind enough to fix our water pump. Mr. Samuels, these are Mrs. Carter Steadman and Mrs. Maxwell Steadman."

After the requisite social exchange, Tyler was relieved to see the women leave. Their speculative glances did more to make him uncomfortable than the heavy bushel of apples he held. These women had just married his cousins. Were they noticing some vague resemblance between him and their new husbands? He wasn't ready for that yet.

He cleared his throat and turned his attention to the matter at hand. "Have you decided where you want these, Ma'am?"

Amy started. "How foolish of me. I'd like you to take them to the kitchen, if you don't mind. My, those are fine apples. Perhaps there'll be enough so we can make applesauce for the church bazaar."

Tyler opened his mouth to protest that the apples were for the girls but never got the chance.

"Oh, Auntie Amy, there's plenty of apples."

"He gots rows of trees!"

"He has rows of trees," Amy automatically corrected.

Tyler chuckled. "We've gathered seven full bushels besides this one."

"Seven more?" she echoed incredulously as they reached the kitchen and he put the bushel basket down.

"I'm sure you'll be able to use them all." He looked around the crowded room. "The branches were so full they were bending, and the apples shouldn't go to waste."

Her luminous eyes sparkled. "Of course we can put them to good use."

"Applesauce!" Marissa and Evangeline sang out.

"Applesauce?" Scorn filled Alys's tone. "No. Apple-Brown-Betty!"

"Aunt Amy," Jessica pled, "let's make apple pie!"

"Oh, please, can't it be apple butter? You know Rebecca bakes the best bread in the whole world!"

"Cider!" the twins cried in unison.

Tyler interrupted them all. "I have a press. I'd be happy to make juice with the apples you girls missed. In fact," he winked, "I'd gladly trade for an apple cobbler. It's my favorite. I'll bring over some straw and extra barrels so you can pack apples for winter storage. I've plenty of extra for you to use."

Amy nodded happily. "Certainly, Mr. Samuels, and why don't you come over for lunch tomorrow? We're having a simple picnic, but it's the least we can do to thank you for your generosity."

He smiled. "I've finished the pump, so you can get all the water you want. I'll bring over the rest of the apples."

After she'd agreed to this plan, he found himself wondering what he could give them for the church bazaar. He'd continue to let them think of him as the caretaker. It allowed him to watch the girls without having Amy fawn all over him when she learned of his wealth.

For he was rich. Even though Uncle Steadman refused to acknowledge him and his sister after their father died, Tyler managed to make something of himself. Of course, all that came too late to save his sister. After Emma died, he'd been adopted by a family who owned a large, prosperous mercantile. Because the owner was getting on in years and didn't have a son, he wanted someone he could train to take over the business. Tyler grew to love his new family; but when he turned seventeen, the man whose name he'd taken passed away. His foster mother followed her husband to the Lord's waiting arms only two years later.

They'd left the mercantile to Tyler, and he'd become a wealthy man. Still, he'd roamed restlessly, having nothing to tie him down but business. He sold the mercantile and bought a controlling number of shares in an international trading company. He traveled for many years. On his last journey, he'd met a Christian sailor who'd reaffirmed the faith Tyler's adoptive parents once shared with him. He rediscovered the Lord, and although God filled his spiritual void, Tyler still lacked something.

Eventually, Tyler felt drawn back to Eastead, where Uncle Ebenezer had refused to acknowledge his own kin, consigning Tyler and Emma to the orphanage where Emma died. Although it was the hardest decision he'd ever made, Tyler knew he needed to forgive his uncle and acknowledge his own Steadman blood before he could close that chapter of his life.

While wandering through town after learning his uncle had died, Tyler spotted Kindred Hearts. Chafing from his inability to confront his uncle and plagued by the memory of how cruel Mistress Lowland killed Emma through years of neglect, he'd realized something: The Lord was giving him what he so desperately sought—a purpose. He sold his shares in the trading company and spent a small fraction of the amount to buy the huge house next door, where he could easily watch over the children.

For now, everyone thought him a kindhearted caretaker. He grinned at the irony. It provided the perfect cover. Since no one knew his true identity and he tended to resemble his mother, this would give him the perfect opportunity to get to know his cousins without the stigma of past differences.

Thinking back over his years in trading had inspired Tyler, and he suddenly knew just what to get the girls for the church bazaar. He could have it by tomorrow if he hurried, and he'd get to see their excited faces during their picnic.

After the day's end, Amy tucked the girls in with nighttime devotions. Her prayer carried an extra note of gratitude: The visit from Mother Ross had gone by more smoothly than she'd dared hope, and the apples were an unexpected boon. The moment she slipped into bed, she fell fast asleep.

Amy awoke the next morning feeling completely refreshed. Today she and the girls would take care of the apples. They'd dry, preserve, and bake them this week. Mr. Samuels was so kind to the children. In fact, he'd done more for the orphanage in three days than most people did all year. She'd make sure they served apple cobbler as dessert for dinner and bake an extra one for him to take home.

After breakfast, Amy and the younger girls washed the dishes. Jessica and Susannah got busy taking in the rest of the laundry since they hadn't managed to complete it all the day before. As soon as they finished, they'd come in and work with the apples would begin.

First, Amy needed to decide what to do with the apples. Since Mr. Samuels promised to make the cider, they hadn't put any apples aside for juice or jelly. Of the eight bushels, she decided to use two for drying, two for packing in straw and keeping, and three more for applesauce. The remaining bushel would be for snacks and today's apple cobblers.

With the youngest girls thinking of sweet treats and the older ones thinking of winter provisions, everyone set to work with a cheerful heart and busy hands. First, they carried the chosen apples to the cold room and packed them in barrels with straw. Back in the kitchen, the littlest girls squeezed lemon juice and readied the drying pegs while the bigger girls peeled, cored, and sliced the apples. Amy supervised everything and started making cobbler for their picnic lunch.

"Many hands make light work, and soon it will be time for our picnic." Amy cheered her girls on.

Soon they'd finished packing the two bushels of apples for winter storage and were well into drying the others. Noting the old grandfather clock in the parlor had already struck eleven o'clock, Amy called to the children, "Alys, Mary, why don't you make some egg salad? Ruthie, bring me some blankets to take out back for our picnic. And, Evangeline, would you please make the lemonade?"

"I'll make the lemonade, Auntie Amy!"

An emphatic "NO!" from everyone present met Prudie's offer. Striving to lighten the rejection, Amy told her, "Let Evangeline make it today, Prudie. I need you and Carolyn to slice the bread and cheese for lunch."

"Yes, Auntie Amy."

Mr. Samuels would be there soon. As Amy took an armful of blankets to spread on the grass, a knock sounded. She reached and opened the door expectantly. No one stood there.

Amy looked down and found baskets full of lace and fine Irish linen with a note lying on top. "For the girls and church bazaar, from a secret friend in the Lord." That was odd. Kathleen and Isabel never left mysterious notes with their gifts, but Amy couldn't think of anyone else who possessed the wherewithal for such a costly donation. There was enough lace and material to make a fine lace collar for each of the girls' Sunday best, with plenty left over.

Thrilled at this unexpected bounty from the Lord, Amy joyfully carried the baskets into the parlor. First the apples, now this. But who could have sent it?

Chapter 5

Concealed behind the chicken coop where he'd sprinted after placing his basket on the steps, Tyler heard exclamations as Amy carried it into the house. He smiled, pleased beyond all reason by their excitement. He'd thought the note an inspired touch, considering how she'd misconstrued his intentions for the bucket of water and the apples on other occasions. This time, he'd specified the gift was for the girls.

Tyler glanced around, making sure no one would see him emerge from behind the chicken coop. Intrigues were fun, but he still needed to prepare for the inevitable questions his gift would bring if it became known he was their benefactor. He'd visited church for the first time the day before yesterday and met most of the community. The way his cousins and their wives didn't snicker when Amy's ribbons ran impressed him. He still felt a bit guilty about that little scene.

He strode quickly to the door and knocked. A very flushed Amy opened it. He smiled at the sparkle in her eyes—it made her look younger.

"Hello, Mr. Samuels. We were just getting ready to set up our picnic when we received an unexpected bounty." She gestured to the parlor, where several girls examined the linen and lace.

He pretended surprise. "Really? I didn't see anyone when I came over. Sure looks like some nice material, though."

A small frown furrowed her delicate brows. "I'm afraid our benefactor wishes to remain anonymous, Mr. Samuels, but it is an answer to our prayers, in any case."

"Oh?" He waited to hear how she planned to use the lace and Irish linen he'd purchased that morning.

"Indeed, yes. It would appear unseemly if we didn't donate something to the upcoming church bazaar, but now we can fashion lace collars for the charity." Her satisfied pronouncement held no mention of the girls benefitting from the gift.

"Is it so very important that the less fortunate give to charity? I mean, shouldn't the girls be able to use at least some of it for themselves?"

A look of reproach met his pointed inquiry. "Of course it is. No matter how hard life may seem, there are always others in greater need. Anyway, the girls needn't deny themselves. There is plenty for the girls to make a collar each and still contribute to the community."

Pleased to hear her say so, and a bit shamed by the look she'd given him, Tyler ventured, "Just so, Ma'am. Is there anything I can do to help with the picnic?"

Her stiff posture relaxed as she inclined her head. "If you could help me lay out these old blankets while the girls bring out the food, we could begin."

He quickly grabbed some of the blankets and followed her to a large shady patch on the lawn. They laid them out in silence, appreciating the fine weather.

When the girls started placing various platters on two large tree stumps nearby, Tyler suddenly became aware that he'd skipped breakfast. "Sure looks good."

Prudie skipped up next to him with a pitcher of what looked suspiciously like lemonade. "Yep. Egg salad sandwiches and lemonade are my favorite," she confided. She held up the pitcher. "Want some?"

Probably seeing the wariness on his face, Amy took pity on him. "Of course he wants some of Evangeline's wonderful lemonade. Why don't you pour him a glass?" She winked conspiratorially at him as he let out a relieved breath and accepted the glass.

He cautiously sampled the brew. Proclaiming it to be just the thing for a hot day, he turned to his hostess. "I've already met most of the girls, but I'll probably need to hear their names a few more times before I can get them all straight, A—Mrs. Ross." That was a close one.

She summoned the girls, and they all obliged him by saying their names and ages. He by no means could remember all the names and faces, but it was a start. He thought of how Mistress Lowland and her husband always called him "Taylor" instead of "Tyler." Apparently, such mistakes did not happen at Kindred Hearts. Amy readily named any of the girls when she called to them. She could even tell the twins apart!

A clear voice interrupted his thoughts. "Who wants to pray today?"

He was a bit surprised when thirty-four eyes all seemed to gaze in his general direction. "I'd be honored to thank the Lord for the fine company I find myself in today and for the bounty we're about to receive, Mrs. Ross."

Why Amy's approving nod pleased him so, he couldn't say, but she seemed fresh and alive, handling the girls with tender skill and organizing their little feast quite capably. She made quite a fetching picture, with a smile on her lips and the sun warming the golden highlights in her hair as she reached for the hands of the two girls closest to her. The other girls followed suit until they all connected in a large circle.

Tyler bowed his head and wholeheartedly gave thanks to God for everything he could think of—the girls, the food, the sunshine, and the promise of more beautiful days to come. Then they all served themselves from the piles of sandwiches.

"This is excellent," he praised, savoring the flavor of the sandwich made from fresh-baked bread. "Who made lunch today?" He looked around expectantly. Everyone seemed to answer all at once.

"I gathered the eggs," young Evangeline volunteered.

"Susannah baked the bread, but I helped!"

Alys and Mary chimed in, "We made the egg salad."

"I sliced the cheese," Prudie proudly informed him.

"Laura made the sandwiches."

The twins finished, "And Auntie Amy made the cobbler!"

Tyler perked up and turned to Amy. "Cobbler?" He knew he

probably sounded like a three year old begging for a favorite treat, but it had been so long since he ate hot-out-of-the-oven apple cobbler.

Amy smiled. "Well, the cat's out of the bag, isn't it? We started work on the apples this morning, and we made the cobbler you requested." She pretended to glare at the girls. "It was supposed to be a surprise."

"We didn't tell him about the other one," Evangeline protested defensively.

"The other one?" Tyler echoed hopefully. He watched as she shrugged in mock defeat.

"You might as well finish telling him, girls."

"Auntie Amy made an extra so you could take it home, Mr. Sam."

"It sure is your lucky day!" Prudie added.

He was inclined to agree with her on that point.

"Can we have some now, Auntie Amy?" the twins chorused, voicing his thoughts. They all turned pleading faces toward her.

"Why don't we let lunch settle for a bit, first?" Her suggestion met with groans. "The sooner we eat it, the sooner our picnic is over, ladies. Then we have to finish work with the apples." The mood suddenly shifted. He bit back his surprise that she actually wanted to give the girls more free time.

"Can we play a game?" one of the more adventurous youngsters questioned.

Soon they began tossing around ideas. After rejecting jackstraws, hide-and-seek, and a few others, they settled on a rousing session of blind man's bluff.

"You're goin' to play with us, too, aren't you, Auntie Amy and Mr. Sam?" Prudie's question was quickly seconded by all the girls.

Tyler raised his eyebrows at his hostess. He was willing to bet she wouldn't do it, but he issued the challenge anyway. "I'll play if you will."

She proved him wrong as she nodded, held up a towel, and gamely answered, "So long as you're 'It' first!" Her smile made her look five years younger, and he couldn't help grinning back as she advanced with the makeshift blindfold.

A short time later, after an exasperated Evangeline gave up trying to catch somebody, everyone collapsed back onto the quilts to catch their breath.

Amy'd forgotten just how much fun the game could be. She looked over her girls, some sipping cool lemonade and others fanning themselves in the heat. The only exceptions were Mr. Sam, Prudie, and the other little ones who waited their turn for a piggyback ride. She couldn't believe how gentle and patient the large man managed to be with her girls. He definitely deserved a reward.

"So," she called out, "who wants to help me clean up and get the apple cobbler?" She bit her bottom lip to keep from laughing as Mr. Sam stopped suddenly, turned around, and galloped over, much to the delight of his tiny rider. The rest of the children eagerly followed.

The dishes and leftovers were cleared away in record time. Soon the warm cinnamon fragrance of dessert wafted over the yard, and everyone was enjoying a piece of the much-anticipated apple cobbler. They all seemed to enjoy it, and Mr. Sam solemnly assured them it was the best thing he'd ever tasted.

He seemed so different today—smiling, laughing, playing with the children. He'd smelled of summer and strength when she'd blindfolded him. The sun glinted off his black hair as he lifted the smaller girls onto his strong back and broad shoulders. He seemed more like a gentle giant than their next-door neighbor.

She watched as he picked up Ruthie and walked toward her, his long stride quickly covering the small distance. The toddler struggled to keep her eyes open. It was no wonder—Ruthie's naptime had usually come and gone by now.

He nodded toward his little bundle, his deep green eyes silently asking for instruction. Amy got up, whispered to Susannah to have the girls pick up and get washed, then gestured for him to follow. Ruthie fell asleep in his arms, and the tender way he held her tugged at Amy's heart.

When they reached the right room, he laid the toddler on her bed and silently backed out. For such a large man, he moved soundlessly. Back in the hall, Amy invited him into the kitchen.

"Here's that apple cobbler we promised you."

He held it up to his nose and inhaled deeply. "Smells as wonderful as the one we just finished. Thank you. You know, the offer for apple juice still stands. Why don't you and the girls come over tomorrow afternoon and we'll get it done?"

Amy told herself she accepted because it was best for the girls—not because she wanted to see him again.

Chapter 6

The girls spent the next few Sundays diligently working with the tatted lace, fashioning delicate collars. Ginger, Isabel, and Kathleen had been invaluable in organizing the girls and containing their excitement about the bazaar. Accompanied by their husbands, the three friends arrived bright and early on Saturday to help get everything packed up for the bazaar.

Amy surveyed her troops rushing back and forth from Maxwell Steadman's wagon, loading the lace collars, old picnic quilts, and the apple cobblers they'd made for the church potluck. Ginger and Lucas joined them, too, and the girls looked forward to the special treat of riding in the wagons designated for the nighttime hay rides. Everyone had bathed on Friday, a night earlier than usual, to prepare for the special event. Amy hoped they would expend some of their energy before Tyl—Mr. Samuels came.

His help since he'd fixed the water pump couldn't be measured. The apples and subsequent picnic made him an unabashed favorite of the girls, and they'd all enjoyed the day spent on his property making apple cider. Even his goose, who'd once again rushed at Amy the second she stepped over the fence to help with the apples, was a hit. Tyler was kind to all her girls, and although she suspected he had a soft spot for her little pick-pocket, he never let it show.

At first she worried about how quickly the children became attached to their first male role model. He was, after all, a caretaker. Who knew how long he intended to stay? But it wasn't until he knocked on the door, surrounded by most of her girls, and showed her their new picnic tables and benches that she realized the level of his commitment to her precious charges. He'd even involved Isabel and Kathleen by commissioning them to work with the girls to make new tablecloths.

Tyler Samuels had earned a place in their hearts—and at their new tables. He ate with them more than a few times but always brought something to alleviate the burden of feeding an extra mouth. His understanding surprised Amy almost as much as the astonishing way the girls obeyed him without question.

A knock on the door interrupted her thoughts. She watched as the subject of her musings strode into the house and shook hands with everyone in reach.

"Since some of the girls are to ride in my wagon, and yours isn't quite full, why don't we put the barrels of apple cider in yours?" he asked Carter.

"Great idea. I'll lend a hand."

The women watched as the men exited purposefully. Isabel

grinned. "Mr. Samuels is a fine man, Amy, and he gets along so well with everyone in town."

"We're lucky he takes such an interest in the girls," she replied. "He's been a godsend."

"I don't think the girls are the only thing he's interested in," Kathleen stated knowingly.

Ginger nodded. "His smile lights his face when he talks to you or the girls."

"Nonsense, there—"

"What's that?" one of the men asked as they reentered the house.

Kathleen smoothly took over. "We were just discussing the seating arrangements for the wagons. Ours is obviously full to bursting, and Isabel's. . ."

Isabel swiftly caught on. "We'll be carrying Ginger and Lucas and most of the older girls, so we thought you could take up Amy and the smaller girls, Mr. Samuels."

They maneuvered so shamelessly their husbands exchanged knowing grins, but Tyler didn't notice anything amiss. "Sounds good to me." He looked around. "Are all the girls accounted for?"

Amy took a swift head count. "Yes. Susannah, Evangeline, Ruthie, Prudie, Alys, Mary, and the twins will ride with us; everyone else will go with Isabel and Carter." The girls divided into two camps and prepared to walk out to the wagons.

"Wait just a minute, there." Tyler's voice halted their progress. He pulled a small bag from his pocket. "As the Bible says, 'The laborer is worthy of his hire,' and I believe all of you helped to pick and juice my apples a little while ago. Am I right?"

The girls nodded, glad to have their help appreciated and remembered but curious as to what was in the bag. They soon found out as Tyler loosened the drawstrings and ordered, "Hold out your hands and close your eyes." He began depositing a bright, shiny nickel in the hands of every single girl. When he finished, he allowed, "You may open your eyes now."

Obviously trying to sound stern and failing miserably, he clarified, "These are for each of you to spend on whatever you want, but it must be used today. It's my way of thanking you for your help and hospitality." He glanced at Amy as he said this.

Amid startled exclamations and a great many hugs, Amy didn't have the heart to object to this unexpected extravagance. Eighty cents equaled two days of a mill worker's wages, and she knew to an ounce how much sugar and flour that money could buy. His generosity overwhelmed her.

After the girls finished their chorus of thank-yous and trekked out the door to pile into the wagons, Amy turned to Tyler. "You didn't need to do that, but I'm glad you did. Thank you."

He nodded, offered her his arm, and they set out for the annual Founder's Day Church Bazaar and Potluck. Feeling the strength of his arm through his blue cambric shirt, Amy felt a sudden spurt of gratitude for her friends' not-so-subtle plot to seat her beside him. She preferred not to ask herself why.

A few minutes later as the wagons pulled away from the

orphanage, Tyler glanced at the woman next to him. Her diminutive stature and worn dress might have made a lesser woman seem plain, but her warmth and generosity were all the adornment she needed. "Beauty should not come from outward adornment. . . . Instead, it should be that of your inner self, the unfading beauty of a gentle and quiet spirit, which is of great worth in the sight of God." His foster mother showed such virtue, and his father often quoted that verse from 1 Peter.

Tyler came to this town to forgive his uncle and lay the past to rest by confronting his kin. Exposing this orphanage headmistress to be as conniving, hard-hearted, and selfish as Mistress Lowland was to give him closure and the assurance that a horrendous wrong wouldn't be repeated. He'd been so locked up in his memories, it had taken him far too long to recognize Amy bore no resemblance to his old nemesis. Now that he realized it, however, he'd make amends.

Coming back to the present, he smiled at his riders' excitement. The wagon pulled into the large grass field next to the church, where tables and booths were already being set up.

Carter and Isabel pulled up alongside them. "Everybody ready to go?" He nodded toward the old trees in the corner of the lot designated as a children's play area and asked Tyler, "Those swings we put up last weekend look pretty good, don't they? Good of you to volunteer at the town meeting."

Tyler shrugged. "I did nothing more than you, Maxwell, and Lucas did. Maxwell even donated the rope—all I did was—"

"Shimmy up the trees faster than I'd ever thought a grown man could," Lucas cut in, smiling.

"All right, enough chatter," Kathleen called. "How 'bout you big, strong men help us out with unloading this wagon?"

Everyone scrambled to follow instructions as the women assigned jobs. Soon Ginger was marshaling the older girls, loaded with foodstuffs, over to the potluck picnic tables. Amy and Isabel helped the little ones carry the lace collars over to the women's booth. The men busied themselves with setting up Tyler's cider booth and the mill's fabric area.

In just a few short hours, the lot bustled with activity, and the girls were trying to decide what to spend their treasure on. The church women's booth overflowed with lace collars, ribbons, and embroidered handkerchiefs. The men's booth burst with the stick horses, wooden hoops, and spinning tops the male parishioners made in their spare time. Along with the rope swings and wooden seesaws set up in the corner earlier, the toys would entertain the little ones for most of the day.

An area reserved for foodstuffs stood a little ways off. Since the potluck dinner was provided by the community, the townspeople were expected to purchase their evening supper. Thankfully, Maxwell and Carter had generously offered to buy this for the girls.

The general store had donated fruit, licorice, and gumdrops. The baker showcased all manner of breads and pastries—including cream puffs. Next to him, the owner of the dairy farm offered slices cut from a few large wheels of cheese. The fishermen offered a multitude of fish and lobster, and a grill stood ready for use.

A small platform had been raised in the corner of the open

picnic area, waiting for the traditional raffle and Mayor Smythe's speech. The raffle prizes were nothing short of decadent: The ladies' sewing circle presented a lovely appliquéd maple-leaf quilt, and Vivian Steadman's generous contribution of a precious silver tea set would surely increase ticket sales. Not to be outdone, Mother Ross offered the pìece de résistance: a small box pianoforte.

None of the townspeople could possibly know the value Amy placed on the instrument. Amy had played that very pianoforte the night she met Jason. She would have loved to own the instrument as a keepsake of that night, and her fingers itched to make music. He'd told her he'd never enjoyed music so much. Only Mother Ross knew its significance, and she would rather see the piece raffled off to someone she didn't know than let her daughter-in-law enjoy it.

Looking at the pianoforte regretfully, Amy resolved not to let the memories she cherished stand in the way of making new ones.

Chapter 7

At one o' clock, after Parson Hull asked God's blessing, the potluck picnic began. Sandwiches, deviled eggs, bread and cheese, shepherd's pie, crab cakes, fried chicken, sauerkraut, and a variety of fresh produce and salads awaited the hungry townsfolk.

Everyone hustled around the picnic area, smoothing old blankets across the summer grass and gossiping about who sat with whom and who brought what. Several people eyed the large group in the northwest corner, speculating about the connection between Amy Ross and the new man in town.

"Don't mind the old biddies," Kathleen advised them with a smile.

Tyler agreed wholeheartedly, hesitant to examine the warm feeling that came from Amy's name being linked with his. "I don't understand the fuss. Why two neighbors can't sit with sixteen girls and three newly married couples without raising eyebrows is beyond me."

"And Davey," added Susannah, sending an adoring gaze to

Isabel's younger brother. The fourteen-year-old girl had become quite attached to the young man who had arrived in town scant months ago.

"David," he corrected good-naturedly, probably resigned to the nickname Susannah persisted in using. Clearly, the attraction wasn't as one-sided as he let on.

Tyler, for his part, tried to ignore the icy stares "Mother Ross" aimed at Amy. He hadn't missed Amy's longing glance at the pianoforte earlier, either. With a little prompting, Isabel quietly revealed the history behind it.

He shook his head, hardly tasting the delectable crab cake he bit into. He knew as well as anyone how anger and blame over unresolved issues could leave a person bitter. Why the older woman felt so toward her daughter-in-law stayed a mystery to him, but her behavior was unconscionable.

He snuck a glance at Amy. The dappled sunlight weaving through the leaves played on the loosened curls around her face, giving her an almost angelic appearance. Her expressive gray eyes appeared almost violet as she laughed at something Ruthie said. Amy wore a light shade of something lavender-pink that flattered her coloring, and he had a sudden flash of her adorable face covered in the dye from her ribbons. He couldn't help grinning at the memory—he didn't know any other woman who could pull off a purple-pink face with half the dignity she'd managed.

His grin slipped when he remembered the raking-down Mother Ross gave her for that little lapse in decorum. It only happened because Gussie had slipped through the fence when he wasn't looking. If the girls didn't love the silly goose so much, he'd cook the bird for dinner for all the trouble she'd caused. Gussie had even tried to run down Amy again the day they'd juiced the apples. Of course, he certainly couldn't fault the fowl for bad taste. Who wouldn't want to be as close to Amy as possible?

Geese were good watchdogs, but their bad tempers and tendency to bring trouble put him in mind of. . .well, Mother Ross. What kind of woman would rather see something that would bring her daughter-in-law joy go to a stranger rather than release a grudge? Amy should have the pianoforte. If only there was a way he could buy a lot of tickets without raising questions about his financial situation. . . .

He looked up to see Kathleen and Isabel watching him. Apparently, he'd missed something.

"I'm sorry, I was paying more attention to my stomach than the conversation." He threw in his best smile for good measure. It didn't work. The two women shared a knowing glance before answering him.

"We just said that you seem somehow familiar. Are you absolutely positive you never passed through town before?"

For a moment he stared at their expectant faces in panic. His tall, broad frame bore similarities to Maxwell's, but he wasn't nearly as tan. Carter was thinner, and Lucas was a bit stockier, but their coloring was lighter than his. All three possessed brownish eyes; his were green. They boasted varying shades of brown hair compared to his black. The Steadman nose might mark him, but he'd broken it long ago and he'd thought the resulting bump would hide its shape. But apparently it wasn't enough to stop his cousins' new wives from recognizing the vague resemblance. The strong Steadman jaw, stubborn chin, and wavy hair probably gave him away. He saw the similarities right away, but he searched for them, so he hadn't expected others to notice just yet.

"I came a few weeks before I moved here, and you might have seen me then. Other than that, I seriously doubt such an. . . observant town would fail to notice if I passed through."

Maxwell clapped him on the shoulder. "If that's not the blessed truth, I don't know what is."

Congratulating himself on his narrow escape, Tyler's gratitude turned to Amy when she asked if they wanted dessert. Watching her lead some of the girls to the picnic tables once again, he found himself wondering whether he should tell her his secret. He didn't think she'd try to charm money from his pockets when she learned his identity, and he'd already decided to make amends for his misplaced suspicions. The idea had definite possibilities.

After a day full of excitement and treats, everyone flocked once again to the picnic area with their supper to hear the mayor's speech and find out who won the raffle. Carter and Maxwell generously purchased supper for everyone, letting them choose whatever they wanted from the many foodstuffs available—so long as it wasn't candy or sweets.

Tyler had been rather busy. He'd found each girl and given her a nickel apiece to purchase two raffle tickets, to be under

Amy's name, then bought a few more for good measure. Yep. Forty raffle tickets should do the trick. He couldn't wait to see the expression on Amy's pretty face when she won that little pianoforte. He'd also enjoy hearing her play it on Sundays, when he maintained a standing invitation to dinner. On Sunday afternoons while the womenfolk sewed, he read Bible parables to the girls and led a short time of worship.

For now, everyone politely pretended to listen to Mayor Smythe's annual, long-winded speech about Founder's Day. The townspeople bore the tradition good-naturedly, knowing that the raffle announcements and "a special surprise, courtesy of the Steadmans" awaited them.

Finally, raffle time came. Peg from the mill won the beautiful quilt, and Parson Hull's wife proudly carried away the silver tea set. A hush fell over the crowd, but Tyler barely noticed it. His gaze glued on Amy's wistful expression as the time for presenting the pianoforte arrived.

The Mayor Smythe dug deep into the third hatbox and dramatically flourished the winning ticket before proclaiming grandly, "Amy Ross."

Amid the shrieks and hugs from all the girls, who carefully protected their secret, Amy stayed seated, her eyes shining in stunned disbelief. She finally stood when the mayor repeated her name, and made her way to the makeshift platform, where he shook her hand. The mayor assured the crowd that no one deserved it more, and the pianoforte would be delivered to Kindred Hearts the very next day.

Tyler nearly burst with pride at the tears shining in Amy's

eyes when she returned. He'd done that, and the wonderful feeling it brought surprised him. When she sat down, he reached out and squeezed her little hand, giving her a supportive nod to let her know he shared her happiness.

When the fireworks began in great, booming sparkles, Tyler barely paid attention. For some reason, his entire focus centered on the dainty hand that lay so sweetly in his.

Amy still couldn't believe what a perfect day it had been—or how much of it had been Tyler Samuels's doing. How had she ever thought him to be disagreeable? From the moment he'd picked them up, giving the girls those coins, to his comforting clasp as they watched the fireworks, he'd demonstrated the gentle warmth and selflessness she'd noticed regularly for weeks.

Why, the only happy spot of the day that couldn't be attributed to him was winning the pianoforte. When Isabel scrawled "Amy" on a ticket, Amy warned herself not to be overly hopeful. The Lord certainly did work in mysterious ways.

She wondered whether Tyler's interest was confined to the welfare of the girls or if perhaps he returned her regard in some small measure. Amy tried to tamp down the requisite feelings of guilt that sprang up at the thought. His warm hand encircling hers surely provided proof that he did.

The removal of that comfortable clasp shook her out of her reverie. Cool autumn rain sprinkled the area. She quickly took charge of the situation, helping the girls gather their trinkets and blankets. They all headed for the wagons.

Amy was still smiling when she said her prayers after sending the girls to bed. In fact, the feeling lasted through the next morning, when she started down the stairs and ran into Jessica.

"Oh, I was just coming to get you," the girl cried. "It's Prudie—she's sick!"

Chapter 8

Hurrying to the remade study where Prudie roomed, Amy realized with a sinking heart that the precious little pickpocket, flushed and shivering under her blankets, was indeed ill. The ride home in the rain last night had taken its toll.

Amy crossed the room to the bed where Prudie lay in the grip of a fever. "Prudie, Sweetie, I'm here." She held her small, hot hand. "Soon you'll be right as rain." Her heart ached at the sweet smile Prudie managed before she gave way to a fit of coughing.

Amy took charge of the situation. "Jessica, I need you to go fetch Dr. Steadman right away and see if Ginger can come help with the young ones. Susannah, cool cloths would be welcome, and have Faith get some applesauce. Alys, please keep the other girls away from this room."

Susannah bustled in with the cold compresses, and after thanking her, Amy sent her back to the kitchen to fetch the teakettle. Inhaling the steam would help the child breathe more easily as they waited for the fever to break. She would do all she could—hopefully Dr. Lucas would be there soon.

Tyler saw Jessica hurry out of the house without her bonnet. The morning was damp from the previous night's rain, so he called her name to stop her. When she turned, he saw her face and dread swept through him.

"What's wrong?"

"Prudie's ill, Mr. Samuels. She caught a chill from the storm last night, and I'm off to fetch Dr. Steadman."

He nodded. "You forgot your bonnet. It wouldn't do to have you get sick, too. Go back inside and help as best you can. I'll get the doctor."

"Ginger, too. Aunt Amy needs her to help with the younger girls."

He quickly agreed and set off, worried about the adorable rascal who'd practically killed him with her lemonade the first day he'd met his precious neighbors.

When Tyler brought Ginger and Dr. Steadman back, Amy was holding a towel over Prudie's head, encouraging her to take deep breaths from the steaming tea kettle.

Ginger immediately set about making the girls breakfast, but Tyler couldn't stop himself from hovering near the doorway with Amy to hear Lucas's pronouncement. After all, it was their fault. He'd promised himself he wouldn't let this happen to another orphan, but he'd been so distracted by Amy last night that he hadn't noticed the gathering clouds.

Neither had she. A surge of male satisfaction at knowing he'd distracted her filled him, but he beat it down. Now wasn't the time.

He gazed at the little lump in the bed until the doctor came to the door and blocked his view.

"She has a chill," Lucas proclaimed. "Unless I miss my guess, the coughing has already improved." He looked at Amy and received an affirming nod. "So I'd like to alternate between the steam treatments and using cool cloths to help bring down the fever. She needs to be drinking a lot of fluids. It seems as though you have things well in hand here. She ought to be fine—and the other girls shouldn't be in any danger. I daresay companionship will help her forget her discomfort and help her recover even more quickly."

Amy relaxed a bit. "Thank you so much for coming, Dr. Steadman."

The kindly doctor smiled. "Glad to do it. But I thought we'd agreed on Lucas?" Smiling, he turned toward Tyler and gave him a nod. Heading for the door, Lucas added, "I'll have to go now, but I'm pretty sure Ginger will want to stay. I'll be by a bit later to check on Prudie."

Tyler turned to Amy. "Do you mind if I see her?"

"Since she's awake, that will be fine. But it's best if we don't tire her out too much. She quite dotes on you—maybe you could get her to eat some applesauce. . . ." Her voice trailed off. Although she obviously found some relief in the doctor's words, Tyler could see Amy still fretted. She should be concerned. This could never be allowed to happen again.

Seeing her questioning look, he quickly stepped into the sickroom. He stood over the bed. "How are you doing, Prudie?"

"I'm better, Mr. Sam," the child whispered. "Thank you so much for yesterday—it was the best day ever."

His heart twisted at her words. It should have been a wonderful memory, untainted by her illness.

"How about some of this great-looking applesauce, hmm? Maybe you could try a few bites? Hey, you could even slurp since you're sick. Slurping," he confided, "is absolutely the best way to have applesauce. Want to try it?" He brought the spoon to her mouth as she dutifully opened up.

Amy joined in. "Oh, come now. That is pitiful. You have to really get into it to make the sound impressive." Prudie's giggle lightened Tyler's mood considerably, and the improved slurp was met with enthusiastic approval from both adults. The game continued until the young patient took another steam treatment, then slipped into a light sleep.

The difference between Amy's concern for Prudie's well-being and Mistress Lowland's complete disregard for Emma's health struck Tyler forcibly. He'd been wrong about her, too easily casting her in the light of a cruel orphanage mistress to give himself a reason to stay. Now he had a completely different reason than he'd ever expected to remain in Eastead.

"Aunt Amy?" Evangeline stood in the doorway. "Ginger sent me to get everyone's clothes from yesterday so we could wash them."

Amy gave her an encouraging smile. "Certainly. Let me just grab Prudie's." She reached for the damp dress on a peg nearby, and as she handed it to Evangeline, something fell out onto the bedcovers.

Tyler didn't miss Amy's concerned glance his way as she ushered the child out of the room, then returned to Prudie's bedside herself. He picked up the golden timepiece—his pocket watch. *How odd. I never misplace this, but this is the second time Prudie found. . .*

It all fell into place. Prudie, talking to him by the pump. Amy's odd behavior as she'd returned the watch. Her hesitance over letting him reward Prudie for her "good deed." It hadn't been because she'd wanted to deny the child; she didn't want to encourage her because. . .

"She's a pickpocket?" He saw resignation on her face as Amy took a deep breath.

"It's really not her fault. Prudie learned to survive on her own before coming to the orphanage. She does her best to stop, but sometimes she slips and does it again. It takes time to break old habits." Her eyes pleaded with him for understanding.

"It's all right. Everyone has secrets." Tyler looked into her incredible eyes and came to his decision. "In fact, I have a few of my own."

Taking a deep breath, he plunged in. "My real name isn't Tyler Samuels—it's Tyler Steadman."

Ignoring Amy's gasp, he continued. If he stopped now, he'd never finish. "I'm the only son of Esau Steadman. His family cut him off when he married my mother, a woman whose social station didn't match his. They moved away rather than be separated, and they had me and a little girl, Emma. My parents died in a carriage accident when we were young. Word was sent to my uncle Ebenezer, but he turned his back on us. We were sent to an orphanage, where my sister died of malnourishment and disease." He stopped for a second, asking the Lord for the strength to continue.

"I was adopted soon after by a kind man, and I took his name. When he died, I set off on journeys, running from my past. Even though my adopted parents taught me the Lord's way, I still blamed my uncle and the orphanage headmistress for my sister's death. Much later I accepted what happened and realized I needed to forgive my uncle. That's why I came here."

Amy had reached out at some point during his speech and now stroked his hand comfortingly. "It's rare that someone forgives so much. I know how hard it is to lose someone. I lost my husband when I sent him out into a storm for the doctor. I still haven't forgiven myself, and I can't imagine how difficult it must be for you to forgive someone who took away your sister. You should be proud of the man you've become, not ashamed. You didn't need to hide who you are."

He took a deep breath, overwhelmed by her understanding yet determined to leave nothing out. "But there's more. When I arrived, my uncle was already dead. I prepared to leave—but then I passed by Kindred Hearts. When I saw all of the girls, I felt as though God had given me a new purpose. I moved in next door to keep an eye on you, to make sure you treated the girls fairly. I knew I would do anything in my power to protect them from the fate of my sister." He could feel her withdrawal.

"You thought I would abuse my girls?"

He rushed on before she could continue, aching to wipe the look of horror off her face. "Yes. I know now that I misjudged you. I've never seen anyone care for others the way you do—you're wonderful with them. That's why I'm telling you this now. I knew I would care for the girls, but I didn't expect to hold you in such esteem. You have made the past months the best in my life, and I don't want any more secrets between us. Can I hope that you will accept my apology and forgive me?"

He held her hand as a drowning man clung to a wooden board. He couldn't bear it if she refused. The tears in her eyes tore at his heart, and he prayed he could regain her trust.

Amy couldn't believe it. What did he want her to say? What did he mean when he said he held her in esteem and didn't want any more secrets between them? Did this mean he saw them as a couple? The combination of Prudie's illness and his confession sent her head swimming. There was so much to think about.

She didn't blame him. It was admirable that he wanted to protect the girls. After all, wasn't that what she'd dedicated her life to? She could even see why he wouldn't want to be known as a Steadman until he got to know the cousins he'd never met. Still, where did that leave her—leave them? Precisely what was he saying about the future now that he knew the girls didn't need him to watch over them? What would he say if she told him she needed him? That last wild thought brought things into perspective. She most certainly wouldn't behave like a giddy schoolgirl.

She looked him straight in the eye. "There's really nothing to forgive. We all make mistakes about others, but at least you can admit when you're wrong."

"Thank you." He looked so relieved, she wanted to hug him. "Where do we go from here?"

The question remained unanswered as Alys rushed into the room, startling them. "Oh, Auntie Amy, Mother Ross is here. She insists she must see you right away!"

Chapter 9

After excusing herself, Amy left the room to face her mother-in-law in the parlor. Since the parlor happened to share a wall with what used to be the study—and now served as the bedroom shared by Prudie and her roommates—Tyler was privy to every word of Mother Ross's harangue. He could only be thankful Prudie still slept.

Dispensing with even the pretense of civility, Hortense Ross started in as soon as the door was shut.

"You wanton. What have you done? Only a shameless hussy would behave in such a manner with a man—in front of the whole town, no less! Everyone is talking about you two. Where did you get the money for those tickets? Payment for services rendered, perhaps?"

Her accusations shocked Tyler. Such profane allegations should never cross a lady's lips. Even as fury boiled in his breast, the harridan raged on.

"I held my tongue about the dresses, the fine china tea sets, porcelain dolls, tatted lace collars—I've even seen fine nightgowns hanging on the washline—but spending good money on a frivolous pianoforte for your own amusement? I will no longer sit by idle, watching you corrupt these girls the same way you ruined my son." Her voice broke, and she paused before continuing.

A sharp pang of guilt shot through Tyler as he realized his gift had sparked this diatribe. This was the second time his actions caused Amy trouble—first the wet ribbons, now the raffle.

"How can you dishonor Jason's memory this way? Wasn't it enough that you took him from me? That then you couldn't even bring my grandson into the world?"

Grandson? Amy had lost a husband and her child? Tyler's heart ached for her, and he began to understand the source of the older woman's bitterness, misplaced though it might be. He could even sympathize with the pain of her loss—until she went on.

"You are the downfall of everything you claim to care about—poisoning all you touch and sullying my family's name. Now you take up with this stranger, flaunting your sin in front of the whole town? No more! I refuse to house and feed such a Jezebel. You have one week to get your things together and leave. No, I'll not hear any of your vile lies. Nor do you need to concern yourself, if you ever really have, over the welfare of the orphans. I'll see to it that they're placed in homes where they'll learn the value of silence, hard work, and all the other virtues you lack. Don't let me see you again. It would be best if you left town altogether."

How could Amy sit quietly through this tirade? Tyler barely restrained himself from storming in there with a few choice words of his own. He'd seethed about how Mrs. Ross had denounced Amy, and her threats to use the children for slave labor only fanned the blaze. He'd never let it happen, and he knew his Amy would lay down her life for their girls. He only wished he could be in there so she knew how much he supported her. What was she thinking?

Amy felt calmer than she had in a long while. She was used to Mother Ross's frequent vituperative attacks, which she'd come to dread. Not any longer. The big one had finally come, and the sense of freedom it gave her was incredible.

Mother Ross might be right that both Jason's death and the loss of their baby were her fault, but for once her mother-in-law was wrong about everything else. Since the axe hovering over her head for so long had fallen at last, Amy could finally tell her so.

If Maxwell and Carter—and now Tyler—didn't care so much for the girls, she might feel differently, agonizing over their welfare. God's providing hand could surely be found in that. Now she could humble herself to her friends and know the girls would be provided for. They'd never be subjected to the slavelike environment Mother Ross envisioned as fitting for the brave girls who had nothing but each other.

As Mother Ross prepared to storm out, Amy quickly blocked her path.

"You've more than spoken your piece. Now I'll speak mine.

You didn't lose Jason. We lost him. I loved him, too."

Mother Ross opened her mouth to speak, but Amy rushed on, cutting off the woman's venomous words for the first time in years.

"As for my child, there isn't a day that goes by that I don't regret losing him, as well. I lost everything in one night, my husband, my babe, my hopes; all of which you throw in my face every time we see each other. Don't you know that I've held my tongue at every harsh word you've said because of my guilt? But that can't ease your sorrow or mine—and I can't bring them back."

Amy paused to blink back the tears that threatened to overcome her. Honestly, it was a marvel she hadn't started bawling long ago. When she saw the tears shining in her mother-in-law's eyes, she almost couldn't continue.

"Be that as it may, I've tried to make something of my life. These girls mean the world to me, and I won't let you hurt them to spite me. As for my relationship to Mr. Samuels, the girls and I are fortunate to have the support of such a wonderful, God-fearing man. He's shown nothing but compassion and generosity to the girls, and I'll be forever grateful to him for it. Nonetheless, that is as far as our relationship goes. We haven't crossed the boundary of friendship, and his conduct is impeccable. You won't cast aspersions on his character."

A sharp pang accompanied the words. How had she come to care so much for the man who'd just assured her his purpose in looking after the girls was over and he had no other reason to stay? Ignoring the pain for the time being, she continued.

"As for my so-called spendthrift ways, everything you've listed—the dolls, tea sets, dresses, and nightgowns—were gifts from the Steadmans. The lace for those collars came from an anonymous donor. The pianoforte was a simple matter—Isabel put my name on a ticket. You have no reason to cast me out. My behavior hasn't been the slightest bit improper, nor have I sullied our family name. You've wanted to do this for some time, and now you're convinced you have good reason so you can sleep at night. Don't bother to deny it. I'll be gone as soon as possible, but you won't get your hands on any of my girls. I'll see to that. Good day, Mother Ross."

Amy held the door open, feeling better than she had in years until her opponent made one last verbal thrust.

"Don't think your high-and-mighty words fooled me, Missy. I looked in the ticket box, and I know there were dozens of tickets with your name on them." With that, she swept through the doorway where Amy stood, dumbfounded.

Tyler only stayed at the orphanage for as short a time as was seemly before beating a path to the elder Mrs. Ross's door. The time had come for the woman to hear a few home truths.

Amy's speech had been gut-wrenching. He ached for her loss and sense of guilt. He knew pride for the dignified way she'd stood up for herself. He loved how she'd championed him and protected the girls. Mostly, though, the hollow ache was due to her faint praise of his friendship. He'd left it up to her, but he'd never imagined she thought he only cared for the children. He hadn't spoken aloud the depth of his regard, but he'd thought she shared his feelings. How had he made such a mess of things?

His mental ramblings came to a halt when he reached the tidy brick house he searched for. Not a thing stood out of place—not even a stray leaf dared mar the premises of Hortense Ross's abode. He squared his shoulders and gave a quick prayer as he went to beard the lioness in her den.

That was the plan, anyway. Apparently, no one was home. About to walk to the church, Tyler heard sounds coming from behind the house. Following the noise, he found Mrs. Ross at the gazebo, massacring a hapless plant.

Tyler took a deep breath, knowing how much rode on what came next. He sent up another prayer, this time in hopes that the woman would be receptive to his words.

"Ma'am, I think we need to talk." *Well,* he assured himself as he received the full force of her formidable glare, *at least I got her attention.*

"I don't imagine that we do, Mr. Samuels. I usually don't speak with persons of uncertain reputation." She eyed him while ruthlessly snapping off another branch. The look she sent his way assured him she wished it were his head she was chopping instead of a bush.

Tamping down the spurt of anger she'd inspired, he concentrated on stopping her from entering her house. He could see no other way.

"The name's not Samuels, Ma'am. It's Steadman."

The look on her face was worth his left foot. Until the glare returned. "Don't lie to me, Boy. I know your name. Everyone does."

"No, only Amy and now you do. I'm the son of Esau Steadman." For once the biddy was silent. He decided that was encouraging and went on.

"You know his father cut him off when he married Mother. Both of my parents died years ago. When Ebenezer Steadman refused to acknowledge my sister and me, we ended up in an orphanage. My sister died there, but I got adopted soon after. Samuels is my foster name."

Surprisingly, he could see her softening. Her shoulders relaxed, and she stopped glaring as if she hoped she'd bore a hole straight through him.

"I'm sorry, Mr. Steadman. I know how horrible it is to lose someone you love." Her voice hardened once more as her scowl returned. "Ebenezer sacrificed your sister's life. Amy did the same to my son. What do you hope to gain by telling me this?"

Remembering how he'd reached her moments before, Tyler knew the woman was more receptive to his words than she wanted him to think. God's will would be done, and Tyler suspected it marched right along with his.

"Mrs. Ross, that's what I've come to talk with you about. I came to Eastead to forgive my uncle after years of hating him. I lost my chance to make things right because he'd already passed on. You still have the opportunity I missed." Seeing her open her mouth to interrupt, he continued.

"I know you blame Amy for your loss, and she holds herself responsible. But you've hurt her deeply over the past years with your actions. I realize you were overcome with pain, and that for a woman as concerned about doing the right thing as you are, you'll come to regret hasty words." She actually looked like she was considering his words. As the saying went, best to strike while the iron was hot.

"The Bible says, 'So that contrariwise ye ought rather to forgive and comfort, lest perhaps such a one should be swallowed up with overmuch sorrow.' You've added to Amy's sorrow, and now is the time to forgive her for what she never had control over. Then you can grieve together properly." He'd said all he could. He couldn't take it back now, even if he wanted to. She could throw him out of her yard or accept his message—it was between her and the Lord.

For the first time in his life, Tyler was happy to see a woman cry. He put his arms around the sobbing woman and waited. Finally it came, a broken whisper.

"I don't know if I can."

" 'I can do all things through Christ which strengthens me.' Shall we seek His help?"

Relief flooded his soul as they knelt in the gazebo together and prayed.

Chapter 10

Amy didn't know what to make of it all. First, Tyler told her about his past and claimed he wanted no secrets between them. In the next breath, he talked about how he didn't need to stay there anymore. Then, as soon as she'd returned from speaking with Mother Ross, he'd up and left with nothing but a hasty good-bye. At least Prudie was feeling better.

What I told Mother Ross must be right. He only cares about my girls, not me. The admission wrenched her heart, so she shifted focus to Mother Ross herself.

After her long-winded condemnation, Mother Ross has just returned to Kindred Hearts. Hadn't she said that she never wanted to see me again? Why has she come back?

Alys had just announced the older woman's return to the house and desire to speak with Amy. Confused thoughts raced through Amy's mind as she took her time reaching the parlor, where her uninvited guest awaited her. Considering that forewarned was forearmed, Amy prepared for battle as she entered the room.

And stopped short.

Mother Ross wasn't standing with rigid posture, wearing a glower that could melt ice as was usual. Instead, she sat on the red velvet settee, nervously fingering the gold filigree cross she wore about her neck.

What was going on? Recalling the image of a coiled snake that could attack with lightning speed, Amy proceeded with caution. "What can I do for you?" She couldn't quite keep the wariness out of her tone.

The older woman rose stiffly to stand before her. "Mr. Steadman came by to see me a little while ago, Amy." It was the first time her mother-in-law had used her nickname since Jason's death.

"Through much prayer and soul-searching, I've come to the conclusion that I've wronged you."

Amy could see what it cost Mother Ross to admit that. A million questions swirled through her brain, but she stayed silent to catch the rest.

"I don't know if I can ever forgive you for taking my son away, but I'm going to try. It was you who sent him for the doctor. . .but it wasn't your fault his horse spooked."

Tears filled both women's eyes.

"I'm sorry for how I've treated you the past five years, Amy. It wasn't Christian of me to try to make you as miserable as I felt. Can you forgive me for my cruel words?" Mother Ross lost the battle with her tears and began to cry at the same moment Amy did.

In that instant, Amy realized her mother-in-law spoke the truth. Jason's death wasn't her fault. Jason had willingly gone into the storm to fetch the doctor when she'd experienced complications with the pregnancy. She hadn't killed him. She'd blamed herself for so long when she didn't have to, and all she'd needed was for the one other person who understood her loss to tell her so. As understanding swept through her, Amy knew she'd forgive her mother-in-law all the horrible things she'd said in the past for the few kind words she'd just spoken.

Reaching out to envelop the older woman in a hug of shared pain and triumph, Amy stopped crying long enough to tell her so. The two women held each other and prayed together, thanking God for His healing gift. Mother Ross was the first to pull away.

"Thank you, Amy, for forgiving a stubborn old woman's bitterness. It's time for me to go. I know I have many amends to make, but I hope this is the first." She pressed a crumpled piece of paper into Amy's hand and left before Amy could say another word.

The tears she'd thought couldn't be left sprung to Amy's eyes when she realized what she held: the deed to her home.

The next Sunday afternoon, everyone gathered in the parlor and dining room for their weekly sewing and Bible study. Amy's heart, which had been flying up to the rafters just the day before when Dr. Lucas pronounced Prudie "good as new," plummeted to the root cellar when she saw Tyler wasn't there. He'd become an integral part of their Sunday sessions, and she couldn't stop wondering if he'd already left town.

She remembered the conversation she'd had with Isabel and Kathleen just the day before. It had begun with her recitation of the astonishing events of the week and her somewhat gloomy conclusion that Tyler was probably just biding his time before he left.

To her surprise, her formerly supportive friends switched camps. "Piffle," stated Kathleen. "If he was just going to pack up and leave, he would have done it without baring his soul."

Isabel, the turncoat, chimed in, "He's a Steadman. Steadmans don't behave like that. We just knew there was something special about him, didn't we, Kathleen?" Encouraged by Kathleen's nod, she continued. "If you ask me, he's more reason to stay now than he ever did. Carter, Maxwell, and Lucas are crazy about him."

Amy couldn't stay silent at that sensitive remark. "Well, that's something encouraging. He'll stay for the men!"

Kathleen's reproachful look shamed her. "No. What it means is, now that he's found his roots, he'll be ready to start a family of his own."

"So when did he tell them?"

"Last Tuesday. He asked them all to meet him, and he explained everything. Carter wanted him to move in so they could get to know each other better, but he said he liked his house just fine. Claimed it had a better view." This last comment was accompanied by a knowing look.

"Do you think that could mean he really wants to stay?"

"For such an intelligent woman, you're being inordinately foolish," Kathleen retorted.

"Excuse me? I told you what he said."

Isabel shot a questioning look at Kathleen, who nodded slowly. They each grabbed one of Amy's hands.

"What's going on?"

Isabel smiled. "We have some good news for you."

"Proof positive." Kathleen actually made something akin to a bounce. "At the church bazaar, we saw Tyler giving the girls extra nickels. We didn't think of it at the time. . . ."

"But after you told us what Mother Ross said about the ticket box, we asked Evangeline about it. She confessed that Mr. Sam had given them all enough to buy two tickets apiece, with specific instructions to write your name on them!"

He did that for me? Amy just knew she was grinning from ear to ear as she and her friends agreed there was hope, after all. Amy sighed. But that had been yesterday, and there was no sign of Tyler today. By all rights, he should be at the head of the dining room table with his big Bible, reading another parable, as he had for months.

She couldn't bear to make small talk with her friends for another minute. Even they were beginning to look around expectantly.

When all three exchanged a heavy glance and simultaneously asked for some water, Amy was relieved. She rushed off toward the kitchen to collect her thoughts. Why had she gotten her hopes up? Everything had been going so well. She shook her head to clear it. It wouldn't do to sulk. She had better just march on out there and act like everything was dandy. But if everything was so fine, why was she still mulling over how empty the dining room looked without him?

Tyler looked at the ring nestled in his hand doubtfully. Isabel, Kathleen, and Ginger had all approved of his plan and assured him it would go well. But was it big enough? Would the girls want him as their father? Would Amy want him to be her husband? There was only one way to find out.

Taking a deep breath, he poked his head through the door in time to see Amy leave the room and Kathleen give him a huge smile and exaggerated wink. Well, that was a relief. If all went as planned, he'd get the girls' support, then ambush Amy when she got back.

He stepped in, prepared to humiliate himself in pursuit of the most perfect ready-made family ever.

Amy had just about convinced herself to trudge back to the parlor when her knees threatened to give way. Was that Tyler's voice, asking her girls if they would let him adopt them? It wasn't enough that he'd stolen her heart—would he leave her completely alone?

She knew he could provide for them better than she would ever be able to. His house alone told her that.

Pushing back tears until she'd stifled them, she commanded herself to move. When she reached the parlor, she thought her heart would break. Tyler was buried under her girls, all of whom were trying to hug him. Even Ginger, Kathleen, and Isabel were sitting on the sidelines, grinning like fools. Didn't they realize what this meant?

She stepped into the room, cleared her throat, and ignored the fluttering in her heart when he turned her way. He gently shook off his living coat of girls and walked toward her. Of course, he'd need her permission to take them away forever.

She could have fainted when he dropped to one knee and held up a diamond.

"Amy. . ."

Ooh, how she loved the sound of her name on his lips.

"When I came here, I'd planned everything. I knew I'd love these girls who've just agreed to become my family. The only thing I didn't expect was to fall in love with you. Would you complete my happiness by becoming my wife?"

There was no helping it. Amy Ross—soon to be Amy Samuels-Steadman—burst into tears as she flung herself at her new fiancé. Being in his arms was every bit as wonderful as she'd imagined, but she had to make sure it was real.

"Are you certain you really want this?"

"I've never been more positive in all my life. Amy, with you as my wife and these precious girls as our family, I'll be the most blessed man in all of Massachusetts. I love you." After the cheers subsided and they'd held each other for awhile, Tyler continued. "Is there anything else you need to know?"

"I love you, too. That's all I need." It was absolutely true. She'd never thought to have a husband again or to lose the guilt she'd carried for so long. As the Good Book said, "Your heavenly Father has plans for you, plans to prosper and not harm you. . . ." Indeed, He'd brought this wonderful man into her life to make her heart whole again, and it was more than she'd ever dreamed. Amy's joy would have been complete if Prudie hadn't chosen that moment to call her attention to one other tiny detail.

"Are we gonna move next door with Gussie 'cuz Mr. Sam's our new daddy?"

Amy suddenly found she needed one other thing. "Yes, we are, Honey. But," she gazed mischievously into Tyler's amazing green eyes, "you'll have to build a pen for that goose."

Epilogue

Tyler surveyed the scene around him with satisfaction. Now that they'd started taking in boys, there was even more activity to deal with. But he wouldn't trade it for the world.

They were having a family picnic, complete with all the Steadmans except Lucas and Ginger, who were at the University of Edinburgh in Scotland, doing research.

Isabel and Amy reclined on some old blankets in the shade while Kathleen chatted with Vivian. The children surrounded them, romping around with high spirits now that school had let out for the summer again.

Maxwell proudly displayed his new son, Baby Max, as Carter and Tyler compared notes on Isabel's and Amy's pregnancies.

"How do you deal with it?" Tyler appealed to Carter. "I just can't get her to sit down and rest. She just smiles and says there's too much to do to coddle her."

Carter nodded sympathetically. "Yes. Isabel was the same

way with Michael. Told me to stop treating her like a porcelain figurine."

Maxwell tossed his two cents in the pot. "It'll change soon enough when they're about seven months along. Then they don't have a choice—getting up is too difficult."

"Whoa, there." Carter's hand shot out to catch Molly from toddling straight into Michael.

Tyler shook his head, grinning from ear to ear. "If you'd told me two years ago that I'd be standing here, talking with my cousins about our coming children, I'd have thought craziness ran in the family."

"Yeah, we sure are lucky, aren't we?" Tyler could always trust Carter to understand what he meant.

"How's business?" Tyler turned to Maxwell.

"Great. Those tips on cheap sugar cane made us a tidy profit. Thanks."

"The mill's accident rate is much lower since we widened the aisles."

"And the young lovebirds?" Maxwell indicated the corner where Davey and Susannah, now seventeen and sixteen, strolled arm-in-arm.

"Just great. The house was a wonderful engagement gift, Tyler." Carter clapped him on the back.

"So long as they wait a bit, first. To tell the truth, it wasn't my idea. Amy wanted Susannah to stay close to home when she married, and the house was just sitting empty since we moved here and took on the boys. . . ."

"Our women have hearts of gold." Carter's comment

met with warm agreement as the men looked over fondly at their wives.

Tyler watched as Amy got up and began hustling some of the youngsters their way. It was naptime. As she neared him, he breathed a quick prayer. *Oh, Lord. Thank You for Your many blessings. I ask for nothing more than I already have, except a long while to enjoy it with my precious family.*

KELLY EILEEN HAKE

Kelly is a recent high school graduate who is fast aspiring to her lofty dreams of writing and teaching by attending college. She is currently majoring in English and spends her free time writing, baking, and playing with her dog, Skylar.

A Letter to Our Readers

Dear Readers:

In order that we might better contribute to your reading enjoyment, we would appreciate you taking a few minutes to respond to the following questions. When completed, please return to the following: Fiction Editor, Barbour Publishing, Inc., P.O. Box 719, Uhrichsville, OH 44683.

1. Did you enjoy reading *Woven Hearts?*
   ❑ Very much. I would like to see more books like this.
   ❑ Moderately—I would have enjoyed it more if ______________

____

____

2. What influenced your decision to purchase this book?
   (Check those that apply.)
   ❑ Cover ❑ Back cover copy ❑ Title ❑ Price
   ❑ Friends ❑ Publicity ❑ Other

3. Which story was your favorite?
   ❑ *Ribbon of Gold* ❑ *A Second Glance*
   ❑ *Run of the Mill* ❑ *The Caretaker*

4. Please check your age range:
   ❑ Under 18 ❑ 18–24 ❑ 25–34
   ❑ 35–45 ❑ 46–55 ❑ Over 55

5. How many hours per week do you read? ______________

Name ______________________________________

Occupation ______________________________________

Address ______________________________________

City ______________ State __________ Zip __________

If you enjoyed

Woven Hearts

then read:

One Woman's Mentoring Shapes Lives in Four Stories of Love

Tumbling Blocks by Andrea Boeshaar
Old Maid's Choice by Cathy Marie Hake
Jacob's Ladder by Pamela Kaye Tracy
Four Hearts by Sally Laity

Available wherever books are sold.
Or order from:
Barbour Publishing, Inc.
P.O. Box 721
Uhrichsville, Ohio 44683
www.barbourbooks.com

You may order by mail for $6.97, and add $2.00 to your order for shipping.
Prices subject to change without notice.

If you enjoyed

Woven Hearts

then read:

German Enchantment

A Legacy of Customs and Devotion in Four Romantic Novellas

Where Angels Camp by Irene B. Brand
The Nuremberg Angel by Dianne Christner
Dearest Enemy by Pamela Griffin
Once a Stranger by Gail Gaymer Martin

Available wherever books are sold.
Or order from:
Barbour Publishing, Inc.
P.O. Box 721
Uhrichsville, Ohio 44683
www.barbourbooks.com

You may order by mail for $6.97 and add $2.00 to your order for shipping.
Prices subject to change without notice.

HEARTSONG ❤ PRESENTS

Love Stories Are Rated G!

That's for godly, gratifying, and of course, great! If you love a thrilling love story but don't appreciate the sordidness of some popular paperback romances, **Heartsong Presents** is for you. In fact, **Heartsong Presents** is the only inspirational romance book club featuring love stories where Christian faith is the primary ingredient in a marriage relationship.

Sign up today to receive your first set of four never-before-published Christian romances. Send no money now; you will receive a bill with the first shipment. You may cancel at any time without obligation, and if you aren't completely satisfied with any selection, you may return the book for an immediate refund!

Imagine. . .four new romances every four weeks—two historical, two contemporary—with men and women like you who long to meet the one God has chosen as the love of their lives. . .all for the low price of $9.97 postpaid.

To join, simply complete the coupon below and mail to the address provided. **Heartsong Presents** romances are rated G for another reason: They'll arrive Godspeed!

YES! Sign me up for Hearts❤ng!

NEW MEMBERSHIPS WILL BE SHIPPED IMMEDIATELY!
Send no money now. We'll bill you only **$9.97** postpaid with your first shipment of four books. Or for faster action, call toll free 1-800-847-8270.

NAME ____________________

ADDRESS ____________________

CITY ____________ STATE ________ ZIP ________

MAIL TO: HEARTSONG PRESENTS, P.O. Box 721, Uhrichsville, Ohio 44683
or visit www.heartsongpresents.com